Noel Brown recently obtained his PhD in Film Studies from Newcastle University. He is currently an independent scholar and writer on cinema.

Cinema and Society series
General Editor: Jeffrey Richards

THE HOLLYWOOD FAMILY FILM

A History, from Shirley Temple to Harry Potter

Noel Brown

I.B. TAURIS
LONDON · NEW YORK

Published in 2012 by I.B.Tauris & Co Ltd
6 Salem Road, London W2 4BU
175 Fifth Avenue, New York NY 10010
www.ibtauris.com

Distributed in the United States and Canada Exclusively by Palgrave Macmillan
175 Fifth Avenue, New York NY 10010

ISBN   978 1 78076 269 2 (HB)
       978 1 78076 270 8 (PB)

A full CIP record for this book is available from the British Library
A full CIP record is available from the Library of Congress

Library of Congress Catalog Card Number: available

Designed and typeset by 4word Ltd, Bristol
Printed and bound by TJ International Ltd, Padstow, Cornwall

CONTENTS

ILLUSTRATIONS

ACKNOWLEDGEMENTS

The seeds of this book were sown some years ago. Like many children in the Western world, I grew up watching Hollywood family films. One of my favourites was *Mrs. Doubtfire*. I was so enamoured of the slapstick clowning and outrageous sight gags that its more 'adult' aspects largely passed me by. However, re-watching the film for the first time as an adult many years later, I was struck by the realisation that this was *not* a children's film – much of its exploration of the shifting social expectations surrounding marriage and family was clearly intended for adult audiences, or at least reflected predominantly adult concerns. This prompted some of the key questions underpinning this book: what exactly *is* a family film? How do Hollywood family films satisfy the requirements of different audience sections? Have their methods of appeal changed over time? How have they attained their current position of commercial dominance? To my surprise, there was no extended scholarly study of the historical, industrial and artistic aspects of the Hollywood family film, despite its great historical tradition. This absence provided a more pragmatic foundation for the development of this book.

More concretely, I would like to extend my gratitude to Bruce Babington for his generosity, advice and support throughout the researching and writing of this book. Kim Reynolds and Melanie Bell – who co-supervised my doctoral thesis – were also generous with their time and offered a great deal of guidance. I also appreciate the courtesy and efficiency of the staff at Newcastle University library, and the BFI reading room.

For various reasons, and in no particular order, I would like to thank the following people: Bill and Nancy Brown, Joe and Irene Cooper, Robin Brown, Philippe Cygan, Peter Clark, Alex Denehy, Andy Bird, Ray Harryhausen and Tony Dalton, Nicholas Sammond, James Annesley and Maria Teresa de Oliveira Corrêa. I am also very appreciative of the enthusiasm and encouragement of Jeffrey Richards and Philippa Brewster, and, indeed, to all the people who contributed in some way to the completion of this book. I hope they will consider their investments worthwhile.

My fullest appreciation and love must go to my parents, Alan and Kate, and to Mauricio Martuscelli. It is to them that I would like to dedicate this book.

GENERAL EDITOR'S INTRODUCTION

The family film has long been a staple of Hollywood production but has received comparatively little attention from cinema historians. This may be because while everyone knows a family film when they see one, the process of precise definition tends to be more difficult. Noel Brown suggests five non-textual manufacturing processes, which together give family films their generic identity: marketing and distribution strategies, rating/classification, critical response, merchandising and television broadcasting strategies. In applying this interpretation to Hollywood's cinematic product he rejects a range of ideas previously advanced by a variety of critics, notably that family films were chiefly intended for and largely consumed by children, that the majority of films in Hollywood's heyday were family films, that family films equate purely with Walt Disney and that the family film as a format originated in the 1980s.

Brown convincingly argues that the family film emerged in the 1930s following the tightening of the censorship rules aimed at curbing the perceived excesses of the early talkies. This was the era of the child star, as every studio tried to emulate the success of Twentieth Century Fox's Shirley Temple, who regularly topped the annual polls of box office winners; of the faithful literary adaptation of a Victorian classic (*Treasure Island, David Copperfield, Captains Courageous*, for example); and of the developing tradition of the Christmas release (*Babes in Toyland, Alice in Wonderland, Snow White and the Seven Dwarfs*). The 1940s saw a change of emphasis with child stars and literary adaptations overtaken by nostalgic celebrations of families in the recent past (*Life with Father, Meet Me in St. Louis*) and child-centred animal films (*Lassie Come Home, National Velvet*).

The rise of television changed the nature of cinema audiences and although Walt Disney went over from animated to live action features and cornered the family market, the search was on for the new family film which would appeal to an audience, the majority of whom fell into the 16–29 age range, but that would also engage older viewers. The studios eventually came up with the 'kidult' franchises, fantasy films that appealed to every generation, and so were born the Indiana Jones, Star Wars, Harry Potter and Narnia series and the apparently endless comic-derived superhero films. In this original, carefully researched and cogently argued book, Noel Brown has provided both a convincing definition and persuasive explication of the history of the family film.

Jeffrey Richards
November 2011

INTRODUCTION

If W. B. Yeats was correct in supposing that the core, essential self is determined by self-perception and aspiration, then the 'family film' is Hollywood in its purest, most unadulterated form. It embodies the impossible dream of universalism – which itself must be Hollywood's exclusive province, because of its unique economic power and global reach – and has emerged, particularly since the late-1970s, as the quintessential mode of production of the Hollywood cinema. No other form of screen entertainment has come close to matching its popularity with international audiences. Indeed, the Hollywood family film has become the most commercially-successful and widely-consumed cinematic entertainment in the world.[1] That this is the case is unsurprising, given that the family film encompasses genres as diverse as science fiction and fantasy to domestic comedy, and in its fullest extension is deliberately constructed to appeal to the broadest audience base, transcending all possible cultural and biological barriers, such as age, race, social class, gender, nationality, and religious and sexual orientation.

This talk of universalism may seem portentous and hyperbolic. After all, most of us have grown up with Hollywood family films and have become accustomed to viewing them as little more than innocuous, diverting amusements for children. Indeed, many family films and franchises evoke feelings of comfort, nostalgia and intimacy, particularly in Western countries. We may recall with fondness such 'family' favourites as *Little Women* (George Cukor, 1933), *Snow White and the Seven Dwarfs* (David

1

Hand, 1937), *The Wizard of Oz* (Victor Fleming, 1939), *Pinocchio* (Hamilton Luske and Ben Sharpsteen, 1940), *Meet Me in St. Louis* (Vincente Minnelli, 1944), *20,000 Leagues under the Sea* (Richard Fleischer, 1954), *The 7th Voyage of Sinbad* (Nathan Juran, 1958), *Mary Poppins* (Robert Stevenson, 1964), *The Sound of Music* (Robert Wise, 1965), *Star Wars* (George Lucas, 1977), *Superman* (Richard Donner, 1978), *Back to the Future* (Robert Zemeckis, 1985), *Home Alone* (Chris Columbus, 1990), *Jurassic Park* (Steven Spielberg, 1993), *Toy Story* (John Lasseter, 1995), *Shrek* (Andrew Adamson and Vicky Jenson, 2001) and *Harry Potter* (2001–11). Whatever our opinions regarding such films, they are very difficult to ignore, from their first showings in cinemas to television repeats, the ubiquity of the merchandise they generate and their home video (re)releases. Such family entertainment figureheads as Charlie Chaplin, Shirley Temple, Mickey Rooney, Walt Disney and Steven Spielberg are similarly indelible in the cultural consciousness. Yet, incredibly, Hollywood family films themselves have received remarkably scant critical attention in spite of their artistic, cultural and commercial prominence.

This may stem partially from the very broadness of the format. The term 'family film' is a vague and unsatisfactory label to describe such a diverse, pluralistic body of films as is covered in this book, but as good a general definition as any has been provided by Andy Bird, Chairman of Disney International:

> 'The Family Film' is a film that can be enjoyed by the whole family together, as well as a film that can be enjoyed by a broad audience demographic. The true test [...] is if a child and his/her grandparent could go together and equally enjoy a film.[2]

Of course, films targeted towards actual 'families' are an industry in themselves, but this book is also concerned with those films which – while purporting to address the 'family audience' – actually attempt to secure a far wider consumer base. The producers of such films employ a range of textual and non-textual strategies in an effort to engage mass audiences, under the cloak of intimacy and respectability offered by the 'family' label. Almost all family films attempt to elicit pleasurable emotional responses in audiences, especially feelings of comfort, reassurance and even happiness. The means through which these emotional cues are transmitted vary from film to film, but Hollywood family-orientated productions almost invariably convey certain ideological values (e.g. the reaffirmation of 'family' and other forms of kinship) attractively packaged in a narrative that fulfils certain structural expectations (e.g. a happy ending).

Mainstream cinema has always sought types of entertainment capable of attracting mass audiences, and it is axiomatic that films capable of playing successfully to all ages and social groups stand the best chance of commercial success. As Ruth Vasey has argued, as early as the 1920s – the period in which it tightened its grip on the world market – Hollywood 'had to formulate a recipe for movies that could play in the North and the South, on the West Coast and in the East, and from Cape Town to Capri'.[3] By 1930, the major Hollywood studios had established a near-hegemonic control over global film distribution, and – assisted further by powerful protectionist policies – their share of feature films in world distribution had reached 80 per cent.[4] The populist aesthetic historically employed by Hollywood producers reflects, to a large extent, the very *ability* to reach mass audiences internationally. Although the mainstream Hollywood family film has always been manufactured for as wide an audience base as possible, dating back to the 1930s, certain post-1970s examples of the format, such as the *Star Wars* and *Harry Potter* franchises, represent clear attempts to unify audiences not merely on a national but a global level. This is not to say that Hollywood producers regard mass audiences as an undifferentiated body. On the contrary, major studios such as Disney test all their films with a variety of different audience groups prior to release. However, the success of a contemporary, mainstream Hollywood family film is measured largely in terms of its ability to transcend such audience divisions as age, gender, class, religion and ethnicity. Because it promises vast audiences and huge economic rewards, such a product is the Holy Grail for commercially-minded producers.

The Family Brand

'Family entertainment' is a term that has been applied to such broad-appeal recreational and escapist pursuits as the theatre, the fairground, the theme park, the live sporting occasion, mainstream radio and network television.[5] In each case, it denotes the intersection of broad appeal, inoffensiveness and a potential mass consumer base, and is actively encouraged by its purveyors. In English-speaking countries, where the term is most prevalent, 'family film' is not merely a descriptor, but a signifier of expense, distinctiveness and a peculiarly North American form of mass entertainment. Over the course of several decades, Hollywood has engineered the term into a hugely lucrative brand. Today, it is widely acknowledged in Hollywood that when a product is success-fully 'branded' as 'family entertainment', its commercial prospects are significantly boosted.

During the 1910s and 1920s – the period during which Hollywood cemented its status as a cultural institution with tremendous interna-tional reach – it was central to its brand identity that it was a 'family' entertainment. In North America, people of all ages and social back-grounds attended movie theatres, which typically offered an evening's entertainment comprising a broad range of amusements. A variety of different types of movie would be shown consecutively; there was usually a feature-length film, bolstered with an array of shorter, often action-orientated subjects. Prior to the late-1920s, all films were silent. Theatres employed their own orchestras to play music appropriate to the on-screen action. According to the propaganda, collectively these amusements would satisfy the entertainment requirements of everyone. Children of both sexes and all ages were important consumers, some-times attending with their families, and sometimes alone or with friends. Yet in spite of persistent claims from civic, religious and educative bodies that films were often morally unsuitable for the consumption of young people, it was widely accepted that cinema in the United States was a 'family' entertainment.

This perception was greatly challenged by Hollywood cinema's tran-sition to sound in 1929. Hitherto, even feature films with clearly adult themes had generally been accepted as suitable entertainment for chil-dren, largely because there was no dialogue through which to transmit salacious content. This no longer held true after the transition to 'talkies'. Hollywood's accepted status as a 'family' entertainment historically had protected it, to a certain extent, from enemies of the medium, but with the increasing proliferation of 'adult' films during the early-1930s, there was an imminent threat of federally-imposed censorship legislation. The industry's response was to establish the Production Code – a pre-emptory form of self-censorship that heavily regulated all films under general release. The Production Code – established in 1930 and made mandatory in April 1934 – ostensibly reasserted Hollywood's self-appointed status as a respectable, universal 'family' institution. Furthermore, during this period the industry also 'invented' a specialised type of feature film specifically intended for 'families'.

Beginning with the release of *Little Women* in November 1933 and continuing with such major productions as *Treasure Island* (Victor Fleming, 1934), *David Copperfield* (George Cukor, 1935) and *A Midsummer Night's Dream* (Max Reinhardt and William Dieterle, 1935), this new format was designed simultaneously to attract mass audiences, to symbolise Hollywood's artistic maturity and to reaffirm its acknowledged responsibilities as the nation's leading recreational attraction. Even at this early stage in its development, the family film was explicitly constituted as an attractive counterpoint to adult-orientated entertainment.

Beyond these affirmative connotations, the generic identity of the family film is extremely fragmented. There is a very basic and crucial dichotomy between productions aimed literally at 'families' (i.e. parents and children co-attending) in which broader audience appeal is a secondary concern, and those which are predicated on more universalistic lines, where 'families' are merely a small – if attractively marketable – element in a wider spectrum of mass audiences. The first category is more commonly associated with lower-budget films, often made by smaller industries (especially in Europe) orientated towards domestic audiences, and unable to match Hollywood's production values and global distribution networks. The second pertains more to mass-appeal blockbusters, usually produced and/or distributed by the Hollywood studios. However, while Hollywood has expanded considerably since the 1930s – both creatively and economically – the rhetorical and ideological appeal of the 'family', in Western societies, at least, has endured. This means that although family films themselves are subject to continual change, the 'family' brand has stood the test of time as a patented antidote to cultural forms marked by contentious material; most notably, graphic portrayals of violence and sex.

Like all successful brands, the 'family' label has often served to obfuscate or mislead consumers. After all, it possesses an intimacy lacking in descriptors such as 'total entertainment' or 'multi-demographic programming'. The family film responds to anxiety-producing social changes in post-industrial societies across the world, in which 'extended' and 'nuclear' families have been supplanted by more fragmented, less permanent social structures. Given that most of the biggest international markets for Hollywood entertainment (Japan, Western Europe and Australasia) are economically-developed and post-industrial, it is unsurprising that films which nostalgically and defiantly evoke utopian family ideals (as seen through the eyes of the majority) retain an immense amount of cultural capital.[6] This association with an image of family unity makes an afternoon at the multiplex with the latest blockbuster seem as warm and comforting as a night in front of a log fire. These connotations appear doubly inappropriate in relation to contemporary franchises such as *Indiana Jones* (1981–2008) and *Pirates of the Caribbean* (2003–), which are propelled by simple but appealing narratives satisfying the senses as well as the emotions, making them more attractive propositions for teenagers and young adults concerned with kudos. A suitable metaphor might be a theme park, in which sensual pleasure takes precedence over sophistication; in which those willing to 'loosen up and have a good time' will have exactly that, and in which the thrills are exhilarating, but safe and inoffensive. The brand, then, is highly flexible. Hollywood family films address Western social anxieties regarding the condition of the 'family', but also appeal to a very different audience group concerned predominantly with emotional uplift and escapism.

What Makes a Family Film?

The 'family' label, then, is widely disseminated by the media industries for commercial purposes. However, there are much broader, uncoordinated processes of negotiation involved in the socio-cultural manufacturing of Hollywood family films. Distributors, marketers, review boards, critics and audiences all play a part in these processes, which take place prior to, during and after cinematic release. There are, I would suggest, five primary *non-textual* manufacturing processes through which family films attain their generic identity:

1. Marketing and distribution strategies. These pertain to how a film is represented to the public by its manufacturers. If a film is seen as having 'family' appeal, it is the job of marketers and distributors to communicate this clearly and unambiguously to the moviegoing public. The costs of marketing and publicity campaigns often run into tens of millions, reflecting the need to raise awareness among

potential consumers and to implant the appropriate impression of the film, based on its perceived selling points.

2. Rating/classification. Since 1968, an independent panel, attached to the trade organisation that represents the interests of the major Hollywood studios, has assigned ratings to all films exhibited in the United States, based on perceived suitability for young audiences. Today, the categories comprise: 'G' (suitable for all ages); 'PG' (parental guidance; some material regarded as unsuitable for children); 'PG-13' (parents strongly cautioned; some material regarded as inappropriate for children under the age of 13); 'R' (restricted; children under the age of 17 require accompanying parent/guardian; and 'NC-17' (no children under the age of 17 admitted). The merits of the ratings system have been widely debated, but many countries globally have similar mechanisms in place.

3. Critical response. Many general interest and specialist entertainment publications provide film reviews, although tone and quality vary enormously. Reviews are not as influential as once they were in determining moviegoing habits, but remain important in categorising films during the formative period of generic classification.

4. Merchandising. Although merchandising licenses have constituted a useful ancillary revenue stream for Hollywood films since the studio era, they have proven most valuable in relation to family-orientated productions; especially since the late-1970s. Such merchandising streams as toys and games are commonly construed as child-orientated, but young adults have become important consumers of such products. Whilst adult films offer comparatively few opportunities for merchandise and other tie-ins, family films are particularly attractive because of their broad audience base and the additional scope for licensable properties accorded by fantastical narratives (of which family films constitute a large percentage).

5. Television broadcast strategies. Television plays a key role in how films are represented to the public in the months and years *after* theatrical release. Viewers are expected to understand that daytime television slots are reserved for programming possessing broad audience suitability, and night-time slots may contain 'adult' elements. Furthermore, the implication of 'family' viewing is particularly intensified during periods of national celebration and family unity, such as Thanksgiving (in the United States), Easter and

Christmas. Entertainment that provides comfort, as well as evoking feelings of community and togetherness, are particularly in-demand during this period.

Most of the time, identifying family films presents no difficulties. *Harry Potter and the Sorcerer's Stone* (Chris Columbus, 2001) is clearly a family film: it provides multiple avenues of access for mass audiences, and contains little or no violent or sexual content; it was released just before Christmas to attract the highest concentration of cross-demographic audiences; it was overtly marketed as a 'family film'; it received a family-friendly PG rating; it was widely-received, critically and popularly, as a family film; and it spawned a huge range of merchandise and other tie-ins. Of course, the definition is not always so straightforward. Many of the qualities audiences now expect from mainstream Hollywood family films – for example, a fast-paced narrative aesthetic; visceral thrills and excitement; spectacle and sensorial appeal, rather than an emphasis on dialogue and sophisticated character motivation – can also be found in productions not socially regarded as acceptable for juvenile audiences (such as high-octane action films). When a film is clearly *appealing* to children, categorisation as a family film depends on a more subjective assessment of suitability.

It is socially accepted – often implicitly – that a family film must possess broad moral and thematic suitability, *and* broad demographic appeal.[7] There are many examples of films which fulfil one of these criteria, but not both. Consider the films of Frank Capra. Their 'suitability' for children, by accepted Western social standards, is not in doubt: they were typically moralistic, contained little violence or allusions to sexuality, and several were adapted for the highly-successful, family-orientated Lux Radio Theatre (1934–55) slot in the United States. On the other hand, they were often talky and sophisticated, containing little to which juvenile audiences could explicitly identify. Similarly, although *It's a Wonderful Life* (1946) is now widely understood as a family classic in the United States and the United Kingdom because of a long-standing tradition of television stations broadcasting it every Christmas, it was neither marketed nor received as such upon its initial release. Conversely, Steven Spielberg's *Jaws* (1975) – which was his last adult movie before diversifying into family films – possesses many of the broad-appeal strategies of his later productions, but its gore and intensity currently precludes 'family film' status. This may well change in the future, if the cultural barriers between childhood and adulthood disintegrate further. As the following chapters suggest, suitability and appeal are not immutable, but are interpreted in accordance with constantly-changing social values.

The Critical Status of the Family Film

Bluntly, as a subject for historical, critical and theoretical analysis, the family film has been woefully under-addressed. Indeed, it must surely constitute the most neglected of *all* the major Hollywood modes of production. No extended history of the format has emerged at the time of writing, a fact which is both astonishing and revealing. Only a handful of academic articles explicitly addressing Hollywood family entertainment have been published.[8] All are useful and insightful, but their brevity enables little more than a scratching of the surface. Furthermore, they are devoted almost exclusively to modern incarnations of the format, ignoring family films produced prior to the 1970s. Other relevant works have generally assumed a textual approach in relation to individual studios (i.e. Disney), franchises (e.g. *Lord of the Rings*) or individuals (e.g. George Lucas or Steven Spielberg). Much of this research, such as Eric Smoodin's *Animating Culture: Hollywood Cartoons from the Sound Era* (1993), Nicholas Sammond's *Babes in Tomorrowland: Walt Disney and the Making of the American Child, 1930–1960* (2005) and Kristin Thompson's *The Frodo Franchise: The Lord of the Rings and Modern Hollywood* (2007), is invaluable. Nonetheless, what studies of this ilk cannot provide, by their very nature, is a sense of the overall historical and generic aspects of the Hollywood family film. The critical neglect of the family film on a broader scale, meanwhile, is the unfortunate by-product of a range of misconceptions and prejudices surrounding its generic and commercial identities.

Firstly, many family films are misleadingly referred to critically and popularly as 'children's films', or even 'kids' films'. Usually these slippages are perfectly innocent, but can also be used in a more patronising sense in relation to their subjects (and, by extension, consumers). Peter Kramer has suggested that 'children's and family films' are widely misconstrued as 'cheaply made', 'simply not very good' and 'not even very important commercially'.[9] Given the enormous budgets afforded many contemporary Hollywood family films, the irony is clear to see. Conversely, it is not unusual to see expensively-produced family films crudely categorised as 'blockbusters', a catch-all term that fails to determine intended and actual audience suitability and appeal. Just as cheap or commercially-marginal family films may be dismissed as unimportant, blockbuster family movies are open to denigration on account of *excessive* commercialism, representing all that is rapacious and cynical in Hollywood's capitalistic identity. Furthermore, the fact that the provenance of the 'family' brand lies with Hollywood itself is, perhaps, a stumbling block for an academy rooted within an independently-minded liberal humanism. Film scholars not only tend to dislike blatantly commercial products, gravitating towards the artistically innovative and commercially negligible, but prefer to identify their own areas for study, and resist having labels imposed on them by non-experts, or worse, commercial cinema itself. The extent of these prejudices is hard to quantify, although a cursory check of the United States' Library of Congress catalogue will reveal literally hundreds of academic books specifically devoted to film noir. Although it is a 'genre' well-known for its position of high critical esteem, film noir is far less commercially or culturally prominent than the mainstream Hollywood family film.

To allude to these prejudices, of course, is not to deny that the family film is a particularly manipulative mode of entertainment. It responds, at one end of the scale, to cultural requirements for optimistic, comforting narratives that provide reassurance and reaffirm often conservative social values; and at the other, to innate desires for spectacle, escapism and release from everyday pressures and anxieties. There is little question that critical estimation of the family film has been affected by several perceived defects; namely, exploitative qualities, excessive sentiment, excessive juvenility, a tendency to be anodyne (leading to boredom), poor production values, style over substance and sometimes even substance over style. Perhaps as a result, artistically significant family films (such as Cukor's *Little Women* or Minnelli's *Meet Me in St. Louis*) have tended to be adjudged in isolation, rather than as existing within the 'family' milieu. In contrast, relatively uninspired productions – such as *Are We There Yet?* (Brian Levant, 2005) or *RV: Runaway Vacation* (Barry Sonnenfeld, 2006) – historically are far more likely to be received as 'mere' family films, associated with a mode known for its creative inadequacies. A truer assessment of the artistic value of the format would acknowledge that there have always been a widely disparate collection of products marketed as family films, some cheap and derivative, some cynical and exploitative, some earnest and worthy, some dumb and escapist, some downright tedious, and some intelligent and sophisticated.

The fact that the family film sits awkwardly in relation to the question of genre is undoubtedly a factor in this neglect. It is generally assumed by theorists that movies residing within a genre will, at the very least, share 'recurrent situations and consistent narrative patterns'.[10] By these criteria, the family film, in itself, is not a genre. There are relatively few formal connections, and family films often inhabit genres of their own: musicals, comedies, fantasies, animations, science fiction films, epics and even westerns. Nor is it easily understood as a genre defined by audience address (rather than formal connectivity), because the target 'family audience' is largely symbolic. The family film is perhaps better understood as a master-genre, within which a broad, formally diverse array of sub-genres operate, while still satisfying certain structural, ideological and emotive expectations popularly associated with family entertainment. Problems arise, I would suggest, when such unifying elements are overlooked purely in favour of semantic commonality (such as the iconographies associated with westerns or crime films). A certain contingent of genre theorists seemingly delight in placing films within easily-digestible frameworks, noting divergences, developments and evolutions corresponding to the established canon, and generally trying to fit pieces together, like parts of a puzzle. There is a convenience to such classifications which sometimes precludes deep analysis of incongruent forms. I would suggest that the fact that the family movie is incoherently, yet tangibly, popularly understood as pertaining to standards of moral decency and emotional relatability – rather than formal unity – undermines totalising interpretations of film genre, as do the overlapping generic elements of many individual texts.

When seemingly every agency involved in film classification *other than* the academy – ranging from producers, trade papers, listings magazines, video stores to the general public – recognise the family film as a coherent generic entity, something is clearly wrong. But the criticism should not be of 'genre' per se. When used as a tool, rather than a rigid doctrine, it is immensely useful. Indeed, several theories of genre (such as those advanced by Steve Neale, which place more of an emphasis on categorisations employed in the industry) are highly insightful, even as others are confoundedly pedantic and constraining. Lately, in film studies, there has been a determined movement away from puritanical or inhibiting interpretations of genre. A recent edited collection argues that generic labels are largely irrelevant, and even detrimental to the works to which they are applied.[11] This assessment is roughly in accordance with my own position. When mighty tomes like Barry Keith Grant's edited *Film Genre Reader* volumes – which purportedly examine all of the key cinematic genres – make no reference to the most profitable type of films in the world, there has clearly been a failure somewhere down the line, whether in process, conceptualisation or understanding. My approach in this book is to treat the Hollywood family film as a reasonably coherent body of films, typically sharing specific ideological overtones, emotive aspects and commercial intent, while corresponding to the processes of socio-cultural manufacturing outlined above. Readers are, of course, free to make up their own minds as to where family films sit in relation to this endlessly contentious site of debate.

As Chapter 1 will show, commercially- and politically-motivated interest in the 'family audience' dates back at least to the beginnings of the twentieth century. In most respects, the specialised family films produced in Hollywood during the early-1930s are recognisable precursors to those that dominate box office tables today. Due to a combination of changes and advances in technology, demographics, lifestyle habits and social and cultural differences – which have led to an increased emphasis on aesthetic modes of appeal and a youth-orientation in general – there are many cosmetic differences between classical and contemporary family films, but their ideological role essentially remains the same. This historical perspective has tended to be overlooked by the few scholars who have chosen to examine Hollywood family films. Robert C. Allen has argued that:

> What was referred to in the trade as the 'family film' emerged in the late 1980s and early 1990s as Hollywood's attempt to exploit the profit potential of the video market, particularly sell-through, as fully as possible.[12]

Obviously, the entire thrust of this book is that the family film is *not* a post-1980s phenomenon, although it is perfectly true that the Hollywood studios stepped-up their commitment to the format during the late-1980s and early-1990s. However, to portray the family film as a recent phenomenon is wholly misguided. In contrast, Kramer has argued – just as inaccurately, in my view – that all Hollywood productions made prior to the 1960s, differences in taste notwithstanding, were 'family movies'. This misconception stems largely from the perceived function of the Hollywood Production Code, which was intended to keep explicitly 'adult' content from the screens. Although the studios initially resisted the Production Code (since it meant abandoning some of their most profitable types of entertainment), the Hollywood establishment put their own positive spin on the matter, representing the Code as inaugurating an era of high-class 'family' films and rendering commercial cinema a truly universal cultural institution.

The first problem, I think, is that some critics have swallowed this propaganda rather too easily, overlooking the fact that adult-orientated films were never truly abolished. The more one interrogates this supposed era (c. 1934–66) of family films, the less it stands up to scrutiny. It might be argued that 1960 was the key year in the movement away from family films, with the release of – among others – *Psycho* (Alfred Hitchcock), *Elmer Gantry* (Richard Brooks) and *The Apartment* (Billy Wilder). However, one might then point to the mid-1950s as an equally valid watershed, as it was the period in which the first serious Production Code violations occurred; in which the intensity of the early youth films began to erode the 'middlebrow' aesthetic dominant since the 1930s; and in which adult-inflected European imports hit US theatres for the first time. One may chip further away at the initial date range by invoking such 1940s film cycles as the crime film, the psychological melodrama and the resurgence of the 'serious' western. In short, the contention that all (or even most) Hollywood Code-era productions were family movies is indefensible. Indeed, I would argue that relatively *few* Hollywood films produced during this period were family-orientated.

Two possible counter-claims are that such adult-orientated productions were exceptions to the rule, or that I am employing excessively strict definitions of family films. However, even if one were to accept the first counter-argument, the second would seem to depend on a definition which construes a 'family' film only as an entertainment *unlikely to inflict psychological harm* on a child, whilst ignoring entertainment requirements. As I have already argued, moral and thematic suitability is only one criterion for defining a family film, and it seems equally important that entertainment value is also considered. After all, party political broadcasts on network television may be *suitable* for children, even as they target prospective adult voters; does this make them 'family' advertisements?

One further likely reason for the scholarly under-appreciation of the family film presents itself: the possible misconception that the format has already been sufficiently explored. For example, many family movies are fantasies or musicals, genres which have been scrupulously surveyed. Meanwhile, a wide range of literature has addressed the *representation* of children and adolescents in popular film, but not how popular films *appeal* to juvenile as well as adult audiences.[13] Others scholars working within the field of children's studies have attempted to plot a coherent picture of children's literature and film from theoretical and ideological perspectives.[14] This is especially problematic because of the deeply divergent commercial imperatives at the heart of these media; most so-called 'children's films' are manufactured equally for adult consumers. Similarly, although there is considerable difference between youth films (which target one *specific* demographic) and family films (which often target the *broadest possible* demographic cross-section), they might easily be associated through their shared interest in pre-adult consumers.

Undoubtedly the major factor, however, is the ongoing scholarly fascination with the Disney Corporation. There have been dozens of excellent studies on Disney's family entertainment output, but not a single one on the family films produced by major Hollywood studios such as MGM, Twentieth Century Fox, Paramount, Warner Bros., Columbia or Universal. Whilst it would be foolish to represent Disney as anything other than the leading purveyor of family entertainment within Hollywood, the family film was already well-established before it made the transition to feature filmmaking, and there have been long periods in which it has struggled to challenge its supposedly less illustrious rivals in the 'family' market. Disney receives more attention in this book than any other studio, but I have determined to view the company and its output in context of a much broader fixation with family entertainment in Hollywood, rather than construing this wider history as little more than an adjunct to the established Disney canon.[15]

The Hollywood family film is a multifaceted entity. It is the clearest manifestation of Hollywood cinema's ongoing pursuit of mass acceptance as a universal democratic art both domestically and internationally; taken as a body of films governed by common entertainment principles, it is a diverse and fascinating form of popular entertainment; as a cultural phenomenon, it is massively significant not only in Western, but increasingly global, cultural history. As a result, my approach considers industrial, material and cultural perspectives in relation to its development. I endeavour to show how the family film has been shaped by attitudes and developments within the Hollywood film industry, constantly-changing socio-cultural values, and the continual need to satisfy the needs of the majority. I also hope to disprove any perceptions that: i) the family film is a culturally-negligible format chiefly intended for, and consumed by, children; ii) family films are a new format; or, conversely, they constituted the majority of studio-era Hollywood productions; and iii) such a diverse, pluralistic format can be understood solely in relation to Disney's output.

Each chapter in this book examines a specific period in relation to the development of the Hollywood family film. Chapter 1 investigates how and why Hollywood began strategically pursuing 'films for the family', and discusses the various 'family' genres designed to attract this conceptual audience. Chapter 2 examines Disney's entry into feature filmmaking with *Snow White and the Seven Dwarfs* (1937), and how its success – and that of subsequent Disney films – impacted on the strategies employed elsewhere in Hollywood. Chapter 3 considers Hollywood's relationship with the family audience during the 1940s and early-1950s, when most of the studios settled on a conservative but highly successful strategy of making lavish, big-budget films *about* small-town families.

Chapter 4 analyses how the family film was affected by Hollywood's uneasy period of transition between the early-1950s and late-1960s, in which audiences declined, television threatened the film industry's dominance, and the teenager emerged as a powerful consumer. Chapter 5 explores how a generation of independent producers – particularly George Pal, Ray Harryhausen, Charles Schneer and Robert B. Radnitz – battled to overcome lack of resources and industry apathy to produce a number of critically- and commercially-successful family films between the late-1950s and early-1970s. Chapter 6 addresses the re-emergence and reconfiguration of the Hollywood family film between the late-1970s and mid-1990s, when the key shift from a predominantly national to a global audience address occurred. Chapter 7 largely eschews a textual approach, instead focusing on the recent development of family entertainment in context of ongoing processes of conglomeration and technological advance. Collectively, these chapters underline the considerable – and ever-expanding – importance of the Hollywood family film across this broad historical period, both culturally and industrially.

THE EMERGENCE OF THE HOLLYWOOD FAMILY FEATURE, 1930–9

For the majority of its silent period – from its mass emergence in the 1900s until its transition to sound in 1929 – it was widely accepted that Hollywood was, as its advocates insisted, a 'family' institution. That is to say, it was construed as an amusement fitted to serve all facets of the general public, including children. This understanding of commercial cinema as a 'family' medium developed in conjunction with its growth in the United States as a near-universal cultural institution, particularly during the 1910s, when Hollywood shook off its slightly seedy, working-class associations and successfully cultivated the middle classes, which brought with them the appearance of social respectability.

It was important to the early film pioneers that their medium should be seen to possess social and cultural legitimacy. There was little that was respectable about the early, bargain-basement nickelodeon theatres, many of which were flea-pits, but which achieved enormous popularity because of their cheapness. The early film moguls, such as Adolph Zukor and Marcus Loew, aspired to the middle-class respectability of vaudeville. As North American commercial cinema began to develop beyond its primitive origins, producers and exhibitors consciously chose to market their medium as a 'family' amusement; this usefully ambiguous word asserted suitability for all members of the family, whilst simultaneously implying appeal for all elements of the broader social sphere.[1] Then, as now, the 'family audience' symbolised respectability, profitability and mass cultural acceptance. The term was apparently used in the trade long before it slipped into common usage. The trade paper *Variety* employed it with regularity from its inception in 1906, but it was not used in *The New York Times*, the nation's most popular daily, before 1917. The key point, though, is that while the nebulous perception of North American commercial cinema as a 'family' institution had long been established by the time Hollywood made the transition to sound, the 'family film' – by which I mean a feature-length production *explicitly* designed for the joint consumption of adults and children, and received as such – was yet to materialise.

For several reasons, any discussion of 'family films' in relation to Hollywood's silent era is far from straightforward. At this point, the feature film – today virtually analogous with the cinematic experience itself – was merely one part of a 'balanced programme' of attractions that constituted an evening's entertainment at the movie theatre. The actual content of the movie programme varied, as it was usually assembled independently by the theatre owner. It was the job of exhibitors to know their clientele, as audiences would respond differently to entertainment based on their location (urban or rural; inner city or neighbourhood) and socio-economic orientation. A typical movie programme during the 1920s would comprise a newsreel, a cartoon, one or more comedy shorts, a live musical interlude and a feature film. The overall programme would typically run for somewhere between 90 and 120 minutes. The composition of the movie programme, however, was often secondary to the drawing power of the theatres themselves, which frequently built up a regular clientele.

At this point, moviegoing was one of the dominant social activities in North America, and a weekly visit to the cinema was a way of life for a large percentage of the population. Exhibitors considered themselves to be showmen, and assembled their movie programmes much in the same way as stage managers assembled their vaudeville (i.e. variety) shows. Movie programmes were designed to offer as diverse a range of attractions as possible to appeal to the broadest audience demographic. The short subjects – especially serials, comedies and animations – were generally escapist fare, with particular appeal to children and adolescents. The feature films were more orientated to adult tastes. For this reason, relatively few features were produced for the explicit consumption of juvenile audiences. Edgar Dale's survey of the content of Hollywood feature films found that 'children's films' comprised a mere 0.4 per cent of the 500 films under review from 1920, a figure which rose only marginally to 0.8 per cent in 1925.[2]

The relative lack of films made specifically for children was a subject of immense controversy. Cinema was still a relatively new medium, and its rise to social and cultural prominence had been nothing short of meteoric. Film exhibition, in its crudest form, began in the USA in April 1896, when Thomas Edison sponsored the first public unveiling of the movies at a prominent New York vaudeville theatre. The mass emergence of commercial cinema during the 1900s owed much to working-class urban patronage of nickelodeon theatres, but it was the subsequent seduction of the middle classes that elevated commercial cinema beyond this socially disreputable milieu.[3] By the mid-1910s, *The New York Times* estimated that 10 million people attended motion picture theatres every day.[4] This, in turn, gave rise to considerable unease regarding its (potentially corrupting) influence upon mass audiences, particularly children.

In 1915, the US Supreme Court found that movies were not protected by the First Amendment – a section of the Constitution's Bill of Rights guaranteeing freedom of speech, particularly in relation to the commercial press. The ruling was a landmark, because it meant that Hollywood had no legal protection on the grounds of artistry, leaving its films vulnerable to state, local and national censorship legislation. At the same time, the Supreme Court ruling institutionalised the development of moviegoing in the USA from a 'poor man's art' and 'salvation of democracy' into an increasingly regulated mainstream 'family entertainment'.[5] As such, it shaped the movies' relationships with child and adult audiences for the remainder of the studio era. With full creative autonomy removed, Hollywood cinema became a site of negotiation between moral and political organisations and censorship boards cognisant of the increasing socio-cultural significance of the medium, and determined to curb its potential for misuse.

One of the key criticisms of the burgeoning film industry at this point was its relative lack of regulation. A wide variety of organised civic, religious and educational groups made it their mission to campaign for Federal censorship of commercial cinema, a motion strongly opposed by industry leaders. From 1909, an independent, New York-based organisation called the National Board of Review 'reviewed' films on behalf of the industry, suggesting possible changes to those which contained questionable material and awarding satisfactory films its seal of approval. Although its role was welcomed by critics, the Board had no legal power to impose changes to the films it reviewed, and its credibility was weakened by its insistence on charging producers a 'fee' to cover overheads. However innocent this financial link may have been, it hinted at a conflict of interests.[6] With the 1915 Supreme Court ruling apparently signalling the failure of the Board as an effective safeguard against censorship, the industry worked to establish a credible system of self-regulation. The first such self-regulatory body, the Motion Picture Board of Trade, was short-lived, whilst the subsequent National Association of the Motion Picture Industry (NAMPI), formed in 1916, was similarly ineffective as an anti-censorship lobby. Throughout this period, a large number of local- and state-sponsored censorship boards were established, and there was constant pressure from reformers for a strong Federal voice in motion picture content.

In desperation, the leading studios and independent producers turned collectively to Postmaster General Will H. Hays as the man to 'clean up Hollywood'. Hays became the first president of the Motion Picture Producers and Distributors of America, Inc. (MPPDA), a new trade organisation formed in March 1922. Hays said many times publicly that the primary role of the MPPDA was to effect higher standards in two ways: 'improving the quality of supply' by encouraging member companies to produce movies of a higher artistic standard; and 'improving the quality of demand' by 'educating' the public and working with interested civic organisations. However, these twin objectives were not self-supporting; although Hays continued to promote 'better films' from moral and artistic standards, and introduced two self-regulatory codes of production aimed at restricting salacious content, neither were mandatory, and so-called 'sex films' proliferated during the late 1920s. Hays repeatedly resisted trying to impose the cooperation of producers in this endeavour; his method, rather, was the 'flower of slow growth [...] I did my best to encourage the flower, but any forcing would have killed it. You can't tell creators how to create'.[7]

Hollywood in the 1920s was marked by an ongoing game of cat and mouse between the industry and the reformers who were leading the campaign for moral, educational and artistic uplift. The MPPDA was not only a regulatory body, but also a propaganda department for the industry, designed to placate the fiercest critics whilst doing little to disrupt the status quo. In 1922, Hays formed a Public Relations Committee comprising many of the most prestigious North American social organisations, such as the General Federation of Women's Clubs, the National

Congress of Parents and Teachers, the International Federation of Catholic Alumnae and the YMCA. Together, these organisations formed a cultural elite that exercised an influence far outweighing its true levels of representation. However, very few of the Committee's activities had much bearing on film content. Disillusioned with their 'inconsequential work' and the apparent lack of progress, various organisations broke rank and the Committee was finally dissolved. Undeterred, Hays formed a Department of Public Relations within the MPPDA in March 1925. Headed by Hays's old friend Jason Joy, the Public Relations Department was far more visible than the behind-closed-doors activities of the Committee, and did a good job of managing dissenting voices. It invited participation from 'every organisation of every description in either this country or any other country which is interested in public betterment' – although, inevitably, the more commercially valuable voices were the most influential.

Because there was no dialogue, Hollywood's silent-era entertainment relied instead on more visual methods of storytelling, some of which – such as action and slapstick comedy – possessed particular appeal to children and adolescents. There is a general lack of substantive data upon which to formulate a reliable picture of the movie attendance habits of children during this period, but three large-scale contemporary studies nonetheless give an indication. In 1923, the Russell Sage Foundation, the National Board of Review and Associated First National Pictures jointly conducted a nationwide survey of 37,000 high-school students across 76 North American cities. In 1929, Alice Miller Mitchell published a survey of 10,000 Chicago children of varying ages, in the form of her book, *Children and Movies*. Finally, Edgar Dale conducted an investigation of the movie attendance habits of young people aged between eight and 18 in Columbus, Ohio, during the spring of 1929, the results of which were eventually published in 1935 as *Children's Attendance at Motion Pictures*. Although piecemeal, the data assembled from these studies correlate in several key areas. Firstly, most boys and girls attended movie theatres at least once a week, and often from a very young age. Secondly, as they entered adolescence, it became increasingly common to attend with friends, rather than with families.[8] Thirdly, although expressing preferences for particular forms of entertainment – westerns and comedies for boys, and love stories and comedies for girls – on the whole, pre-teen, adolescent and teenage audiences patronised and enjoyed all kinds of movies.[9] The social experience was as great a lure as the movie programme itself.

Because of the way the balanced movie programme was designed, relatively few silent-era features were family films in the way that they are understood today. The feature films of Charlie Chaplin and Mary Pickford might leap to mind, but comedian Harold Lloyd (whom Richard Koszarski has dubbed 'the Steven Spielberg of silent comedy') and western star Tom Mix were more prolific and popular with children.[10] Whereas slapstick comedy shorts were ideal cross-demographic entertainment, various producers of short films explicitly targeted children, such as Hal Roach, whose *Our Gang* series covered 221 shorts between 1922 and 1944. There were also serials, which were distinguished by cliffhangers designed to draw back young viewers week after week. Many were comic-book adaptations, colourful in tone if not (because of their cheapness) in appearance. Celebrated *New York Times* columnist Andre Sennwald looked back fondly on serials as 'the most sheerly [sic] exciting movies [...] which I recall for their phenomenal ability to conclude each week's instalment on a note of overpowering suspense'.[11]

Serials emerged at a time when working-class patrons dominated movie audiences, and initially, as Raymond William Stedman suggests, they were consumed by children and adults alike.[12] As the composition of audiences changed, children became the main consumers. Because of the popularity of cheap neighbourhood theatres ('nabes') – which often catered predominantly to children – and the constant demand from young audiences throughout the 1920s for such products, this was perhaps the only period in its history when Hollywood produced 'children's films' (as opposed to family films) on a broad scale. The silent movie experience in general was far more sensual and unsophisticated before the transition to sound. Indeed, legendary mogul Adolph Zukor averred in 1926 that the intelligence of the average moviegoer was that of a 14-year-old.[13] Even adult-themed movies, such as crime films and sex comedies, worked chiefly through visual appeal and therefore remained accessible to juvenile audiences.

Demand for thrills 'n' spills-type products created a virtual sub-industry of shorts tailored to the child audience, often series films and serials manufactured by independent producers. Such largely escapist fare failed to meet the approval of moral reformers, who continued to campaign hard for production of specialised, educative and morally-pure children's feature films. In 1922, the Chicago Board of Education determined to find a new breed of educative movie to replace 'the wild West and blood and thunder movies in the affections of the young folks', and were disappointed when their educational test films were poorly received.[14] One influential lobby was the National Juvenile Motion Picture League, a subsidiary of the National Board of Review. The Board of Review had long campaigned for a 'better class' of movie that was both educative and family-suitable, and persistently pointed to the adult-orientated nature of Hollywood's films. It argued that 'there must [...] be recognition of the fact that *most film dramas are made for the consumption of adults*' (my emphasis).[15]

In 1920, *The New York Times* quoted from an open letter addressed to the Hollywood studios from the President of the League, Adele F. Woodard, appealing for more family films:

> Some pictures are made, [Woodard's letter] says, 'but [Hollywood] producers are not alert to the necessity of wholesomeness in every detail. They inject all sorts of civil suggestion, attempting to smother out the evil effect of these details with a moral tacked on at the end or a severe spanking for the offender'. It adds that 'another serious mistake is the inane picture, which children call "goody-good"' and it insists that 'clever, wholesome pictures artistically produced are in demand and will succeed'.[16]

Woodard went on to suggest texts ideally suited for adaptation, such as 'Peter Pan', 'The Ginger Bread Boy' and 'Red Riding Hood'. Producers achieving hits with sex films considered such saccharine fare unappetising commercial propositions. A recurring mantra in 1920s movie discourse was that audiences wanted movies that were 'passionate but pure'.[17] There was a tangible cultural appetite for salaciousness which, although firmly regulated and restricted, was clearly contrary to the long-standing association of Hollywood filmmaking as 'family entertainment'. Indeed, in 1927, the MPPDA estimated that as much as 80 per cent of its total business was subject to censorship, both domestic and international.[18] The industry would continue to supply such films as long as they were supported by the moviegoing public, and troublesome elements could be placated.

Some reformers – especially PTAs, local boards of education and women's clubs – came to realise that the best short-term policy was providing child-friendly alternatives to the standard movie programme, by organising matinees. The first children's matinees emerged during the early 1910s, but were constrained enormously by the basic short-fall in child-orientated films, which was exacerbated by the scrupulous selectivity of matinee organisers. In 1915, Helen Duey, then editor of the *Woman's Home Companion*, argued that a mere 150–200 'photoplays' under general release dating back to the beginnings of commercial cinema were 'suitable and adaptable to the child's mind from entertain-ment, educational, and moral standpoints'.[19] Another difficulty was the lack of industry support. Theatre managers were concerned with the possibility of losing money, and the matinee movement would never have taken off without the sponsorship and persistency of voluntary organisations. Nevertheless, by the mid-1910s, children's matinees had become widely-recognised and relatively organised, with established programmes in such cities as Boston, Louisville, New Orleans, Grand Rapids and New Rochelle. Content differed from region to region, but 'educational' films were a vital component. Most educational films were adapted from commercially-released movies, while some were made-to-order.[20] Having failed in their repeated attempts to stimulate production of family films, the Board of Review also tried to establish nationwide 'family nights' and children's matinees. The Board did not envisage that such programmes would be financially self-sufficient, but suggested – rather optimistically – that local communities could subsidise exhibitors in order to cover expenses.[21] As such, these matinees were viewed as a public service, rather than a commercial enterprise. The Board main-tained that a 'well-considered system of education of parents to develop a public sentiment both for finer family pictures and for selected pictures for young people must be carried on'.[22] Although supposedly supported by the industry, the initiative did not catch on with the general public.

Between 1925 and 1926, however, the MPPDA put its considerable weight behind a nationwide programme of children's matinees. Launched by the MPPDA's Committee for Public Relations, the venture was moti-vated not only by PR, but also by profit. As Richard deCordova explains:

> During 1924 and 1925, the committee completed a survey of the films in the vaults of the MPPDA's member companies. They identified those films that were suitable for children to view and constructed a series of 36 programs for special matinees. By the fall of 1925, 52

programs were available to any organisation or theatre – a full year's supply of movies for weekly matinees. Each program consisted of a feature film, a two-reel comedy, and what was referred to as a semi-educational short, usually a scenic or industrial film.[23]

As had been the case with the earlier, locally-run matinee programmes of the 1910s, these films were substantially cut and sometimes re-titled 'to make them appropriate for a child's psychological needs'.[24] In part, these cuts were designed to truncate the films in accordance with the shorter attention span of children. By late 1925, weekly MPPDA-sponsored matinees were playing in 30 major US cities, with plans for expansion in smaller localities.[25] The major obstacle, however, was the lack of sufficient children's fare to support the programme, and organisers were forced to rely on films 'that had long since had their first run...[and] were usually in poor condition'.[26] This lack of suitable programme material perhaps explains why the project was abandoned only one year into a projected three-year run. Nevertheless, these industry-approved matinees succeeded temporarily in appeasing critics. The plan also served to reassert traditional distinctions between the child and adult in a period where a 'levelling' of movie content suitability was being widely and vociferously mooted.

The Emergence of the Specialised Family Feature Film

Writing many years later in his memoirs, Will Hays looked back on the late 1920s with fondness, as a time when

> the American motion picture industry [was] happily absorbed in its world mission of entertainment and mass education. Its films, though silent, were full of action, humour, appeal. Then came the world-shaking discovery: motion pictures could also speak.[27]

The transition to sound, which occurred on a wide scale in the USA in 1929, was a watermark not only in the broader history of Hollywood cinema, but also in the development of specialised family films. Had movies remained silent, Hollywood would never have come under such intense pressure to reform. As it was, the MPPDA was cognisant that the transition to sound would upset the uneasy alliance with movie reformers, and this prompted

Hays to organise and address a National Conference on Motion Pictures, which was held in New York in September 1929. The forum was attended by dozens of religious, educational and community organisations from around the country. A similar conference had taken place shortly after the MPPDA's formation in 1922. In both instances, the 'party line' was that Hollywood was essentially a benevolent and respectable cultural institution, and although the odd undesirable movie slipped through the net, progress was continually being made towards universal audience suitability. Hays insisted that the industry had largely succeeded in 'improving the quality of supply', and that it was up to community workers to 'improve the quality of demand'.

To this end, one of the most significant products of this conference was the MPPDA's sponsorship and distribution of *The Neighborhood and its Motion Pictures: A Manual for the Community Worker Interested in the Best Motion Pictures for the Family* – a handbook with contributions from, amongst others, the World Federation of Education Associates, The General Federation of Women's Clubs, The International Federation of Catholic Alumnae, and several Better Films committees under the auspices of the National Board of Review. Arguing that 'the training of our people for wholesome recreation and intellectually profitable entertainment is a matter of tremendous importance', the publication outlined how community organisations and individuals could successfully solicit the cooperation of local exhibitors for the establishment of children's matinees and 'family nights'.[28] Readers were advised to give feedback to exhibitors with such comments as 'I liked the picture today. It is the sort my family approves', and encouraged to pass lists of approved films to theatre managers.[29] Hays told the MPPDA in 1932 that 'inviting the public into consultative partnership' in this way solved 'the ever present dilemma of how to maintain adequate adult entertainment and at the same time give due weight and response to the entertainment needs of the child'.[30]

However, the days in which the MPPDA could appease critics through good public relations in the face of blatantly salacious movies were finally over. Talkies were seen as far more potentially damaging than silent films. Pre-emptively, the MPPDA introduced the Production Code in April 1930. Written by two prominent Catholics, it was designed to placate potential enemies by restricting certain 'adult' content, notably depictions of violence, sexuality, profanity, obscenity, vulgarity and other 'repellent subjects', whilst upholding the sanctity of the law, religion, family and national honour. In a speech announcing the Code, Hays affirmed that:

> The Motion Picture, as developed for the primary purposes of the theatre, is a universal system of entertainment. Its appeal has broken through all barriers of class distinction. It is patronised by the poor man, the rich man, the old and the young. It is a messenger of democracy, and the motion picture industry is sensible of the great public responsibility.[31]

Whilst the Code was considerably more restrictive than previous, half-hearted attempts at self-regulation, contemporary reaction was sceptical. As trade writer P. S. Harrison noted: 'some of the papers have attacked the producers and Mr. Hays; some have ridiculed them. But not one of the worthwhile papers has taken them seriously'.[32] Many guessed the truth: that the Code was brought in not to reform the industry, but rather to protect it from pressures exerted by 'women's clubs' and 'ministers', who possessed

> the power in many communities to hurt the motion picture business. It is this fact, rather than any love of virtue for its own sake, which has inspired [Hays] to assemble in one code all the known counsels of perfection.[33]

Without any real mechanism of enforcement, this voluntary Code paled into insignificance when faced with the promise of the box office.

The majority of the major movie cycles in the immediate aftermath of the transition to sound – 'trial films, musicals, society dramas, social realist, then gangster films' – were predominantly adult-orientated.[34] Talkies were a remarkable novelty during 1930 and 1931, and there was a brief but significant spike in attendances before receipts settled back roughly to their pre-sound levels. Nevertheless, there was widespread concern among critics, reformers and even some producers that this swing towards adult-orientated entertainment would alienate and ulti-mately drive away juvenile audiences. For a time during the early 1930s, trade paper the *Exhibitors' Herald-World* published a regular feature, written by exhibitors, offering advice to their peers on ways to attract children back to the theatres. In November 1930, C. Graham Barker, associate executive at First National studios, advised that the industry 'cannot afford to let the adolescent taste divorce the motion picture from its list of preferences, and there are a hundred other interests to engage them'.[35] By this point, Paramount's head of production, Ben Schulberg, no doubt mindful of the public-relations as well as box office value of plugging this production shortfall, had already announced his intention to pursue the 'kiddie' audience. Schulberg – later described appreciatively in Hays's memoirs as a 'code co-operator' – was a long-term friend and ally of the MPPDA head, who, no doubt, brought whatever influence he could muster to bear on the issue.[36]

Nevertheless, there was enough advance publicity and anticipation surrounding the release of *Tom Sawyer* (John Cromwell, 1930) to suggest that this production strategy might pay considerable dividends. Paramount previewed the film heavily in the trade press prior to release. A cover-page advert placed in the *Exhibitors' Herald-World* announced: 'You yelled for a great big picture that would bring the kids back – Here it is! "Tom Sawyer" – BOOK IT! GET BEHIND IT! CLEAN UP WITH IT!'[37] Another ad described the film as 'A fine, big, clean motion picture without a divorce, speakeasy or gangster', exhorting exhibitors to book the film 'For the good of your pocketbook...for the reclaiming of your juvenile patronage...for the glory of the picture business' and thus 'Be happier than you've been for years!'.[38] A more restrained advert in *Photoplay*, meanwhile, proclaimed the film 'Fun for everyone from 6 to 60!', whilst stressing the charm and acting ability of its young leads: Jackie Coogan, Mitzi Green and Junior Durkin.[39] The reviews were similarly positive, with the New York *Mirror* affirming it as 'a wow for children and a honey for anybody', whilst the *Herald-Tribune* thought it 'a tribute to everyone concerned, including the picture industry'.[40] However, probably the most rapturous review *Tom Sawyer* received was in the highly influential fan magazine *Photoplay*:

> Come on, kids – from five to eighty-five! Let's go to the pitcher show! For three years the country's youngsters have been missing many of the delights of the movies. The talkies, with their stage conventions and their lack of action, have almost lost the greatest audience of film fans. Now Paramount fires one of the first guns in the battle to bring back the happy boys and girls of old. Gun? It's a barrage!
>
> This great Mark Twain yarn has been brilliantly done. Made into a whirlwind of real entertainment for everybody.[41]

Comedy producer Larry Darmour regarded *Tom Sawyer* as 'the first big production made for youth' and felt that it had outdistanced 'any silent ever made for juveniles'.[42] Judged by these lofty criteria, the film's rather modest pleasures are rather beside the point; it was a solid box office hit. Paramount's follow-up, *Skippy* (Norman Taurog, 1931), received similarly warm reviews and, in a measure of industry approval, garnered a Best Director Oscar for Taurog, and a Best Picture nomination. During the summer of 1931, Loew's – MGM's parent company and, alongside Paramount Publix, one of the largest theatre chains – were aiming for a piece of the action by organising 'vacation shows' (essentially matinees) for schoolchildren, in partnership with parent-teacher groups.[43] Even more notably, the children's adventure serial – which for many years was restricted to nabes and second-run houses – returned to the prestigious picture palaces in late 1930 and early 1931.[44] It seemed that the Hollywood establishment – producers and exhibitors alike – were finally realising the age-old propaganda testifying to North American commercial cinema's universal, democratic, 'family' identities.

This illusion did not last long. The publicity surrounding Paramount's programme of 'kiddie' films failed to distract reformers from the fact that adult-themed films were still dominating production schedules. Furthermore, none of the other major studios had shown any inclination towards abandoning production of adult movies – least of all Warner Bros., which, with such gangster films as *Little Caesar* (Mervyn LeRoy, 1931), was rapidly cultivating a reputation as a purveyor of adult entertainment. Martin Quigley, publisher of the *Motion Picture Herald* and co-writer of the 1930 Production Code, had this to say on the subject in April 1931:

> A principal factor in what's wrong with the motion picture business at this time is an unfortunate choice of story material.
>
> Much of the product which recently has issued from the Hollywood studios is plainly and uncompromisingly adult entertainment. We are quite aware that it is not the business of Hollywood to confine itself to juvenile entertainment, nor to gauge its product to appeal exclusively to 12-year-old intellects.
>
> Rather, it is the business of Hollywood to make product for the motion picture theatres. And that it certainly is not doing when it pulls out a succession of pictures such as 'Millie', 'Strangers May Kiss', 'Illicit', 'Stolen Heaven' and 'A Lady Refuses'.[45]

The MPPDA's public relations drive received a further setback in late 1931, when *Variety* reported that 'kid pictures' were 'practically washed up' as a result of the disappointing box office performances of Paramount's summer releases, *Skippy* and *Huckleberry Finn* (Norman Taurog, 1931).[46] The theatre circuit was apparently disappointed by the levels of adult patronage, believing that these films had lacked the sort of mature appeal that had made MGM's *The Champ* (King Vidor, 1931) a sizable hit.[47] Consequently, *Sooky* (Norman Taurog, 1931) was Paramount's final 'kiddie' release, and the last significant production purposely aimed at juvenile audiences for some time.

Until the early 1930s, as suggested above, Hollywood's supposed commitment to 'family entertainment' was represented largely through the 'balanced programme', which offered a range of attractions designed to appeal collectively to all audience sections. Indeed, Hays once remarked:

> Not only the cornerstone but the foundation of the success of the American motion picture enterprise may be summed up in the phrase, 'one program for one audience'. Here, pictures are not rated for showing to children or adults, theatres are not graded and films are not made for different classifications of audiences.[48]

However, for a variety of reasons, during the early 1930s, the balanced programme was superseded in many theatres by alternative modes of exhibition, further eroding Hollywood's claim as a 'family' institution. One of the major catalysts for changes in the exhibition sector was the Great Depression. Until 1931, cinema's centrality to the North American way of life had insulated it from the effects of the Depression. The first signs of economic downturn were attributed by some to the artistic restrictions of the Production Code, but by the following year, theatre attendances were down massively, and the scale of the losses bankrupted several of the major studios, which were saved only through Wall Street investment.[49] Desperate for films that would make a healthy profit, producers relied increasingly on populist and often salacious genres, such as sex comedies and gangster films. In September 1932, Joy and Hays found that 24 out of the 111 films in production dealt with 'illicit sexual relations'.[50] Exhibitors pursued any means at their disposal to attract audiences, and one of their most popular innovations was the double feature. The premise of the double feature was simple: instead of a varied programme of shorts, animations and one main feature, two feature-length films were shown back-to-back. Whilst the second film was often inferior action-adventure fare (which, ironically, proved popular with juvenile audiences), the rise of the double feature came partially at the expense of the short film, which had long been widely construed as ideal children's entertainment.

By 1932, films possessing specific 'family' appeal were scarcer than ever. Universal made an abortive attempt to lure children and their parents to the theatre with *Destry Rides Again* (Benjamin Stoloff, 1932), the first talking picture to feature silent-era cowboy star Tom Mix, while Mary Pickford insisted that the public was tired of sex and gangster films, and spoke of her desire to star in a Walt Disney-produced animated version of *Alice in Wonderland* or *Peter Pan*.[51] In general, however, the consensus among producers and exhibitors appeared to be that the 'kiddie' film cycle had been a failure. Critics and reformers, on the other hand, continued lobbying hard for the industry-wide production of specialised 'family' films capable of appealing equally to adults and children. Trade papers such as *Boxoffice* explicitly supported this drive. In 1932, Ben Shylen, owner and editor of *Boxoffice*, established the Blue Ribbon award for 'The Best Picture of the Month for the Whole Family', as voted by the members of the National Screen Council, a nationwide body created and sponsored by *Boxoffice* itself to assess the merits of all theatrical releases, both for artistry and family suitability. The National Screen Council was said to comprise hundreds of individuals from the fields of exhibition, journalism, broadcasting, and civic, educational and religious organisations. When announcing the initiative, Shylen argued that:

> For nearly two years any picture, however poor, which presented the miracle of sound and talk, drew the public like flies are drawn to a bigger and better puddle of spilled molasses. Within the last year, however, theatre patrons have resumed their discriminating attitude. They demand GOOD pictures. And, as before the deluge of sound and talk, they are demanding a larger proportion of good pictures containing a powerful appeal to the WHOLE FAMILY.[52]

The monthly Blue Ribbon award winner was afforded a full page of what amounted to free advertising, as its artistic, moral and educational virtues were extolled alongside a plot synopsis, cast list and promotional photograph of the chosen film. It is a measure of the esteem with which the Blue Ribbon award was held that for many years, a still from the winning film was included on the front cover, accompanied by the symbol of the ribbon. Extraordinarily, the Blue Ribbon scheme lasted until 1979.

The actual impact of such initiatives in the long term is hard to gauge, but in the short-term, at least, any perceptible benefit was negligible. Rather embarrassingly, for Hays, Alice Ames Winter – an MPPDA representative of various women's clubs personally appointed by Hays in 1929 – sent a report in May 1933 to various civic organisations advising that the majority of current Hollywood releases were unsuitable for family patronage.[53] After the many public promises he had made regarding Hollywood's maturation to respectability, Hays was no doubt mindful that its current trajectory did not reflect particularly well on him. At an MPPDA crisis meeting in March 1933, he informed the studio heads that he would no longer tolerate Code violations, and threatened to instigate litigation personally against offending studios unless the situation improved.[54] Inevitably, perhaps, the seeds of change were sown not from within the industry, but by an increasingly organised external array of lobbies and pressure groups.

The Catholic Legion of Decency, the most powerful and vociferous voice in the battle for movie reform, was formed the same year. It was founded for the express purpose of reforming commercial cinema. Reformers were given ammunition by the Payne Fund Studies, a comprehensive series of sociological and theoretical works published between 1933 and 1935, and organised by the Motion Picture Research Council. The head of the Council, the Reverend William Short, was an activist who was convinced that movies were socially damaging. He secured funding for these studies from the Payne Fund, a private foundation concerned about the educative implications of commercial cinema. The studies themselves were written by professional social scientists, but the enterprise was undermined by its implicit hostility towards the medium. This was exemplified by Henry Forman's *Our Movie Made Children* (1933), a publication intended to summarise the findings of the various reports, but which reduced these serious studies to the level of crude, anti-movie moralising.[55] While the publication may not have accurately reflected public feeling towards adult-orientated movies, its populist message acted as a call-to-arms for advocates of reform.

Matters reached a head in early 1934. The Catholic Church threatened a nationwide boycott of the cinema from its 20 million members unless effective self-regulation was established, with Jewish and Protestant leaders backing the campaign.[56] Although some executives questioned public support for the so-called 'Pollyanna Pictures' regulation apparently portended, the industry was forced to bow to overwhelming pressure, and the Studio Relations Committee under Joy was reconstituted in July 1934 as the Production Code Administration (PCA) under Catholic Joseph I. Breen.[57] Breen argued upon his appointment that:

> If the screen doesn't clean itself up [...] three things will happen: theatres will be boycotted, Federal censorship will be instituted, and every State and city with depleted revenues will establish censor boards for the taxes that will result. If we clean up there is little to worry about, but if we don't we might just as well forget Hollywood.[58]

Breen had the power to enforce changes on any film falling foul of the Production Code, with a $25,000 penalty for non-compliance.[59] Thereafter, the Hollywood studios usually ensured that their films met the strict standards demanded by the PCA.

With the introduction of the Production Code, Hollywood no longer had an obvious mass audience for the cleaned-up fare now being demanded. Its response, as Richard Maltby has argued, was to 'discover a "new" audience who had previously not attended'.[60] Hitherto, industry leaders had tended to publicly propagate the notion that North American cinema audiences were simultaneously pluralistic and monolithic; that people of all ages and backgrounds attended the movies, but were symbolically unified by their shared enjoyment as part of the cinematic experience. Although the idea of Hollywood cinema as a 'family entertainment' had always been challenged by reformers, the backlash against the overtly adult-orientated films of the early 1930s forced the industry to reconstitute the concept of the 'family audience' as a previously-dormant but vast contingent that was now, finally, being given its due. The idea of the family audience, and the formulation of an all-inclusive type of popular film, represented a concerted effort on the part of the MPPDA – on behalf of the entire industry – to reconfigure the status of commercial cinema within the US cultural consciousness.

Although the Production Code (and the pressures which led to its tightening) was a major factor in Hollywood's embrace of family-orientated fare, it was only one of a number of catalysts. Also important was North

America's embrace of 'middlebrow' culture in the late 1920s and early 1930s, as Joan Shelley Rubin argues:

> In the three decades following the First World War, America created an unprecedented range of activities aimed at making literature and other forms of 'high' culture available to a wide reading public. Beginning with the Book-of-the-Month club, founded in 1926, book clubs provided subscribers with recently published works chosen by expert judges [...] Colleges and universities, accommodating an expanding student body, augmented their curricula with extension programs in the humanities and other disciplines, some offered on the new medium of radio.[61]

There were also internal pressures upon producers, mainly from the MPPDA, but also from such influential figures as market researcher George Gallup (whose Audience Research Institute was employed by RKO and Disney during the 1930s and 1940s), who pointed out that literary adaptations had a built-in audience because of the popularity of the adapted material.[62] Hays had campaigned for greater production of a more middle-class, universally-suitable product since the mid-1920s.

The third major factor in the Hollywood studios' strategic embrace of the family movie was more directly commercial. During the late 1920s and early 1930s, a series of educational reforms were implemented by the National Education Association and the National Council of Teachers of English, which introduced new elements to high school syllabuses based upon 'critical appreciation' of motion pictures.[63] Soon after the initiative began in 1928 in Newark, New Jersey, educators approached Hollywood executives to solicit the specialised production of child-friendly, educational films, but producers were unresponsive, allegedly insisting 'that the label "educational" would spell "failure" at the box office'.[64] The tide changed dramatically in 1933, when, after a successful trial period, representative teachers from 17 states voted in favour of new curriculum units featuring film study, and consequently educational study of the movies was rolled out in approximately 2,500 schools nationally.[65] Every week, students would watch a Hollywood feature film and write a 600-word piece of criticism in response. Not only was this expected to have an immediate impact on the box office, but 'the shaping into critical formation of adolescent minds' was seen as 'having important bearing on future production policies'.[66] Educationalists and producers suddenly found that cooperation was a matter of mutual self-interest. Teachers wanted 'better films' for pedagogical, moral and artistic reasons, and the major studios were the only credible supplier. Producers, meanwhile, suddenly had easy access to a vast, unexploited audience group. The result was a dramatic upsurge in productions of literary classics easily adaptable for the classroom, which in turn prompted the wider integration of family movies into Hollywood production schedules.

Little Women, released in November 1933, was the breakthrough film. Many of its attributes – the historical setting, the focus on the family, the coming-of-age narrative, the atmosphere of gentility and the particular appeal for women – set a successful template for subsequent family-friendly literary adaptations, and, indeed, for family films throughout the studio era. Unlike Paramount's earlier roster of 'kiddie' films, *Little Women* was clearly directed predominantly at adults. Indeed, one of the most important assumptions underpinning the selection of styles and stories for family films henceforth was that wives and mothers represented their families. Although various trade papers estimated that females comprised

Little Women (1933)

between 60 and 80 per cent of the domestic cinema audience, the telling statistic, as Melvyn Stokes suggests, was that housewives 'made 80 to 90 per cent of all purchases for family use'.[67] Rightly or wrongly, women were seen as driving the family's leisure activities. *Little Women*'s emphasis upon family values and unity in a time of social fragmentation – in this case, the US Civil War – neatly parallels social anxieties surrounding the country's future during the Depression. It was the fourth most successful movie of the decade at the US box office.[68] In March 1934, Hays spoke of his belief that moral and artistic standards were continually improving, praising the efforts of better-film movements in their mission to raise artistic standards. He quantified this belief by noting that, in 1933,

> seventy-two pictures were endorsed by previewing groups as suitable for children between the ages of 8 and 12 years, as against the endorsement of fifty-one such pictures for the year 1932.[69]

These 'improving' standards, Hays ventured, could lead to 'an era of literary films' – although he was quick to add that 'intelligent movies [...] need intelligent audiences' – a coded warning that such films would endure for only so long as they remained profitable.[70] Hays did, however, understand their uses as propaganda. The genre was designed to attract mass audiences and rehabilitate the cultural reputation of the movies in one fell swoop.

Literary Adaptations and the Family Film Strategy

Although prestige literary adaptations were becoming prevalent by the time *Little Women* was released, its popularity confirmed in the minds of producers their immense commercial potential. It was, as Tino Balio notes, 'considered the first picture of the decade based on a literary classic to be turned into an artistic and commercial success', and he places the literary adaption within the broader cycle of the 'prestige picture', which was 'far and away the most popular production trend of the decade'.[71] Hays hoped that it 'may open a new type of source material' capable of galvanising 'a new movie-going public recruited from the higher income earning classes [...] which better pictures would transform from casual to regular patrons'.[72]

Because of their prominence in classrooms, public libraries and private bookshelves, literary classics seemed to producers and reformers to be the epitome of 'family' material. Although novels and plays by the likes of William Shakespeare, Charles Dickens, Jane Austen, Charlotte Brontë, Louisa May Alcott and Robert Louis Stevenson may not have been widely consumed, at least by the common man, they were almost universally known. Between 1933 and 1940, many literary classics were brought to the screen, including *Little Women*, *Treasure Island* (Victor Fleming, 1934), *Great Expectations* (Stuart Walker, 1934), *David Copperfield* (George Cukor, 1935), *A Midsummer Night's Dream* (Max Reinhardt and William Dieterle, 1935), *Little Lord Fauntleroy* (John Cromwell, 1936), *Romeo and Juliet* (George Cukor, 1936), *Poor Little Rich Girl* (Irving Cummings, 1936), *Captains Courageous* (Victor Fleming, 1937), *The Prisoner of Zenda* (John Cromwell, 1937), *The Adventures of Tom Sawyer* (Norman Taurog, 1938), *The Little Princess* (Walter Lang, 1939), *The Wizard of Oz* (Victor Fleming, 1939) and *The Blue Bird* (Walter Lang, 1940). All of the major studios, except Paramount, produced these family-friendly literary adaptations, which were respectable and inoffensive; the kinds of canonical texts appointed to school syllabuses and regarded as material children *ought* to be consuming, but which were mainly enjoyed by the adult middle classes. Indeed, these family-friendly literary adaptations succeeded, in the main, because they were explicitly marketed towards parents. The child was rarely viewed as an autonomous consumer; the implication was that children went to see the films that their parents selected for them. In a good deal of cases, this was no doubt true, since many children even attending alone would require the financial support of parents. On the other hand, many children apparently made their own entertainment choices. Nonetheless, several family films from this period were previewed to parent-teacher groups in the hope of soliciting support, while family film trade ads explicitly addressed parents, exhorting them to send their children, and, if possible, come along themselves.

1935 saw the release of two of the most significant family-orientated literary adaptations of the decade: independent producer David Selznick's adaptation of *David Copperfield*, and Warner Bros.' adaptation of *A Midsummer Night's Dream*. Not only were they lavish, star-studded productions, but they were among the most faithful adaptations of literary classics ever brought to the screen. The key to successful literary adaptations, according to Selznick (who later produced *Gone with the Wind*), was ensuring that deviations from the source material were nothing more than omissions; *changes* to plot and character, he suggested, ran the risk of alienating audiences familiar with the original texts.[73] The producers, though, ensured that all bases were covered by making these adaptations attractive to general audiences.

Aside from polished production, the main weapons in this endeavour were big stars. *A Midsummer Night's Dream* featured popular Warner Bros. contractors such as James Cagney, Dick Powell and Joe E. Brown, all of whom made their name in overtly populist genres such as gangster movies, light comedies and musicals. Selznick pulled off a significant coup by casting comedian W. C. Fields as Micawber in *David Copperfield*; it mattered little that Fields had to clumsily read his dialogue from cue cards placed just off camera – his presence alone guaranteed box office value. Both films introduced up-and-coming child actors – namely Mickey Rooney as Puck, and Freddie Bartholomew as young David Copperfield – thereby offering some level of identification for younger viewers. Such was *A Midsummer Night's Dream*'s public-relations value that *Variety* suggested that Warner's would not have been perturbed with a $500,000 loss on the venture.[74] As it was, both films were enormous box office hits.[75]

Most contemporary reviewers tended to agree with Hays's claim that such films appealed to 'the highest common denominator of public taste'.[76] What few reviews acknowledged was that the majority of Hollywood literary adaptations released during this period were essentially cleaned-up films for adults, rather than amusements carefully constructed for the dual enjoyment of adults and children. Film reviews in the mainstream press – especially that bastion of the middlebrow, *The New York Times* – often validated the MPPDA propaganda by implying that through sheer, unequivocal excellence, productions such as *Little Women* or *David Copperfield* managed to efface divisions in age, class, race, gender and even taste. Conversely, the reviews in trade publications, such as *Variety*, the *Motion Picture Herald* and *Boxoffice* – which were written to assist exhibitors in making bookings – tended to assess movies more in terms of projected audience response. For instance, although the *Motion Picture Herald* thought *Little Women* to be 'clean, sweet and beautiful all the way through to the point of being ideal', it acknowledged its particular suitability for women and conceded that:

> The handicap, if there is one, is whether the show will appeal to the hey-hey modernes – the 18 to 25 year old gang which seems to be yelling for something snappy, spectacular and jolting in all its entertainments. There is no modernism in 'Little Women'. There are no sock-in-the-jaw smashes to knock 'em out of their seats.[77]

Similarly, *Variety*'s review of *Alice in Wonderland* (Norman Z. McLeod, 1933) pointed out that 'like most of the other supposed children's classics, "Alice" is really a distinctly grown-up book. Juvenile patronage probably won't be the choice of the kids themselves, but possibly under grown-up duress'.[78]

Many other specialist journals and popular magazines looked beyond the propaganda of 'universal entertainment' and sought to inform readers about playability for different audiences, as well as moral suitability. Several trade papers, such as *Boxoffice* and *Harrison's Reports*, and various general interest publications, including *Parents' Magazine*, *The Rotarian* and *Christian Century*, offered a suitability rating with each review. *Boxoffice* arranged films into 'A' (adult), 'F' (family) or 'J' (juvenile) – although in practice the 'J' rating was never used – whereas *Parents' Magazine* divided films between 'adults', 'youths' and 'children'. In the absence of any formal system of assessment, such judgements were arbitrary; Harrison, for instance, ludicrously viewed *Little Big Shot* (Michael Curtiz, 1935) – a Warner Bros. child-star vehicle starring Sybil Jason – as 'unsuitable for children [or] adolescents'.[79] Nevertheless, it is significant that none of these publications accepted that even cleaned-up Hollywood fare was automatically suitable for juvenile consumption, or, indeed, appealing to their various tastes. Indeed, *Parents' Magazine*, which contained a special section called 'Family Movie Guide', argued forcefully that 'children under eight years of age should not be permitted to attend regular motion picture performances'.[80]

Nevertheless, Hollywood's survival during this period depended greatly on its ultimately successful attempts to prove that it had matured as a respectable, socially-aware 'family' institution. Hays was determined to legitimise commercial cinema by proving that movies possessed pedagogical value. The extensive programme of 'study guides' which accompanied many of the family-orientated literary adaptations of the mid-1930s served to facilitate the easy integration of these films into the classroom. These guides were designed to foster students' 'critical appreciation' and were distributed in schools nationwide, based on films such as *Little Women, David Copperfield, Alice in Wonderland, Treasure Island, A Midsummer Night's Dream* and *Little Lord Fauntleroy*.[81] As Richard Ford explains:

> The average guide (they are called 'Photoplay Studies' or 'Group Discussion Guides') is an illustrated booklet of 16 pages. It deals with the story, historical or literary background, and film treatment of the theme; it includes a number of questions for discussion, and suggestions of books for reading. Bought in quantities the Guides cost three cents each.[82]

Initially, the studios sponsored these guides.[83] Later, the industry maintained its support by providing schools with film posters, stills, pressbooks and free movie tickets for 'underprivileged children'.[84] Hays later claimed that 'no single project in our program did more to raise a generation of discriminating fans' than study guides.[85] Some were enormously profitable: the *David Copperfield* guide sold around 200,000 copies, and *A Midsummer Night's Dream*'s apparently as many as 500,000.[86] During the mid-1930s, then, motion pictures possessed a pedagogical dimension to an extent never seen before or since, although economic interests were also well served by the venture.

For the teachers, higher movie standards were part of a broader educational drive. Educationalists seemed to regard Hollywood as a necessary evil. William Lewin – a representative of the motion picture committee of the National Education Association and author of the new curriculum – suggested that:

> Through the classrooms of the high schools, where during the school year 6,000,000 adolescents are daily in session, the present drive is securing changes looking toward a finer type of audience in the coming generation. Before we can have an era of great photoplays we must have great audiences, and to develop them is the task of the schools.[87]

By late 1935, according to Lewin, producers were spending 'six times as much as they did two years ago on films likely to be of interest to teachers and students. Included are some of the most costly pictures of the coming season'.[88] Lewin also pointed to a recent survey indicating that 'all the studios, major and minor, recognise that there is an effective demand for films worthy of classroom discussion'.[89] It was still an uneasy compromise: studios were unable to sacrifice profitability for the sake of fidelity, but educationalists demanded that adaptations preserve at least the 'essence' of the original texts.

Fortunately for Hollywood, the Legion of Decency was more than satisfied with the changes imposed by Breen's Production Code Administration. Father Donnelly, associate editor of *America* (then the leading Catholic weekly), agreed in October 1935 that 'the producers have lived up to their promises with admirable fidelity' and had 'shown a splendid spirit of cooperation'.[90] Mrs. James F. Looram, chairman of the International Federation of Catholic Alumnae's Motion Picture Bureau, concurred, observing that:

> Motion pictures have improved not only morally but dramatically and culturally as well, and this higher type of picture has attracted a new audience which, in the past, has considered screen entertainment below the standard of literature and the legitimate drama.[91]

Furthermore, despite initial resistance from producers to the prospect of 'Pollyanna Pictures' and 'sweetness-and-light films' – macho expressions of distaste for sentimentality and juvenility from a predominantly patriarchal institution – there was widespread industry support for family films once their box office value became apparent.[92] In April 1935, *Boxoffice* editor Ben Shylen observed:

> Gone forever is the day when selection of a 'family' film was narrowed to the 'westerns and homespuns'.
>
> It is ushered into oblivion by producer awareness that ultimate success depends not alone on sophisticated patronage. This realisation of the monetary importance of the by-and-large attendance of the great American Family is building to a renaissance of the motion picture.
>
> The motion picture flowered and grew as entertainment for the masses. And who are the masses but Mr. and Mrs. America – and their children? [...] Fear recently gripped Hollywood that pictures could not be entertaining if they were sophisticated and 'smart'; if their dialogue did not crackle with double entendre; that pictures

combining adult and juvenile appeal would please neither and consequently end their careers in the 'flop' list. That fear has abated. Hollywood studios are turning out the finest product in the history of motion pictures. Producers have learned how to make pictures that entertain without offending good taste.[93]

For the most part, the popular press – which had, after all, given impetus to the Legion's crusade through the sheer intensity of coverage in the months before the formalisation of the Production Code – also expressed its approval. However, not all media reaction was positive. Some prominent critics, most notably Andre Sennwald, were concerned with artistic standards. Noting that 'it is the ironic misfortune of the screen that its universal popularity as an entertainment medium is its undoing', Sennwald conceded that 'even the finest of the films manufactured in the Hollywood studios are occasionally too adult for the contemplation of children'.[94] Yet he insisted that a better system of screen regulation was needed to prevent the cinema being 'scaled down to the lowest common denominator both of taste and intelligence'.[95] Sennwald was ahead of his time; it was soon apparent that despite a general 'levelling' in suitability, which saw suggestive sex and violence largely eliminated, films remained thematically tailored to adult audiences. However, few critics cared whether films were *entertaining* children; as long as they were not corrupting, the Production Code was doing its work.

By maintaining close ties with educative and religious groups such as the National Education Association and the Legion of Decency, the Public Relations department of the MPPDA worked to embed the concept of the 'family audience' within the popular consciousness. Between 1934 and 1938, the MPPDA published a monthly 'newspaper' called *The Motion Picture and the Family* for free distribution in theatre lobbies. Marketed as 'a bulletin for all who are interested in better motion pictures', it featured contributions from teachers, educators and 'community leaders'. Aside from constituting another useful PR exercise on the part of the film industry, this was yet another attempt to keep potential enemies close at hand. In his end-of-year report for the 1934 season, Hays congratulated the industry for a job well done, and promised more of the same. Pointing to the success of the newly-established Production Code, Hays noted:

We are more than satisfied with results attained during our period of self-regulation. Theatre attendance has increased approximately 20 per cent throughout the country. Our analysis shows that this increase is due to three elements – old patrons going to the theatre more often, the winning of a new audience that had stayed away from pictures in the past, and improved general conditions.[96]

The family-friendly literary adaptation's true value was in redefining the relationship between Hollywood and its audiences. The limited evidence we have at our disposal suggests that it was less effective in changing actual viewing habits. As a spectacular adventure-horror film, *King Kong* (Merian C. Cooper and Ernest B. Schoedsack, 1933) was always likely to be a strong draw for children and teenagers (especially boys), but apparently many adult female patrons found it 'too horrible'.[97] Similarly, Universal's cycle of early 1930s horror films exerted a strong appeal to these demographics, despite their supposed unsuitability on the grounds

King Kong (1933)

of frightening content. One baffled theatre owner said of *The Bride of Frankenstein* (James Whale, 1935):

> I advertised it as a picture not suitable for children and explained it to them when they bought tickets. Many parents even sent written permission for the youngsters to see it alone, so I give up. Why do they holler for family pictures?[98]

The obvious practical obstacle to mainstream family films during this period is that they attempted to construct a unified audience from a diverse, pluralistic moviegoing public. A large percentage of children, in all probability, had as little interest in *Little Women* or *David Copperfield* as the majority of wives and mothers had in *King Kong*. Then again, the main targets of this 'family' drive were religious leaders, women's groups and educators; not children. What the movement *did* accomplish was embedding the idea of the 'family film' tightly within the national consciousness, protecting Hollywood from the threat of censorship, and establishing a public tide of goodwill towards the industry.

The Child-Star Film

Over the next couple of years, there was a progressive increase in the quantity of films abiding by the moral prescriptions laid out by the Production Code. In 1935, approximately 80 per cent of Hollywood feature films were rated 'Family' by *Boxoffice*; this figure increased to 90 per cent in 1936, and to 96 per cent by 1937.[99] Although the popularity of the afore-mentioned literary adaptations undoubtedly kick-started this trend, the growing proportion of family-suitable films also reflected the emergence of additional family film cycles, most notably the child-star vehicle. The child-star film ran concurrently with the family-friendly literary adaptation, becoming big business in 1934 and remaining so until around 1938. Unlike the literary adaption movement, it stemmed not from careful planning and cooperation, but as a rapid response to social affairs – in this case, the Great Depression. Prefaced by the Wall Street Crash of 1929, the Depression damaged the film industry considerably in the short term, but it also galvanised the North American public and further cemented family movies within the popular consciousness. Whilst child-stars such as Mary Pickford and Jackie Coogan enjoyed celebrity status during the silent era, the unprecedented popularity of Shirley Temple transformed the format for the 1930s. Just as Disney's features during the 1950s, and the *Harry Potter* franchise at the time of writing, seem to epitomise the Hollywood family film in their respective eras, so Shirley Temple has become fixed in the popular consciousness – for better or worse – as the poster girl of 1930s family entertainment.

After she rose to prominence in *Bright Eyes* (David Butler, 1934) at the age of six and captured the public imagination, several major studios attempted to cash-in on Temple's popularity by signing promising child performers and by placing them within specialised vehicles designed to showcase their particular talents (whether singing, dancing, precocious cuteness or capacity for mischief). During the mid-to-late 1930s, MGM had Jackie Cooper, Judy Garland, Mickey Rooney and Freddie Bartholomew under contract; Twentieth Century Fox contracted Shirley Temple and Jane Withers; Warner Bros. contracted Billy and Bobby Mauch, Sybil Jason and Bonita Granville; Columbia contracted Edith Fellows; and Universal contracted Deanna Durbin. Although various child actors were under contract to Paramount and RKO during the 1930s (such as Jackie Searle and Virginia Weidler), neither studio embraced the child-star vehicle. Nevertheless, the 1930s was the golden age of the child-star movie. Temple's persona, more than any other, was tailor-made for Depression-era audiences; it is a measure of her immense popularity that she was the top US box office attraction between 1935 and 1938.[100]

Hollywood survived the Great Depression, in part, because of the social and recreational importance of the cinema. Average weekly attendances in 1933 stood at 60 million; at this point, the film industry had an 84.1 per cent share of spectator amusement expenditure, and 21.9 per cent of all recreation expenditure.[101] Moviegoing remained one of the dominant social activities for young people, and their sizable injection of capital partially offset the potentially catastrophic effects of the Depression.[102] It helped that the major studio vehicles of Shirley Temple, Jane Withers and Deanna Durbin, whilst tailored towards adults thematically, had a sizable juvenile fan-base because of the cross-generational appeal of the performers themselves. Overall, though, child-star films generally responded to adult concerns. Graham Greene controversially argued that Temple's 'admirers' were 'middle-aged men and clergymen' who appreciated the 'adult emotions of love and grief' she displayed, an assessment which – when combined with scandalous references to her 'well-shaped and desirable little body, packed with enormous vitality' – provoked legal retribution from her studio.[103] Biographer Norman J. Zierold more diplomatically described her as '[meeting] all the requirements: height, curly hair, bright teeth, an infectious smile, and a definite, distinctive personality'.[104]

However, the true value of these attributes can only be appreciated in context, and whatever dubious sexual appeal Temple may have possessed, her films functioned as a powerful countervailing force against Depression anxiety. Such movies as *Bright Eyes*, *Our Little Girl* (John S. Robertson, 1935) and *Poor Little Rich Girl* (Irving Cummings, 1936) operate almost as licensed public propaganda, directly addressing adult anxieties concerning economic hardship and the hope of recovery. Appearing as a staunch figure of optimism, she enables the extraordinary as she moves through the narratives of her films, transforming the lives of those she meets through sheer force of goodness.

Poor Little Rich Girl is, perhaps, the clearest distillation of these attributes. Temple plays Barbara Barry, the daughter of a successful soap manufacturer (Michael Whalen). Simultaneously the successful businessman and the devoted, overprotective father, Mr. Barry keeps Barbara home-schooled and away from possible harm. Barbara takes the first opportunity to break out of her ivory tower, travelling around the city and helping a variety of down-on-their-luck individuals. The paradox, which sees Barbara/Temple idealised as a priceless object but also exploited for the use value implicit in her social ability to galvanise, is articulated on-screen in an early exchange between Mr. Barry and Barbara's nurse:

> **Nurse:** Did you ever consider that the constant piling-up of precautions and attentions was bad for the child? Why, she's pampered and watched-over and babied to death.

The contrary positions of the nurse, pleading for a loosening of a constrictive domestic structure, and Mr. Barry, obstinate in his precautionary attitude, reflect a wider dichotomy between the need to preserve the child from interference and danger, and the need to universalise her ineffable talents.

Mr. Barry's professional importance highlights the duality of the early Temple figure: the happy marriage between working class and business class, and its implicit reaffirmation of Depression recovery ideology. Her affinity with the working class and desire to project outwards into the wider social sphere are heavily mediated by her middle-class social status, and her ultimate return into the arms of her penitent father as the film draws to a close. Ultimately, Mr. Barry comes to realise the harmful consequences of his behaviour. It is suggestive that his business is the profitable but wholesome profession of soap production – by its very nature clean and unsullied. These films were produced at a time when big business was widely distrusted – particularly in rural areas – because of the believed metropolitan origins of the global Depression.[105]

This distrust promoted ideologies of anti-industrialisation counterproductive to Roosevelt-era recovery policies, which stressed the importance of national unity and downplayed political and class divisions.[106] Because (as contemporary economist Lionel Robbins noted) 'the first essential of any recovery from the position in which the world now finds itself is a return of business confidence', it was crucial that broad-demographic films portrayed big business as innocuous and approachable.[107] If the connection appears fanciful, it should be noted that (as Mark Roth has shown in his analysis of Warner Bros.' flag-waving early 1930s musicals) the spirit of the New Deal transcended normative frontiers between political legislation and popular ideology, infiltrating Hollywood in sometimes explicit ways.[108]

Reflecting a similar set of ideologies, Deanna Durbin's late 1930s vehicles were similarly successful. In *One Hundred Men and a Girl* (Henry Koster, 1937), Durbin stars as Patricia, the daughter of an unemployed musician (Adolphe Menjou). Realising that the Depression has disenfranchised many other talented members of society, Patricia decides to form an orchestra of 100 unemployed musicians. In order to stage the massive, publicity-generating show she envisages, she must court the services of world-renowned conductor Leopold Stokowski, who is sympathetic to the cause, but has already pledged his services to a high-profile tour of Europe. During the course of this narrative – overtly constructed to emphasise as strongly as possible the unifying charm and singing prowess of Durbin – Patricia manages to infiltrate Stokowski's house:

Stokowski: How do you get into places where you should not be?
Patricia: I don't know. My daddy says it's a gift.

Astonished by her impudence, but clearly impressed by her talents, Stokowski agrees to conduct the orchestra of the unemployed. Having obtained the cooperation of a wealthy backer who realises the public-relations potential of the enterprise, the show goes ahead to wild success. The film ends with the promise of financial security for Patricia and her father. As with Temple's early films, Durbin here functions as a galvaniser of the dispossessed. A sharp contrast is established between rich and poor; only through the magical abilities of Patricia/Durbin is the situation improved. If the 'One Hundred Men' of the title represent the wider mass of unemployed and disenfranchised, then the 'one girl' suggests an organisational figure; a leader (paralleling Roosevelt). The affirmative qualities of the film are glaringly apparent: for such individuals, Durbin and Temple offer hope of a brighter future, while for the business class, they render safe potentially subversive factions. Were it not for their mediatory presence, the down-on-their-luck figures they encounter might easily be intimidating or even communistic in their proletariat overtones.

By the late 1930s, the ideologies of social and economic recovery in North American society had changed attitudes towards the Depression. With the New Deal operating in heavily reduced form by 1938, Depression narratives became anachronistic.[109] Temple's studio, Twentieth Century Fox, responded by gradually manoeuvring her into more fantastic, displaced territory. *Wee Willie Winkie* (John Ford, 1937) is set in India, and *Heidi* (Allan Dwan, 1937) in Switzerland. *Susannah of the Mounties* (William A. Seiter, 1939) is located in the nineteenth-century Canadian frontier, whilst *The Little Princess* is set in a picture-postcard Victorian England during the Boer War. Finally, *The Blue Bird* takes place in a mythical land evocative of fairy tale mythology. Even in a film as displaced as *Susannah of the Mounties*, though, Temple's political function – no longer as a galvaniser but still an arbiter of popular morality – remains apparent. At one point, Susannah (Temple) chastises the 'Indian' chief:

> I don't see why you want to fight the white people anyway. They haven't done anything to hurt you.

North America's gradual recovery from the Depression, ironically, disempowered Temple's symbolic properties. The key to her popularity was

Wee Willie Winkie (1937)

never her ability to articulate a conservative ideological position, but rather, as Charles Eckert argues, the positive relationship between her filmic persona and recovery from the Depression.[110] Temple's movement away from dramas located in contemporary North America towards the more blatantly artificial, displaced terrain of literary classic adaptation coincided with a gradual but noticeable cooling in critical and commercial response. The increase in prestige and budget in her films – eventually enabling her movement into colour in *The Little Princess* – served almost as distractions from her comparative social impotence. The balance between ideological and aesthetic appeal unsuccessfully shifted towards the latter.

The New York Times' Frank S. Nugent – a noted admirer of Temple in her earlier films – suggested that, by the time of *Little Miss Broadway* (Irving Cummings, 1938),

> the devastating Mistress Temple is slightly less devastating than usual [...] It can't be old age, but it does look like weariness [...] Although she performs with her customary gayety and dimpled charm, there is no mistaking the effort every dimple cost her. And perhaps even Shirley couldn't feel enthusiastic about the [...] script.[111]

Moreover, both metropolitan and small-town exhibitors, who once regarded a Temple film as a guaranteed cash cow, found they could no longer fill their theatres. One Columbian theatre owner had this to say about *Susannah of the Mounties*:

> Fox's darling is going the way of all child stars. Each picture she slips a little more. Shirley is still her own sweet self, but all the scenes are so palpably fed to her and we see a definite falling-off of the adult patrons that used to go to her. Fox, I think, is finding it increasingly hard to find stories that the adult public will accept [...] She is doing only just average business where we used to stand them out on her pictures two years ago.[112]

Although *The Little Princess* was well received, *The Blue Bird*, Fox's Temple-starred riposte to MGM's *The Wizard of Oz*, performed poorly at the box office. Like all child-stars, Shirley Temple had a limited shelf-life, and even she could not resist impending puberty. Like many adolescent child-stars, she was never a natural adult performer. In any event, critical approval for child-star films was rarely founded upon appreciation of plot, narrative, characterisation or other representational elements. In fact, many such reviews emphasise the role of the child performer in propping-up flimsy or clichéd storylines. Narrative plausibility and textual depth, then, were less important than the signifying presence of the child-star.

The Emergence of the Small-Town Family Film

Small-town US audiences were integral to Hollywood's revenues. At the start of the decade, as high a proportion as 65 per cent of the population – or 80 million people – lived in small towns.[113] Until the mass migration to the suburbs in the late 1940s, the North American small town wielded considerable influence over production strategy, and many films and genres were tailor-made for this sector. Even so, Hollywood was repeatedly criticised for disregarding the requirements of small-town audiences, and favouring more urban-centred entertainments adapted from the Broadway stage. New York-based exhibitor Arthur L. Mayer argued that most films were 'consciously directed to metropolitan audiences eager for the unconventional, the subtle and the artistic'.[114] Small-town patrons, conversely, were 'more appreciative of human, conventional stories and of conservative technique in their presentation'.[115] Margaret Farrand Thorp went even further, suggesting that 'the subtle, the exotic, the unexpected [small-town audiences] do not like at all, and they are frankly annoyed by costume pictures'.[116] In 1934, just prior to the mandatory enforcement of the Production Code, *The New York Times* lamented Hollywood's propensity to

> read what the trade papers said and what the New York critics thought, ignoring the opinion and even the box-office receipts of the small-towns. Hollywood was concerned only with the receipts on Broadway, forgetting that production cost comes from the cities and profits from the towns.[117]

One of the problems facing Hollywood during the mid-1930s was balancing the moral and educational requirements of the movie reformers with the entertainment needs of the vast small-town and rural clientele. Popular and profitable as it had been in the cities, the literary adaptation – which had catered to a largely metropolitan interest in middlebrow culture – was simply too chaste and sophisticated for rural and small-town patronage. One Texas theatre owner acknowledged that *David Copperfield* was 'the cream in entertainment' but that it 'will undoubtedly prove too rich for many patrons'.[118] Another theatre owner from Louisiana argued that a better name for *A Midsummer Night's Dream* would be 'Midwinter Night-Mare', adding that some patrons walked out whilst the film was still playing, and advising 'country' exhibitors to steer clear.[119]

In 1935, producers began addressing this problem by methodically targeting small-town audiences with family-orientated material. MGM's adaptation of Eugene O'Neill's only comedy, *Ah, Wilderness!* (Clarence Brown, 1935), was the first major production in this area. Billed quite overtly as an exercise in sweet nostalgia, carrying the subtitle 'A Comedy of Recollection', it centres on a quiet family in a pre-industrialised small town at the turn of the century, and possesses many of the tropes that would come to dominate Hollywood family films throughout the remainder of the studio era: a large, extended family; the depiction of a simple, ritualistic but spiritually rewarding pastoral lifestyle; the misadventures of an adolescent protagonist on the cusp of adulthood; the pronounced importance of the parents, especially the father; the fallibility, sexual temptation and first love of the adolescent protagonist; and the ultimate transmission of wisdom and experience from the father to the son. What MGM achieved with *Ah, Wilderness!* was a successful repackaging and rebranding of the traditional small-town family drama, a sentimentalised but still adult-orientated genre which reached a commercial peak during the early 1930s, with such Will Rogers-starred vehicles as *State Fair* (Henry King, 1933) and *Judge Priest* (John Ford, 1934). While retaining the humour, sentiment and avowed sincerity from such films (David Thomson has called Rogers 'the marketable noble savage'), *Ah, Wilderness!* broadens the genre's appeal by adding greater child identification.[120] In this way, it taps the respectability of the family movie – and its metropolitan origins – whilst retaining the values that made the small-town drama popular in rural locations.

Ah, Wilderness! became a template for a succession of long-running, cheaply-made family series spanning the late 1930s and early 1940s. Fox was the first studio to exploit the potential of this format, with a series of low-key, earthy comedies centring on the Jones family (1936–40). MGM responded with the most famous and long-running series in the genre, the Hardy family comedies (1937–46), starring Mickey Rooney. Warner Bros. produced a series of three comedy films starring the Lemp family (1938–41), and Paramount adapted their Henry Aldrich comedies from the radio into a family-orientated film series (1939–44). Meanwhile, Universal

Andy Hardy Meets Debutante (1940)

tried and failed to develop a series based on their Pierce family from *The Family Next Door* (Joseph Santley, 1939), and independent producer Harry M. Popkin attempted to reproduce the success of the Hardy family series with a black family – the Browns.[121] Clearly aimed at the so-called Negro theatres, only one film – the now-lost *One Dark Night* (Leo C. Popkin, 1939) – was ever produced.

The Hardy family series was the most famous, critically favoured and longest-running example of the genre. Over the course of 16 cheaply-made instalments, it brought in around $25 million for MGM.[122] Beyond simple economics, the series was close to the heart of studio head Louis B. Mayer. Mayer was notorious for his excessive love of sentiment, and is said to have considered the Hardy family series his masterpiece.[123] Set in the fictional town of Carvel, the family itself consisted of Rooney's Andy; Judge Hardy (Lewis Stone), the benevolent, upstanding head of the family; Mrs. Hardy (Fay Holden), the doting mother; occasionally Andy's sister Marian (Cecilia Parker); and the spinsterish Aunt Milly (Sara Haden). The family was strongly patriarchal, centring mainly on the communication of wisdom and experience from Judge Hardy to his son. Because of the centrality of this didactic theme, there was little narrative variation across instalments.

Like the small-town communities they approximated, these narratives were relatively uneventful. They emphasised a cyclical way of life; ritualistic daily routines and conventions which offered a bulwark against the forces of social change. The lack of overall development in the series, and the importance of repetition, therefore served ideological functions. Indeed, on two occasions where the series steps away from the conventionality of the small-town milieu towards a more metropolitan lifestyle, the results are disastrous. In *The Hardys Ride High* (George B. Seitz, 1939), the family comes into a $2 million inheritance and moves to Detroit. Long before the end, it has become clear that the corrupting power of excess wealth, and the lack of community spirit, necessitates a return to Carvel. When the inheritance falls through, this apparent misfortune is presented as a blessing in disguise. Excessive wealth is presented as concomitant with a decline in the cohesive properties of community spirit within the social sphere; values at a premium in the USA during the 1930s.

In *Life Begins for Andy Hardy* (George B. Seitz, 1941), undoubtedly the most unusual entry in the series, Andy moves to New York to 'find his fortune'. Unable to find a job and reduced to sharing a tiny bedsit with a young dancer, the narrative takes a surprisingly dark turn with the apparent suicide of his roommate. Distraught, but somehow wiser, Andy moves back to Carvel with the promise of maturity. Normality, however, was resumed in time for the next instalment in the series. Increasingly, the main critical complaint was the series' unwillingness to develop beyond its original remit. Reviewing *The Courtship of Andy Hardy* (Seitz, 1942), Bosley Crowther observed, with obvious frustration, that 'the Hardys emerge from the picture no different from what they were when it began'.[124] The following year, Crowther argued that 'the quality of the Hardy pictures seems to be on an obvious decline', and complained that 'the ageless juvenility of Mr. Rooney as Andy is beginning to wear'.[125] Nevertheless, the Hardy family series, unlike, say, the Jones family films, did succeed in transcending its core small-town audience base with strong returns in metropolitan areas.

Some critics stressed the importance of retaining the uniqueness of the cinema, and its sanctity as the pre-eminent national entertainment medium. For such observers, the family series constituted a threat. In February 1940, Nugent argued that family series had become 'too familiar':

> There is great danger now of the family and series film getting completely out of hand and reducing the screen to the level of news-paper comic strip or radio 'soap operas'. Both of these have their addicts, of course; but if the screen is placed too predominantly at their service, millions of others, of less elementary taste, may forget they ever had formed the movie-going habit.[126]

The increasing prominence of soap-opera material appeared to be taking Hollywood cinema in a very different path to that established by the 'Better Films' movement. By the late 1930s, Hays had relaxed his rhetoric attesting to the cultural respectability of the movies, and the clamour of the movie reformers had largely subsided. In his annual report to the MPPDA in 1938, Hays casually accepted the charge that the Hollywood product was 'unreal and escapist', adding that such a 'soft impeachment' was tolerable, given that the industry was flourishing both economically and culturally.[127] Indeed, aside from the brief period in the 1930s when Hollywood was actively attempting to prove its social value and cultural respectability, this desire to be regarded as purely harmless and escapist is its default mode of self-representation. The 'Better Films' movement, we can conclude, was expedient, its value commercial rather than artistic. There was a growing consensus in cinematic discourse by the late 1930s, largely as a result of the Production Code. Whilst this consensus had positive effects, it also resulted in a spate of films pitched at the 'lowest common denominator', just as Andre Sennwald had predicted.[128] Some critics blanched at the growing preponderance of such anodyne mate-rial, and repudiated the small-town family series. By the early 1940s, the format was already in decline, and Hollywood was turning its focus towards more prestigious, less mimetic small-town productions such as *Meet Me in St. Louis* (Vincente Minnelli, 1944).

The Christmas Film

The growing acceptance of family films within studio production sched-ules can be gauged from the development of the Christmas family movie.

Many of the most successful and memorable family films of the 1930s were released for yuletide, which was not only considered an ideal period for family attendance (a public holiday; a 'special' time of year, etc.) but also heralded a temporary suspension in Hollywood's generic and stylistic modes of production. Among the notable family films of the decade released for the festive period were *Tom Sawyer, Little Women, Alice in Wonderland, Babes in Toyland* (Gus Meins, 1934), *Bright Eyes, Ah, Wilderness!, Three Smart Girls* (Henry Koster, 1936), *Snow White and the Seven Dwarfs* and *A Christmas Carol* (Edwin L. Marin, 1938). Such films were often marked, alternately, by a pantomimic or carnivalesque spirit (*Alice in Wonderland; Babes in Toyland*) or by an idealised evocation of small-town family unity (*Little Women; Ah, Wilderness!*). In some cases, a Christmas release was simply a means of maximising 'family' attendances (*Snow White*), but in other cases (again, *Alice in Wonderland; Babes in Toyland; A Christmas Carol*) the festive spirit was reflected in the tone of the film itself. Among Hollywood's 1930s Christmas films, *Babes in Toyland* – a Hal Roach all-star production featuring the producer's biggest stars, Laurel and Hardy – is perhaps the most interesting, because of the clear contrast with the duo's non-festive vehicles.

Roach bought the rights to Victor Herbert's 1903 operetta in 1933, obviously realising the potential of a feature film adapted from the massively popular stage versions (a New York run of 192 shows from 1903–5, and a similarly successful Broadway revival in 1929–30). As an operetta, the production was heavily reliant on music, rather than dialogue, to progress the narrative. Roach wrote his own screenplay, later heavily revised by Laurel, which retained some of the songs but developed prominent roles for Laurel and Hardy. The theatrical trailer – as was usual during this period – addressed parents rather than children, exhorting them not to 'send the kiddies' but to 'BRING THEM! You will enjoy it as much as they will!'. *Babes in Toyland* was released in mid-December, 1934, in time for Christmas bookings. The film was moderately successful at the box office and received some excellent reviews, even from *Variety* – notorious among Laurel and Hardy aficionados for its aversion to most of their features.

There are various similarities with Paramount's 1933 adaptation of *Alice in Wonderland* (not least that the star of that film, Charlotte Henry, plays Little Bo-Peep). These two films are the most child-friendly major Hollywood productions of the period in their calculated juvenility and fantastic themes. Such films would not have found favour at any other point in the calendar, but for the festive trade, these characteristics were deemed acceptable, in much the same way that parents might take their children to a Christmas pantomime as a treat. Hal Roach Studios was probably the most family-orientated in Hollywood at this point (with the exception of Disney), with Laurel and Hardy, Harold Lloyd, Charlie Chase and the *Our Gang* series on its books. Yet even Roach stopped short of making out-and-out children's films, cognisant that adult audiences were necessary for box office success, and that the middlebrow and reformist doctrines of the period disparaged entertainment marked by purely escapist rather than educative content. Moreover, the same audiences that made *Babes in Toyland* a solid festive hit would probably only tolerate pantomimic content but once a year – and not even that in the case of Paramount's *Alice in Wonderland*, which, in spite of a large-scale publicity campaign, was a notable failure.

By the late 1930s, family films were no longer a visible aberration in studio production schedules and, due in large part to the year-round success firstly of child-star vehicles and subsequently family series, they began to fit in seamlessly with routine, non-seasonal studio products. Production of specialised Christmas family films declined commensurately, but did not disappear entirely. Twentieth Century Fox's *Miracle on 34th Street* (George Seaton) was a tremendous hit during the run-up to Christmas 1947, and was viewed by the studio as an 'annuity film' with potential for re-releases every subsequent yuletide.[129] During the 1950s, television networks similarly recognised audiences' requirements during public holidays for screen entertainments that promote powerful feelings of family and community.

Children's Films in 1930s Hollywood

While the major studios concentrated on producing broadly adult-orientated family movies, lesser producers often had a much clearer juvenile emphasis. The main factor behind their greater embrace of child viewers was commercial practicality. Mainstream major-studio offerings responded to the concept of a vast, demographically-unrestrained audience that was tangible and accessible. Smaller, 'poverty row' studios such as Republic and Monogram, and mini-majors such as Universal and

Columbia, adapted to the market by accommodating areas ignored by the majors, resulting in a spate of child-orientated series and serials throughout the late 1930s. Such releases tended to be cheap, usually lacked significant star power, and were generally positioned on the bottom half of a double-bill. Their reputation for inferiority ensured that they rarely transcended cult audiences, yet poverty-row children's entertainments were creatively diverse, encompassing science fiction epics and domestic rural dramas, child-star series and ensemble adventure stories.

The Johnny Weissmuller-starred *Tarzan* series – which began at MGM in 1932 as a high-profile, adult-orientated initiative under the auspices of Irving Thalberg, and ended up as low-budget, largely child-orientated matinee fare produced by RKO – is a fine example of how the 1934 mandatory enforcement of the Production Code imposed changes in Hollywood's modes of address. MGM's first Tarzan film, *Tarzan the Ape Man* (W. S. Van Dyke), was not only conspicuously expensive, but downright racy, with a high quotient of violence and near-nudity from former Olympic swimmer Weissmuller and his co-star, Maureen O'Sullivan. Nevertheless, it was a significant box office success, and a sequel, *Tarzan and his Mate* (Cedric Gibbons), emerged in April 1934.[130] Like its predecessor, it was explicitly adult-orientated, and was widely recognised as such. *Time* magazine's reviewer, for instance, observed that Tarzan and Jane appeared to be 'living in natural frivolity, ignoring the precepts of Tsar Hays, and obeying no civilised conventions except, perhaps, those of birth control'.[131] One infamous sequence sees Tarzan and Jane swimming underwater, Tarzan's modesty protected only by a loin cloth, and in some cuts, Jane absolutely naked – albeit in long-shot.[132] After the tightening of the Code, the series retained its emphasis on action and adventure but introduced a lighter, more inoffensive tone to proceedings. The playful, overtly-sexual relationship between Tarzan and Jane was reconfigured to one of domesticity, particularly after they adopt a 'son', Boy (Johnny Sheffield), in *Tarzan Finds a Son!* (1939). Boy's introduction constituted a clear attempt to engage more with younger viewers. When the franchise was taken over by RKO in 1943, the series embraced an even more fantastical, juvenile tone. In *Tarzan's Desert Mystery* (Wilhelm Thiele, 1943), the hero is no longer battling hostile tribesmen or crocodiles, but man-eating plants, dinosaurs and giant spiders. The two elements that probably attracted Depression-era adult audiences to the first two Tarzan films – the hard-edged style and sexual allure of the two leads – had long since been phased out, and the comic-book style that replaced it was far more attuned to juvenile audiences.

Most series and serials were low-risk, low-return ventures. Pretentions towards art were reserved for the major studios; in contrast, the serials represented themselves overtly – perhaps centrally – as disposable. Serials were distinguished by fantastic situations, heavy use of melodrama and exaggerated characterisations. A typical serial comprised around 13 episodes (although some were longer), with an average length of about 20 minutes.[133] Although they were at their height in the pre-sound era, serials were still produced well into the 1950s as they remained attuned to the requirements of children. Many series and serials were exploitation releases tapping the commercial Zeitgeist. Rarely did they operate in the 'adult' world of Depression anxiety and rural/urban tension, so they were less overtly political. This, too, made them ideal escapist entertainment for children. Serialised adaptations of *Tarzan*, *Buck Rogers*, *Zorro* and *Flash Gordon* were amongst the sci-fi productions released by serial specialists Universal, Republic and Columbia in the late 1930s.

One of the more popular child-orientated series of the period was *Nancy Drew*, based on the adventure books of 'Carolyn Keene', and produced by First National. Four instalments were produced between 1938 and 1939, each centring upon the exploits of an adventurous teenage girl, played by 15-year-old Bonita Granville. Although Granville was almost the same age as Deanna Durbin and was Oscar-nominated for her role in *These Three* (William Wyler, 1936), she was soon appearing in second-feature material. What is most interesting about this series is its naturalistic representation of the central child figures. Nancy is independent, resourceful and brave, and clearly more competent and formidable than her male sidekick, Ted Nickerson (Frankie Thomas). *Nancy Drew* was produced in a period where the teenage protagonists in mainstream films were often subject to the will of their domineering parents, within tightly-prescribed family units. Here, Nancy is the obvious star of the show. The focus, then, is less upon generational continuity than teenage adventure, inevitably filtered through adult eyes, but directed squarely at teen and pre-teen viewers.

Nancy's father, Carson Drew (John Litel), makes frequent appearances in the films, and in common with most contemporary family productions, the family is wealthy and socially respectable (Carson is an eminent attorney). Crucially, though, Carson's occasional, tongue-in-cheek attempts to impose didactic authority upon Nancy are instantly reproved. One sequence in *Nancy Drew, Reporter* (William Clemens, 1939) sees Carson, bored of fielding Nancy's enquiries regarding legal procedure, picking her up into his arms, intent on taking her to bed. Indignantly, Nancy struggles to get free:

> **Nancy:** Daddy, put me down! I'm not a baby!
> **Carson:** You'll always be your daddy's baby.
> **Nancy:** I won't be anybody's baby!

This exchange underlines the fact that whereas Andy Hardy required the persistent direction and intervention of his father, Carson is compelled to leave Nancy to her own devices. Her competency is never in question, as the roles in the titles of the first three films – 'Detective', 'Reporter' and 'Trouble Shooter' – indicate. Another divergence from the Hardy family movies is the absence of the awkward 'adolescent condition'; the exaggerated point of teenage crisis underpinning the transition from childhood to adulthood. The representation of this transition as a bitter-sweet, melancholy passage is a common feature of adult fiction, yet its absence here is unsurprising, given the intended youthful audience of these films. Second-feature movies were a rare escape from the adult fixation on childhood evanescence implicitly present in the child-star films and mainstream family series. Instead, they tended to regard their core consumers as young adults capable of relative self-sufficiency, rather than as bumbling, incompetent hobbledehoys in the vein of Andy Hardy.

Monogram was one of the most prolific producers of low-grade children's and teenage fare. Perhaps Monogram's most enduring film series during the late 1930s and early 1940s was the Frankie Darro-starred ensemble comedy-drama, which can be seen as a precursor to the teen films of the 1950s. Darro was an archetypal B movie actor, appearing in dozens of productions of variable size, budget, form and quality. Comprising stand-alone light-comedy instalments featuring many of the same actors, but with variations on plot, situation and character, the Frankie Darro films served as a kind of clearing-house for fading and emerging talent. Aging child-stars Jackie Moran and Marcia Mae Jones – then in their late teens – made several appearances, as did Keye Luke, also known for playing the title character's eldest son in Twentieth Century Fox's 1930s *Charlie Chan* series. Gale Storm, who became Monogram's biggest star before a successful singing career in the 1950s, joined the series at the launch of her film career in 1941. *Let's Go Collegiate* (Jean Yarbrough, 1941), a typical instalment, sees the protagonists embroiled in a plot to replace a star athlete, who has just been enlisted by the army, on the college rowing team. They enlist the paid help of a burly, none-too-bright trucker to impersonate the athlete until they can find a replacement, but learn to their amazement that he is a naturally-brilliant rower who manages to win the day for the team in the closing stages. P. S. Harrison's review of the film was scornful:

> This program college comedy with incidental popular music is strictly for the younger picture-goers. It holds little appeal for adults, since the plot is somewhat silly, and the actions of the leading characters [are] extremely juvenile.[134]

Harrison's disdain perhaps reflected the fact that most of the cast were either teenagers or in their 20s – this was a rarity in feature films of the period, but was far more permissible in low-budget offerings tailored towards the youth audience.

Other youth-orientated Monogram films included *Barefoot Boy* (Karl Brown, 1938), a second-feature film barely an hour in length. In this film – 'suggested' by John Greenleaf Whittier's poem of the same name – the credits are explicitly divided between child actors and 'the grown ups'. The parents of Billy (Jackie Moran), the male protagonist, only make fleeting appearances, but wisdom and astuteness nonetheless resides with the sympathetic father. Like Judge Hardy, Billy's father is grey-haired and pipe-smoking, slow-moving in body but mentally agile. The film, set on a country ranch, concerns the exploits of a small group of children who uncover, and eventually foil, a prison-break. The pastoral setting elicits a greater play towards romantic 'realism' in the representation of the child figures. Marcia Mae Jones, who appeared as the bratty antagonist of Deanna Durbin in *Mad about Music* (Norman Taurog, 1938), plays Pige, a feisty girl with aspirations to be an 'adventuress'. Such a character would indicate malfunction within the context of later mainstream family films, such as *Meet Me in St. Louis*, but here, she operates as the central focus of a narrative in which rebellious spirit is celebrated, rather than marginalised or resolved. Action, adventure and youthful spirit suitable for both young metropolitan and rural viewers sustained such films, in which the material was wholesome and guileless. The crucial point of difference between these lower-level offerings and the mainstream child vehicles is that these central child actors are subordinate to narrative. Moran and Jones never attained the level of fame to rise *beyond* the pleasures of narrative, in the fashion of Coogan, Temple and Durbin.

Seeking the Family Audience in Late 1930s Hollywood

'The pearl of great price' to the Hollywood film industry, as Margaret Farrand Thorp observed in 1939, 'is the picture that pleases everybody'.[135] However, very few movies produced by Hollywood were capable of pleasing 'everybody'. Appeal remained extremely fragmented. Whilst the term 'family film' might be pressed into service to describe inoffensive, nostalgic literary adaptations such as *Little Women* and *The Little Princess*, as a label it is somewhat inadequate. These films were products of middle-brow culture, reflecting adult social concerns, such as the effects of the Depression and the pernicious impact of industrialisation and global capitalism upon contemporary society. They were designed to appeal to middle-class adults who responded to cute, precocious little girls, pleasing sentiment and nostalgic evocations of a mythologised past. Children had screen entertainment of their own: action-heavy series and serials, comedies, animated shorts, westerns – matinee fare in general. In this sense, we can see that the barriers erected between children and adults in the aftermath of the transition to sound remained largely intact. Despite the notion of the 'great audience' – which circulated widely in industry propaganda and subsequently in popular critical discourse – the concept was illusory. Many more films became morally and thematically *suitable* for children and adults to view together, but few possessed mass *appeal*.

In late 1930s Hollywood, there were perhaps three types of film possessing broad suitability *and* appeal, capable of galvanising a cross-demographic audience. None of these were developed into wider industry production strategy. The first type was the Charlie Chaplin slapstick comedy; the second was the Disney animated feature; the third the prestige fantasy. These various forms require some analysis, as they each possessed qualities thought to be unique, and impossible to replicate on a production-line basis. Chaplin was one of the 'pearls of great price' to which Thorp alluded.[136] He was surely the *most* unique figure operating within Hollywood during the studio era: almost everything about his movies and his methods delineated him as irreplaceable; a one-off. The slowness of Chaplin's work-rate was legendary: he made only ten features in a career spanning 50 years, partly because of a need to fulfil 'every creative function on a film, whether it is scripting, composing, or directing actors'.[137] His level of creative autonomy was unrivalled, mainly because nobody else had the power to operate so independently. Although his release rate was intermittent at best, and his later films heavily criticised for pretension, Chaplin's early-to-mid period work was beloved of critics and mass audiences alike. He successfully tapped into a multilayered mode of appeal which operated, at its base level, on slapstick, yet was framed by a keen eye for social critique and tragicomedy. With the release of *Modern Times* in 1936, James Shelley Hamilton wrote:

> For something like a quarter of a century Charlie Chaplin has been the delight of ordinary movie-goers, the masses who in the beginning were articulate only with their nickels and dimes, with which they set huge fortunes a-building. In later years the literati, the dilettanti, the cognoscenti and the rest of the esthetes [sic] hailed him as artist and genius [...] he creates something of a feeling that perhaps our mortal eyes are looking upon a bit of immortality.[138]

Chaplin was a social phenomenon whose filmic persona, 'the tramp', was perhaps even, as David Thomson suggests, 'the most famous image of the twentieth century'.[139]

Disney films also quickly acquired cultural significance transcending the ephemerality of typical Hollywood entertainment. The studio's development into feature filmmaking with *Snow White* was integral to this process of capturing a broad cross-demographic audience, and, as I will argue in the following chapter, its implicit development from child- to family-orientated programming. It would also seem impossible to write in depth about 1930s family films without examining *The Wizard of Oz*. However, the adoration this film has received over the years risks ahistoricising the conditions of production and response, for it was neither a critical nor commercial success.

When it became apparent that *Snow White* would be a major hit, there was 'a wild search for producers for comparable fantasies'.[140] Clearly, when MGM purchased the rights to L. Frank Baum's 1900 novel, *The Wonderful*

Wizard of Oz, for $75,000, it was hoping for similar success.[141] The movie was regarded as a prestige production, costing just under $2.8 million, but it only returned about $2 million and failed to return a profit until its 1948–9 re-release.[142] The *New Republic*'s Otis Ferguson noted its similarity to *Snow White* but criticised its lack of humour and subtlety.[143] The *New Yorker*'s Russell Maloney lamented a lack 'of imagination, good taste, or ingenuity'.[144] This indifference served to confirm the Hollywood maxim that fantasies were bad business at the box office. The subsequent failure of Fox's stylistically similar production, *The Blue Bird*, underlined this point, and the fantasy genre was once again relegated to second-feature fare. Aljean Harmetz argues that the movie's exalted reputation can be traced to the mid-1950s, when television network CBS purchased the rights and began an enduring tradition of broadcasting it annually at Christmas.[145] As she observes, 'distance would do many things to *The Wizard of Oz*. The over-produced quality that was so offensive to critics in 1939 has [...] later lent a hand to the picture's being seen as significant'.[146] Whilst modern observers of family entertainment may regard *The Wizard of Oz* with misty-eyed approval, its reception in 1939 was far more ambivalent.

Nevertheless, each of these three forms possesses both suitability *and* appeal for cross-demographic audiences, and also, to employ a much over-used epithet, a 'timeless' quality that enables what is now called 'repeatability'. To be more precise, their appeal is not limited to the socio-cultural conditions of production and initial release. However, Hollywood's inability to replicate these forms prevented their widespread integration into the broader 'family' strategy. Chaplin was unique, and pointed towards the past, and although Disney pointed towards the future, he was widely-regarded, like Chaplin, to be a one-off. Meanwhile, *The Wizard of Oz* – as with other contemporary fantasies – was impeded not only by technical limitations but by contemporary distaste for excessive juvenility. *The Thief of Bagdad* – a British fantasy film released the following year and loosely based on the Arabian Nights – was a box office failure in the USA despite its incredible spectacle and evident technical virtuosity, which arguably eclipsed *The Wizard of Oz*. What it lacked, aside from a white, North American child protagonist (its juvenile lead, Sabu, was Indian), was a strongly moralistic and sentimental slant; it was not sufficiently middlebrow. *Snow White* may have been charming and iconoclastic, but it was also a middlebrow morality play, which helped its cause with domestic adult audiences.

WALT DISNEY AND THE BEGINNINGS OF FEATURE ANIMATION

In the months prior to theatrical release in late 1937, *Snow White and the Seven Dwarfs* was widely known in the film industry as 'Disney's Folly'. It was Hollywood's first ever feature-length animated film, and as such, posed considerable logistical difficulties. The average short required between 10,000 and 15,000 separate images, but a state-of-the-art feature-length animation demanded something in the region of 2 million. Clearly, a project of such magnitude also entailed an incubation period of hitherto unprecedented proportions – in this case, approximately three years. There was also the tremendous financial strain, which included the building of an entirely new studio, and the need to recruit and retain the relevant artistic personnel. An even more potent cause for concern than the various practical obstacles in bringing such a venture to successful fruition was the prevailing mistrust and condescension with which animations – or 'cartoons' as they were commonly known – were viewed. Between 1928 and 1937, although doubtlessly enjoyed by adults, they were still generally regarded as children's entertainment. In terms of production, as Eric Smoodin argues, Disney 'achieved success by marketing his product as ideal children's fare'.[1] Leon Schlesinger, the head of Warner Bros. animation, maintained that 'we cannot forget that whilst the cartoon today is excellent entertainment for young and old, it is primarily the favourite motion picture fare of children'.[2] Whereas shorts traditionally succeeded by appealing to children as part of a balanced programme of entertainment, a feature

65

film of such prestige and expense could only succeed by appealing equally to adult patrons.

Nevertheless, the Disney Company had good cause to believe that making the transition from animated shorts to features was not merely logical but essential for its continued profitability. Although all the major Hollywood studios had their own animation divisions by the mid-1930s – and those of Warner Bros. and Paramount were particularly well-regarded – Disney had been the leading force in this sector since the late 1920s, when it released the first major animated talkie, *Steamboat Willie* (Ub Iwerks, 1928). Although Disney secured a distribution deal with Columbia and later United Artists for the 'Silly Symphonies' series of musical shorts, the company spent the early part of the 1930s vying for supremacy with Warner Bros.' copycat 'Merrie Melodies' and 'Looney Tunes' series, and the Fleischer brothers' Betty Boop character, whose coquettish adult appeal during the early Depression years prefigured that of Shirley Temple. Disney, though, had the biggest success with *Three Little Pigs* (Burt Gillett, 1933) – an eight-minute Technicolor cartoon that yielded the Depression-era anthem 'Who's Afraid of the Big Bad Wolf?', and became the most profitable short in Hollywood's history. This success, welcome though it was, doubtless further encouraged Walt Disney to expand into feature filmmaking, because the organisation of the United States' distribution system ensured that shorts made relatively little money in comparison with features.[3] Disney's one significant advantage over its rivals was its merchandising operation. In 1932, Disney signed a contract with salesman Kay Kamen to exploit the merchandising potential of all of the company's licensable characters, most notably Mickey Mouse. This partnership netted Disney millions of dollars over the following decade.[4] In 1934, buoyed by his success in shorts but eager to transcend the financial and artistic constraints of the medium, Disney began work on *Snow White*.

Until now, in this book, I have barely mentioned Disney in relation to the family-orientated feature film. The reason for this, to be blunt, is that in spite of its reputation, Disney was largely incidental to the emergence of this format. Admittedly, the company's position in the animated shorts market was highly prominent (although by no means monolithic), but animations were merely one of various types of short film, and shorts always occupied a relatively lowly position on the movie bill in relation to feature films. Furthermore, shorts and features were produced largely independently of one another, with little direct interaction or interdependency. All of this was to change with the release of *Snow White*. Although Hollywood's first feature-length animation had received considerable scrutiny prior to release, and there was a palpable sense of anticipation in the industry-at-large (obvious even by reading through contemporary trade and general-interest publications), the general tenor was one of guarded scepticism. This quickly evaporated when the film was released to universal acclaim in November 1937. *Boxoffice* was not atypical in its assessment of *Snow White* as 'the most important picture, from a production perspective, since the advent of sound', adding:

> One may not make the bromidic observation that it is the greatest picture ever produced – since nothing of its kind has ever before been attempted.
>
> One thing is certain. Every man, woman and child who regularly patronises pictures will desire to see it, as will untold thousands who rarely or never attend motion picture theatres; for it has a universal appeal, seldom, if ever before, attained in the realm of celluloid entertainment. And everyone who sees it will feel he has been abundantly repaid for his investment in time and money.[5]

Exhibitors were similarly delighted with the picture. One Nebraskan theatre manager enthused:

> Hats off to Walt Disney. Here is possibly the grandest thing offered to the public for entertainment. It appeals to every living person from the ages of 2 to 102. After personally viewing this picture sixteen times, I regretted to see it leave the town.[6]

The commercial success of the film – especially striking, given its particular appeal for children – was unprecedented. *Snow White* was comfortably the second most profitable film of the decade, behind *Gone with the Wind* (Victor Fleming, 1939). Disney was swiftly heralded as an outstanding, one-of-a-kind creative 'genius', and his productions nothing short of 'art' – in contrast to the animated shorts of MGM, Paramount and Warner Bros., widely considered to be 'mere cartoons'.[7] As with many of Disney's adaptations of classic literature, the story is little more than a warmly-familiar pretext for the film's aesthetic qualities. *Snow White* is perhaps the only major family film of the decade – with the possible exception of *King Kong* (1933) – predicated almost exclusively on spectacle and novelty. The richness of the colour, and the depth and detail of the illustrations, was unprecedented in mass entertainment of the period.

Although, as a modern viewer, it is impossible to divorce oneself entirely from a cultural context in which technically-superior animated features have become routine, *Snow White* remains highly impressive to this day. Its impact on contemporary audiences evidently was enormous. Given its immense critical and commercial impact, and various predictions that it would fundamentally alter Hollywood's production methodology, the response from rival studios was little short of bathetic. Admittedly, none of the major studios possessed the resources required to immediately replicate Disney's success with feature animation. However, Paramount – which had a long-standing distribution deal with Fleischer Studios – was the only other producer to even attempt such an initiative during the remainder of the studio era.[8] Furthermore, the relative failure of its two productions – *Gulliver's Travels* (Dave Fleischer, 1939) and *Mr. Bug Goes to Town* (Dave Fleischer, 1942) – spelled an end to the venture, leaving Disney the sole presence in this market.[9] Because Disney's position, by this point, was unique, there seemed little obstacle to continued expansion.

However, animated features remained complicated to manufacture. By the 1950s, the necessary financial outlay, the amount of time needed to bring them to the screen and the attendant risk all led Disney to conclude that such films were almost more trouble than they were worth.[10] Furthermore, finding stories suitable for adaptation was a constant difficulty.[11] More fundamentally, there was widespread distrust of Walt Disney and his medium. Animation still carried pejorative connotations (for adults) with the children's matinee. Moreover, the appeal of animation, it must be remembered, was primarily sensual, and was viewed by the Hollywood establishment as unsophisticated, despite – or perhaps partially because of – its enormous mass appeal. As Schickel argues, Disney spent most of his career 'tolerated by *haute* Hollywood as an enigmatic eccentric whose presence was "good for the industry"'.[12] Nonetheless, during the early 1940s the man and the studio could scarcely have been held in higher regard. The period 'signalled Disney's apotheosis as a media hero', and his reputation as a creative genius grew further with the release of *Pinocchio* (Hamilton Luske, Ben Sharpsteen) in February 1940.[13] *The Board of Review*'s James Shelley Hamilton felt

Fantasia (1940)

that it went 'far beyond anything Disney and his studio have ever done before'.[14]

At this point, the studio's subsequent difficulties could hardly have been anticipated. However, like several Hollywood moguls from this period, Walt Disney wanted simultaneously to expand the reach of the motion picture to a position of commercial dominance, whilst courting cultural acceptance and the approval of the middle classes. Disney's features seemed to offer both, by virtue of their massive critical and commercial success, and yet its early feature films occupied a some-times equivocal position between 'art' and 'entertainment'. They were a curious halfway-house between the lowbrow connotations of the chil-dren's matinee and the relatively highbrow connotations of the prestige production. Disney's dissatisfaction with his personal and professional status within Hollywood was certainly a factor in his desire to produce *Fantasia* (1940), which fuses an episodic series of animated narrative segments to classical music, conducted by Leopold Stokowski. When Disney produced *Fantasia*, he was riding the crest of a wave of critical and popular adoration. It was his first and last attempt at making a model family film – an amalgam of the apparently irreconcilable elements variously considered essential to good family entertainment: sophistication, educative value, broad suitability, escapist quality, spectacle, and a seamless melding of the popular and the middlebrow. The film bombed at the box office, and suffered the same fate as various other 'sophisticated' family films in the small towns. One rural Canadian theatre owner likened the film to 'a poison gas attack':

> If you want to kill your business in a small town, play this one. May be ok for city business. I played this one at a high rental, killed a weekend business. One of the remarks passed by some of my best patrons: 'What is this?' More walkouts than any picture I have ever shown.[15]

This failure taught Disney that trying to please everybody was impossible. It was a valuable lesson, but a costly one: the studio spent much of the remainder of the decade attempting to recover, commercially and artistically.

Fantasia's poor reception had two notable consequences. Firstly, the studio was plunged into financial difficulty resulting from the failure to recoup the production costs. Secondly, the studio reactively abandoned the technical and aesthetic innovation distinguishing its early feature films. Steven Watts has argued that Disney's creative output fundamentally changed after 1941, evidencing

> a new instinct to identify and uphold American values rather than playfully to probe or lampoon them. Individual achievement, consumer prosperity, family togetherness, celebratory nationalism, and technological promise became the beacons of the new Disney corpus.[16]

Although the studio's next two feature animations – *Dumbo* (Ben Sharpsteen, 1941) and *Bambi* (David Hand, 1942) – are amongst its most technically accomplished productions, they nonetheless evidence greater ideological and narrative conventionality. They are allegories of the family socialisation process, in which the symbolic child figures – a baby elephant and a fawn, respectively – learn to overcome their vulnerabilities and make their way in the world-at-large.

From this point onwards, Disney broadcasted his disdain for 'art' at every opportunity.[17] Shortly before he died, he revealed: 'I've always had a nightmare. I dream that one of my pictures has ended up in an art theatre. And I wake up shaking.'[18] During the studio's financial crisis, Disney's output was largely confined to government-contracted training and propaganda films, most notably the part-animated *Saludos Amigos* (1943) and *The Three Caballeros* (Norman Ferguson, 1945), produced as part of the US government's so-called 'good neighbours' policy with South America.[19] Although these contracts provided financial ballast to the ailing studio, overall the 1940s were not a successful period for Disney. By 1945, the studio was in financial difficulty and Walt Disney's personal reputation as a godlike arbiter of democratic art had taken a sizable hit.[20] The *Saturday Review* claimed that the 'genius' in the earlier work was an ability to appeal 'to what is childish in adults and adult in children'.[21] With the turning of the critical tide, Disney came under attack for failing to reconcile 'the disparate groups in the movie audience'.[22] By the end of the decade, the Warner Bros. animations department had overtaken Disney as the leader in cartoon shorts, and in the late 1950s Disney abandoned shorts altogether.[23] Walt Disney later admitted that the unsuccessful post-war years had been marked by crippling indecision.[24] During the early 1950s, the studio successfully embraced live-action as its run-of-the-mill product, with production of the riskier, more time-consuming animated features cut back and formally conventionalised. It was a long road to recovery.

THE MIDDLEBROW FAMILY FILM, 1940–53

While Hollywood's interest in 'family entertainment' during the mid-to-late 1930s led to a preponderance of family-orientated genres, this surge had largely abated by the early 1940s. Instead, the decade as a whole was marked by relative stability and uniformity, reflecting the fact that many of the pressures exerted on producers to orientate their releases to the 'family audience' were no longer being felt. Indeed, this loosening of external pressures resulted in a progressive increase in the quantity of adult-orientated productions as the decade progressed. Furthermore, two of the most popular 'family' cycles of the 1930s – the classic literary adaptation and the child-star vehicle – had petered out, partly due to an exhaustion of story material, partly because of the desire to appeal jointly to metropolitan and small-town audiences, and partly because of the particular need for mass entertainment closely to reflect changes in the socio-cultural environment. For instance, it was widely felt that the Depression had directly resulted from the United States' embrace of industrialisation and urbanisation at the expense of a simpler but more virtuous small-town and rural existence. This belief led to a 'return to the soil' ideology during the late 1930s and 1940s, marked by a form of nostalgic parochialism heightened by the country's inclusion in the Second World War in December 1941. While the war film was one of the dominant Hollywood production types during the early 1940s, the impact of the war on the family film was relatively displaced, but nonetheless perceptible in the quantity of productions offering idealised, nostalgic evocations of the quintessential small-town family, which served to remind audiences of what the country was fighting to protect.

The early 1940s was a period of continued consolidation and expansion by Hollywood in general. Movie admissions increased yearly between 1940 and 1945, reaching their peak in 1946.[1] The small-town family comedy-drama was sufficiently popular to survive long after the end of the war, and became increasingly extravagant in terms of production treatment. Because of its popularity and time-span, and because its central image of a happy, functional nuclear family exerted such enduring power over Hollywood family entertainment in the decades to come, it is this cycle – which includes such films as *Meet Me in St. Louis*, *Life with Father* (Michael Curtiz, 1947) and *Cheaper by the Dozen* (Walter Lang, 1950) – with which this chapter is chiefly concerned. Another key family genre during the 1940s was the animal film, which, like the small-town family comedy-drama, offered a nostalgic snapshot of mainly rural life, but with a clearer juvenile identification, with its usual focus on the relationship between a child and (anthropomorphised) animal. As with mainstream family films of the previous decade, though, all of these films reside within an overtly adult, middlebrow aesthetic. This not only corresponded with the lowly status of children and adolescents as consumers of mass culture, but also reflected the long-standing industry propaganda that Hollywood was a 'democratic' institution. This perception was not merely accepted but was actively celebrated by writers such as Gilbert Seldes, who argued that on the subject of 'Majority and Minority Audiences', 'minority audiences [do not] have any rights at all'.[2] If these words seem to echo Will Hays's seemingly inescapable affirmations of Hollywood as a 'universal system of entertainment', it is no coincidence, for this was a period during which the unifying power of the cinema was at its height.

The further inference, of course, is that while vulnerable audiences (i.e. children) had a right to moral protection, as a supposed 'minority' audience they had no claim to special treatment from the point of view of entertainment. Children were expected to attend the movies not independently but with their families, as part of their joint social routine. However, what Hollywood provided in its so-called family entertainment was not amusement for families per se, but rather entertainment in the service of the constructed *idea* of 'the family' as a socially-venerated institution. The mini-majors and 'poverty-row' studios continued to make films intended largely for children throughout the 1940s in the form of

B-grade series, serials, cartoons and second-feature material exhibited in matinee slots, but even this practice was slowly phased out during the early 1950s, when B movie production was largely abandoned. Nevertheless, for all MPPDA president Will Hays's propaganda attesting to Hollywood's universal reach, certain mainstream genres were clearly marked by particularly adult themes, especially noirs and A-westerns. In fact, movie reformers continued to petition fruitlessly throughout this period for greater production of 'children's films'. However, movies spanning various genres – amongst them *Citizen Kane* (Orson Welles, 1941), *Gaslight* (George Cukor, 1944), *Duel in the Sun* (King Vidor, 1946), *Out of the Past* (Jacques Tourneur, 1947), *Gentlemen's Agreement* (Elia Kazan, 1947), *Rope* (Alfred Hitchcock, 1948) and *Red River* (Howard Hawks, 1948) – give lie to the fallacy that most studio-era productions were family films.

Hollywood's experimentation during 1939 and 1940 with productions foregrounding aesthetic innovation and dazzling spectacle – notably *The Wizard of Oz, Fantasia, The Blue Bird* and *The Thief of Bagdad* – proved to be a false dawn. No doubt the North American public's apparent revulsion to overly escapist (i.e. 'childish') or fantastic productions, when combined with the preference in small towns for homely, earthy stories, contributed to their downfall, and Hollywood family films were quickly set back on a more mundane trajectory. In retrospect, the most significant family-orientated production of 1940 was Paramount's *The Biscuit Eater* (Stuart Heisler), a story about two boys and their relationship with a bird-hunting dog – the runt of a litter – from a novel by James Street. Like many Hollywood productions of the period, it attempts to evoke sentiment through its depiction of the small triumphs and tragedies implicit in rural life. It is a well-made, if low-key, offering, but as with Paramount's 1930 production of *Tom Sawyer*, its qualities were magnified in the eyes of critics (and presumably audiences as well, given its commercial success) through the timeliness of the values it extolled. *Variety*'s review of the film observed:

> Here is a film which to extraordinary degrees captures the common touch and touches the common heart. No picture within recollection deals with the troubles and problems of early youth – both in humour and heartbreak – more appealingly and with greater understanding. Its grace and charm, its fine artistry in keeping the relationship of two youngsters and a dog very simple but unerringly tender and

sincere, rank 'The Biscuit Eater', for all its production modesty, one of the outstanding features to come out of Paramount or any other studio in a long time. It will hold its own with any running mate, from the loftiest to the lowliest theatre, for entertainment of the masses.[3]

The Biscuit Eater became a popular inclusion on children's matinee programmes for many years thereafter. However, its perceived success did not immediately lead to a cycle of animal films, either from Paramount or its rivals. Indeed, the quantity of family films as a proportion of the major studios' overall output fell dramatically during the early 1940s, indicative, no doubt, of the paradigm shift within North American popular culture away from 'literary'-type material, which was still heavily associated with family fare.

One of the major points of discussion at the December 1940 National Board of Review's annual conference were the effects of horror and gangster films upon juvenile audiences. Surprisingly, the joint conclusion of prominent attendees such as Walt Disney, Judge Stephen S. Jackson, director of the New York Bureau of Juvenile Delinquency, and Mrs. Ralph T. Edwards, film editor of *Parents' Magazine*, was that such traditionally 'adult' material was not harmful for older children and did not lead to anti-social behaviour.[4] However, Disney reiterated that his own production *Fantasia* – which had been criticised upon release for supposed scariness – had been produced for children over the age of ten, and that 'I've seen many children being taken to the movies who, in my opinion, were too young to see any picture'.[5] This statement allegedly received a round of applause from the 500-strong audience. Furthermore, Edwards averred that:

> A milk-and-water diet weakens children in later life. A completely de-shivered existence might well disarm a child for the future. Parents should know their own child's capacity for thrills and recommend a movie diet accordingly. More pernicious than Cagney killing and getting killed in the end is the story of the parasitic hero who wins success and wins the girl and never has to work.[6]

Nevertheless, Edwards added that family films were being released irregularly, and that on occasion she had only a selection of clearly adult films from which to make recommendations for good family viewing.[7] One possible inference we can take from such statements is that attitudes had changed since the establishment of the Production Code in relation to producers' responsibility to ensure films remained morally suitable for children. If attitudes on the subject were, indeed, relaxing – and bearing in mind the tension between the perceived status of children as a 'minority audience' with Hollywood's mission to satisfy the highest concentration of patrons – this would perhaps explain the relative scarcity of family films during this period.

Throughout the early 1940s, family audiences were nonetheless provided with regular instalments from the Jones and Hardy family series. The Jones family never attained much success beyond the 'sticks', but MGM's Andy Hardy series (as it came to be known, when Mickey Rooney's popularity outstripped that of his co-stars) transcended the rural/urban divide. Given the popularity of the series and especially Rooney himself – whose hyperactive, mugging but sympathetic all-American persona made him a magnetic on-screen presence and Hollywood's top box office attraction between 1939 and 1941 – it was only a matter of time until MGM released a prestige picture based on the same model. The result was *The Human Comedy* (Clarence Brown, 1943), which preserves the small-town setting and Rooney's confused-but-well-meaning adolescent identity, while the plot deals with the impact of the war on the local community. Perhaps the only major Hollywood family film which deals explicitly with the issues surrounding the war, *The Human Comedy* essentially remains, as the *Motion Picture Herald* observed, 'a super-Hardy type of picture', augmented 'with tears and laughs for the theatregoers of all kinds and ages everywhere'.[8] *Variety* concurred, describing it as 'a brilliant sketch of the basic fundamentals of the American way of life'.[9] It is a measure of the perceived significance of the film that the MPPDA promoted *The Human Comedy* as the 'greatest motion picture' ever produced.[10]

1943 also witnessed the beginnings of a more coherent cycle of animal films, starting with *My Friend Flicka* (Harold D. Schuster, 1943) and continuing with *Lassie Come Home* (Fred M. Wilcox, 1943), *Home in Indiana* (Henry Hathaway, 1944), *National Velvet* (Clarence Brown, 1945), *Black Beauty* (Max Nosseck, 1946) and *The Yearling* (Clarence Brown, 1946). The animal film was conceived on what now appears a rather condescending and Victorian assumption that sentimental films starring children and animals were ideal family entertainment. Nevertheless, the immensely strong box office performance of many of these films – even when bolstered by strong marketing campaigns targeting parents and teachers – gives lie to such cynical reservations. Although the decline in quantity of child-orientated B movies and shorts goes some way to explaining this commercial success, such films undoubtedly exerted a strong pull for adults and children alike. According to *Variety*, 'producers have learned that customers too old and too young for live animals are pushovers for dog and pony stuff'.[11] We might surmise that animal films were particularly appealing to young children, while small-town family dramas were a stronger draw for adults and, perhaps, teenagers. Apparently, animal pictures were regarded in the industry as

> an index to possible coin which may be garnered from the recently almost neglected family trade pictures, especially the trade depending upon the younger children accompanied by elders.[12]

My Friend Flicka was followed by *Thunderhead – Son of Flicka* (Louis King, 1945) and *Green Grass of Wyoming* (Louis King, 1948), while *Lassie Come Home* generated six sequels between 1944 and 1951, and was one of MGM's most enduring properties. By the time Universal's parodic 'Francis the Talking Mule' series (1950–6) emerged, the animal film cycle – traditionally characterised by naturalism as well as down-home sentiment – had largely run its course.

By this point, a clear production trend towards 'basic values in film entertainment' had emerged, but the film that introduced glamour to the small-town family was *Meet Me in St. Louis*.[13] Unlike most subsequent films in the small-town family cycle, *Meet Me in St. Louis* began life not as a stage play, but as a series of stories written by Sally Benson for the *New Yorker* in 1942, centring on the experiences of a St. Louis family at the turn of the century. Although the film takes many liberties with the original stories, the main point of departure can be inferred from the production treatment. Produced by Arthur Freed and directed by Minnelli, *Meet Me in St. Louis* was designed as a prestige picture; a Technicolor musical with a budget of around $1.5 million and starring Judy Garland, one of MGM's biggest stars. The primary plotline concerns the conflict that arises when businessman and patriarch Mr. Smith (Leon Ames) decides to move his entire family to New York. Ultimately, Mrs. Smith (Mary Astor) is able to persuade her husband against the move, but not before each member of the family has expressed their

Meet Me in St. Louis (1944)

misgivings concerning abandoning the pastoral arcadia of St Louis (as it is presented), with its close-knit community, for the complexities and loose social ties of the big city. *Meet Me in St. Louis* is perhaps the first family film that consciously blurs the boundaries between town and city in order to provide an idealised composite that is attractive and recognisable for small-town and metropolitan audiences alike. Although ostensibly located within a big city, the impression of small-town life is always maintained, even at the end of the film, which sees the much-heralded arrival of the World Fair. As Bruce Babington and Peter Evans argue, the arrival of the World Fair should have offered a disturbing portent of the unwanted encroachment of advanced capitalism into the semi-pastoral small-town community; but instead, its hazy colours and distant ambience merely becomes

> the most extreme example of a metaphor that holds together both the past and progress in an impossible image, in spite of reason's claim that the world of the city, by entering the small-town, must destroy it.[14]

Meet Me in St. Louis – and the cycle of imitators that followed – signalled the abandonment of the sincerity and authenticity that had previously marked the small-town family film, from *Ah, Wilderness!* to *The Human Comedy*.

Meet Me in St. Louis was a sizable box office hit that generated almost universal critical acclaim. Unsurprisingly, rival studios attempted to emulate MGM's success with prestige films made in a similar style. A selective list of such films includes *National Velvet* (an instance where the pastoral family drama and animal film intersect), Fox's *Centennial Summer* (Otto Preminger, 1946), Warner Bros.' *Life With Father*, MGM's *Summer Holiday* (Rouben Mamoulian, 1948), RKO's *I Remember Mama* (George Stevens, 1948), Fox's *Cheaper By The Dozen* and *On Moonlight Bay* (Roy Del Ruth, 1951), and its sequel *By The Light of The Silvery Moon* (David Butler, 1953). This genre is defined not only by its broad-based audience suitability, but typically by strong production values. Usually filmed in Technicolor and featuring minutely-observed period detail, these movies often utilise a musical framework to deepen the pleasurable association. Beyond these basic aspects, however, they trade upon social nostalgia for a bygone age, with the period around the turn of the twentieth century recurring time and again in storylines. Equally, there is little historical substance beyond the tokenistic; the cheerful invocation of the Stanley Steamer in *Ah, Wilderness!* and *Summer Holiday*, or the Negro statue in the front garden in *Meet Me in St. Louis*. Put simply, there is a pronounced tendency, as Babington and Evans suggest, to reflect 'reality through its most pleasing representations'.[15] Magnifying and commodifying nostalgia for a period of relative social stability, before widespread industrialisation, global warfare and economic depression, the genre posits an overriding tension between past and present.

The narratives themselves are clearly influenced by the long North American literary tradition of pastoral valorisation, and the writings of Tocqueville, Mark Twain and Booth Tarkington, as well as the Eugene O'Neill play *Ah, Wilderness!* (1933) and the Thornton Wilder play *Our Town* (1937), are obvious reference points. A more contemporary influence was *Life with Father*, a Broadway play (1939–47) subsequently adapted by Warner Bros. and based on turn-of-the-century family life, which became the biggest hit in the history of the stage.[16] In these films, the central families almost invariably comprise a strong, financially solvent and community-respected father figure, a pragmatic, influential, housewife, and a large selection of children of varying ages. Unlike most of the family films from the 1930s, the modes of address in these productions are explicitly differentiated. *Meet Me in St. Louis*, for example, features a full extended family – two parents, a large group of children of varying ages, and even a grandparent – co-habiting. These films, then, operate within a broad cultural understanding of motion pictures as 'family entertainment'. Positioned as fun for all the family, they aim to bring families together through the exhibition experience, even as they offer pleasing evocations of the institution on the big screen.

This ongoing filmic preoccupation with the institution of the middle-class, small-town family reflects not only the continued need to appeal independently to separate demographics in a varied audience base, but also bourgeois anxiety concerning its ongoing survival. The 1930s 'return to the soil' paralleled a reversion to a unified, middlebrow conception of 'the family' as protective private realm, which, as historians such as Stephanie Coontz have noted, is a characteristic response during periods of social anxiety. When Thomas Jefferson talked about 'the pursuit of happiness', Coontz argues, he referred not to 'a subjective or private state of mind, far less to a retreat into the family', but rather 'a public happiness which is measurable'.[17] Therefore, the privileged position of the family as a private realm is not a 'traditional' ideology. Rather, Coontz argues, it was inaugurated 'little more than one hundred years ago' by 'a middle class that had retreated from larger ethical concerns', and this shift towards the private sphere 'may be a symptom of socioeconomic and moral fragmen-tation, not a remedy for it'.[18] With the elevation of the private, supposedly self-contained family unit to an exalted position in North American society, it was 'only a small step [...] to the conclusion that building a comfortable home life was the most morally worthwhile act one could undertake'.[19]

Whereas earlier entries in the pastoral family film – such as *Ah, Wilderness!* and *Our Town* (Sam Wood, 1940) – responded to social ideologies of anti-industrialisation, by the time *Meet Me in St. Louis* was released in 1944, the preoccupation with the private realm of the family had become largely a nostalgic indulgence, reflecting the steely grip middlebrow culture held over North American popular entertainment at that time.

The Family and the Small-Town Community

Two significant aspects of the 1940s domestic family comedies correspond with this institutionalised model of the family. The first is the positioning of the family within the wider community; almost exclusively, 'community life' is portrayed favourably. It is crucial that this way of life is rendered innocuous and unthreatening to the inner realm of the family unit. Far from the invasive connotations of urban living, such affirmative representations of community reflected a lamented wider belief that its positive aspects – familiarity, congeniality, social cohesion – were disappearing. The male protagonists in 1940s family films are usually well-known publicly; they are hard-working members of the business class, widely respected and admired. This relates to the second dominant trope – the representation of the father as symbolic leader. Nat Miller (Lionel Barrymore), the father in *Ah, Wilderness!,* is the local newspaper editor; Frank Gilbreth (Clifton Webb), from *Cheaper by the Dozen,* is an internationally-renowned inventor; Clarence Day (William Powell), from *Life with Father,* is a well-known stockbroker and man-about-town; George Winfield (Leon Ames), from *On Moonlight Bay,* is a senior bank executive. The persistence of this family structure suggests didacticism, revealing the kinds of families that were considered socially desirable, as well as representing an idealised vision of the USA that might be profitably sold to audiences at home and abroad.

These patriarchs share a number of attributes. Aside from the physical similarities – they are imposing and well-dressed; each has an authority-denoting moustache – they are the socially-upstanding, mannered and slightly blustering heads of large families, over which they appear to wield complete control. Despite their exaggerated rigidity, they ultimately defer to the authority of their nagging wives. The matriarchs play a crucial role, providing a pragmatic counterpoint to the often intemperate belligerence of their husbands. The comedic battle of the sexes is a major theme in *Life with Father*, where much of the humour derives from Clarence's failure to realise that he is constantly being manipulated by his long-suffering wife, Vinnie (Irene Dunne). In one sequence, the fastidious Clarence attempts to balance the family housekeeping accounts. After enquiring how Vinnie has spent a small sum of money, he is eventually befuddled by her evasive and long-winded replies to the extent that, unwittingly, he ends up giving her *more* money. Clarence likes to think that he is in full and proper control, but it is Vinnie who holds the real power.

It is a persistent and long-standing trope in Hollywood movies, particularly from the classical era, that apparently meek, subservient wives slyly control their domineering husbands through subtle, gentle emotional manipulation. Sometimes this takes the form of simple level-headedness in the face of the impetuosity or buffoonery of the patriarch. In *Life with Father*, this reaches its apotheosis when Vinnie, after hearing the shocking news that her husband was never baptised, immediately swoons with an apparently serious (but possibly bogus) malady. Hearing Clarence's desperate agreement to mend his ways and get baptised – made in an unguarded moment in the hope that it will cure his supposedly dying wife – Vinnie immediately makes a miraculous, comically unlikely recovery. Such humour has its origins in the recognition that for a matriarch to exercise control over her family in a more straightforward, authoritarian manner would be unfeasible and absurd.

While such presentations are undoubtedly intended to offer amusement through mockery of the intransigent authority figure, the patriarch is always presented with obvious fondness. In *On Moonlight Bay* and *By the Light of the Silvery Moon*, Mr. Winfield (credited simply as 'Father Winfield', emphasising his supposed universality) displays an interest in marrying-off his daughter (Doris Day), which verges on the obsessive. He is told by Margie that he is 'so old-fashioned'; the point is underlined in the sequel, where Mr. Winfield tells his wife:

> Don't make it sound as if I'm trying to get rid of Margie. Being a responsible father, I happen to be old-fashioned enough to want to

see our grown daughter take her rightful position in the institution of marriage.

Given that the movie is virtually a paean to the joys of a mythologised past, Father's 'old-fashioned' outlook is scarcely a negative trait. Instead, it is acknowledged with indulgent patience. *The New York Times'* review of *Life with Father* emphasises the reviewer's receptiveness towards the figure of Clarence: 'While father goes into a towering rage at the slightest provocation [...] he is at heart a very kind, tolerant and sympathetic old man (and we use that term most affectionately).'[20]

As the small-town family comedy descended further into self-parody, a musical framework was often employed. Although the popularity of the musical elements in *Meet Me in St. Louis* was undoubtedly a major factor in this trend, the increasing prominence of song-and-dance numbers also suggest an attempt to sustain the small-town family film beyond its 'natural' life cycle via structural and aesthetic innovation. These musical aspects serve to broaden appeal without dispensing with the conventional attractions of narrative. *Summer Holiday*, for instance – a late 1940s remake of *Ah, Wilderness!* – introduces a number of new elements to the basic story. The vibrancy of the colour stock, which showcases bright but earthy tones, the addition of sprightly musical numbers, even the inclusion of Mickey Rooney in the pivotal role, suggest an attempt to compensate for the excessive familiarity of the material, whilst confirming the abandonment of naturalism. In this sense, the genre's increasing proclivity towards diegetic song-and-dance numbers was not disruptive, but a logical, commercially-driven development. The increasing infiltration of 'unreality' constitutes the cinematic manifestation of the changing social factors that had helped popularise the form. In *Meet Me in St. Louis*, *Centennial Summer*, *Summer Holiday*, *On Moonlight Bay* and *By the Light of the Silvery Moon*, there is a gradual trend of leaving behind some of the motifs and received values of the past, as they begin to enter into rather too fundamental a conflict with the present.

Another repetitive trait bordering on self-parody is the setting of the narrative during a public holiday, which overemphasised what was, in reality, a restricted, ritualistic aspect of rural life.[21] *Ah, Wilderness!* and *Summer Holiday* take place against the backdrop of the 4th July celebrations; *Meet Me in St. Louis* is partly set at Halloween, partly at Christmas; and *By the Light of the Silvery Moon* features both Thanksgiving and

Christmas family scenes. In the first three films, at least, there is a palpable suggestion of the carnivalesque, where usually upstanding figures temporarily behave outside the usual bounds of decorum. This serves neatly to circumvent the hard work and productivity ethic in rural life, instead reinforcing parallel associations of its positive recreational qualities. Urban-centred narratives are not usually able to offer such a polarised opposition between 'hard work' and 'hard play'. The carefully-signalled, rhythmical shifts in time projected in *Meet Me in St. Louis* and *Our Town* emphasise cyclicality, rather than progress. The commercial value of these narrative settings is considerable. Public holidays themselves formed a role in families being able to watch movies together, and movies offering romantic, sanitised depictions of small-town life undoubtedly offered additional vicarious appeal for audiences seeking escapism. Additionally, the structural strategy of locating stories around public holidays – occasions of supposed unity off-screen as well as on-screen – provides ballast to narratives which, by their very nature, are based on mundane, determinately 'normal' experiences and events.

Youth Appeal and the Socialisation Process

Whilst these films are clearly largely interested in adult middlebrow audiences, they do make various concessions for pre-teen and teenage audiences. *Meet Me in St. Louis*, *Summer Holiday* and *On Moonlight Bay* prominently feature child figures, whose vaguely amoral adventures are injected into the narratives in the form of brief, self-contained, episodic subplots, usually extraneous to the dominant plot lines. In *Meet Me in St. Louis*, the mischievousness of the child figure, Tootie (Margaret O'Brien), is reiterated various times during the course of the narrative. One particularly well-known sequence shows the neighbourhood children erecting a large bonfire, and enacting a Halloween ritual, in which the children are dispatched to various households to throw flour in the faces of the adult who opens the door – symbolically 'killing' them. When Tootie 'kills' the particularly feared Mr. Braukoff, she is heralded, to her delight, as 'the most horrible of us all'. In another sequence, she sabotages a rail line, an act which initially provokes condemnation, and then amusement, from her older sisters, Esther (Judy Garland) and Rose (Lucille Bremer). *On Moonlight Bay* offers child appeal in the character of Wesley (Billy Gray), who, like Tootie, comically disrupts 'adult' behavioural norms. As if to pre-empt intimations that the film does not have a sense of fun, a po-faced graduation address delivered by young hero Bill Sherman, ruminating on the passage of boyhood to manhood, is interrupted by repeated assaults from Wesley with a pea-shooter. Earlier in the film, Wesley falsely tells his teacher that Father is a drunk; Bill later becomes convinced that George beats his family, resulting in a comedic altercation. In *By the Light of the Silvery Moon*, Wesley is responsible for the unfounded rumour that George is having an affair with a French movie star. Farcically, in both cases it is the child that is responsible for undermining the almost exaggerated strength of the patriarchal head of the family. Importantly, though, these children are designed to be received with humour and understanding; their behaviour, after all, is never seen as a prelude to delinquency, but merely an extreme, comedic representation of childish play.

Within the small-town inflection, these apparently disruptive aspects carry deeper suggestions of down-home authenticity and naturalness. In narratives in which non-conformities and dissention are usually effaced, Tootie's behaviour is received with benign tolerance, as the actions of an artless child yet to learn codes of adult morality and decorum – but she will do so, by-and-by. Similarly, Wesley's mischievous antics seem permissible within the tonal and generic framework established by the film. The figure of Wesley, and indeed the persona of Billy Gray, consciously recalls the famous 1930s child-star, Jackie Cooper. However, whereas Cooper's young hoodlum persona verged on parody, Wesley's actions are intended to evoke the realities of childhood. This distinction underpins an important, broader trope in the pastoral drama – the conscious rejection of the extraordinary. *Meet Me in St. Louis* and *On Moonlight Bay* both draw heavily upon Booth Tarkington's *Penrod* tales of childhood experience and misadventure. Despite this influence, the blend of anarchism here is too calculated, too sanctioned to bear comparison with reality, and repre-sents an attempt to appeal to younger viewers while operating within the overall adult inflection of the narrative. This adult emphasis is maintained by the representation of the various child and teenage characters, which invariably progress logically and obediently from childhood rebellion to adult responsibility.

Martha Wolfenstein and Nathan Leites identified a general trend in classical-era Hollywood cinema – reflecting a broader societal expec-tation – that 'children should surpass their parents'.[22] In this genre, the expectation is reversed: children simply reproduce the success, beliefs and lifestyle patterns of their parents. To *surpass* one's parents, after all, may tacitly imply that there is something unsatisfactory or incomplete with previous generations, or indeed the past as a whole, and in these films, such an implication would be counterproductive. The one notable exception is *I Remember Mama*, which centres on a poor Swedish immigrant family in the USA, and which sees the Americanised children surpass the social and economic position of their foreign parents. Although the film presents the parents – particularly the mother – as wise and benevolent, their community standing is relatively lowly. It is a structural inevitability that the eldest girl, Katrin, and eldest boy, Nels, achieve bourgeois acceptance by becoming a successful author and college student, respectively. In all instances, within this narrative tradition, the older generation is regarded with deference, as the arbiters of a deeper knowledge, wrought by experience. Nearly all of these texts have post-adolescent, pre-adult characters in the pivotal role. The fundamental point of tension in this tradition is the period where 'childhood' and 'adulthood' converge – sometimes expressed colloquially as 'that awkward age'. These pre-adult figures are usually presented with some conflict on the journey to adult responsibility, often manifested as a choice which will determine the ideological correctness of their adult trajectory. Although the parents – particularly the father – remain symbolic figures of authority, their ultimate role is guiding their progeny and passing on their experience, allowing the pattern to continue in future generations. In *Meet Me in St. Louis*, we see a hierarchy of socialisation, beginning with the amorality of Tootie and ending with the prim chastity of Rose. It suggests a form of reversal and integration of childhood rebellion, reminiscent of the ultimately conventionalised, domesticated trajectory of Alice in *Through the Looking Glass* (Lewis Carroll, 1871).

In *Life with Father*, based upon the semi-fictional accounts of Clarence Day Junior (the post-adolescent figure in the movie), the narrative is predicated upon the literal and symbolic qualities of the authoritarian father. Early in the film, we witness Clarence Jr. (Jimmy Lydon) receiving an old cast-off suit from his reluctant, thrifty father. Humour is derived from a number of sequences showing the young man wearing the suit, comically behaving in the same way as his domineering father, particularly towards his romantic interest, Mary. In desperation, Clarence Jr. tells his mother:

> Very peculiar things have happened to me since I started to wear this suit. I can't seem to make these clothes do anything father wouldn't do. Mother, I've got to have a suit of my own!

When he finally receives his own suit (through tricking his father, financially), it represents a finding of his own voice, subtly circumventing the possibility that he is simply a carbon copy of his father. He remains, however, tightly bound by the structures and traditions of his previous generations, comically underlined by the fact that all four boys – each of a slightly different age – have, like their father, red hair. Similarly, although such films often conclude with scenes promising love and lasting marriage between the young protagonist and the love interest, these sequences are largely based upon a structural expectation, or a symbolic token of fulfilment, rather than genuine romantic interest. With the re-enacting of such romantic aspects, continuity is again reaffirmed with the promise of children, future plenitude, and the passing-down of hard-earned experience.

The Decline of the Small-Town Family Comedy

Although Hollywood cinema was at its commercial peak during the mid-1940s, it was once again subjected to criticism for failing to adequately cater to juvenile audiences, and for allowing adult-orientated material to reach the screen. In September 1946, MPAA (formerly the MPPDA) head Eric Johnston announced the creation of an industry-sponsored Children's Film Library, which would make significant family films from all the leading Hollywood studios since the early 1930s available to exhibitors nationwide for use in Saturday matinee shows. Previously, children's matinee organisers had always encountered the problem of lack of availability of suitable material. The initial list of 28 films added to the library included *Alice in Wonderland* (1933), *A Midsummer Night's Dream* (1935), *Poor Little Rich Girl* (1937), *The Adventures of Huckleberry Finn* (1939), *Young Tom Edison* (1940) and *The Human Comedy* (1943), and the programme was designed to cater predominantly to the 6–12 age bracket.[23] When announcing the library to the press, Johnston emphasised the pedagogic qualities of the films made available:

With the opening of the school year, we are making available for Saturday showings some of the ageless juvenile stories by Mark Twain, Lewis Carroll, Rudyard Kipling, Alice Hegan Rice, Kate Douglas Wiggin, Charlotte Bronte and others.

A whole generation of children has reached school age since these pictures were produced. A motion picture film, unlike a book, isn't always available on a shelf. In a relatively short space of time a motion picture goes out of circulation [...] I have had assurances from many theatre operators that they will make their theatres the Saturday morning headquarters for children in their communities.

If parents will encourage the screening of these pictures as Saturday shows, their children, I believe, will be enriched in litera-ture, adventure, fantasy and fun.[24]

In spite of this positive spin, there is little doubt that the creation of the Children's Film Library represented a tacit admission on the part of the MPAA that the majority of films were unsuitable for juvenile audiences. Nevertheless, like his predecessor Will Hays, Johnston ensured the public relations value of the initiative by forming a jury of civic and educa-tional organisations to decide on the future inclusions in the Library.[25] By September 1947, approximately 2,500 theatres were participating in this matinee programme.[26]

More films were added to the Children's Film Library over the next few years, but again, it was little more than a token gesture on the part of the MPAA, which was doing its best to mitigate the impact of the profitable but adult-orientated productions slipping through the net. Although the annual report of the Protestant Motion Picture Council argued that 'Hollywood turned out more films in 1949 suitable for general family entertainment than in any previous year', the Catholic Legion of Decency found that 'morally objectionable' films had reached an all-time high of 19 per cent during the same period.[27] At the United Parents' Association's annual conference in April 1950, Jack Glenn, president of the Screen Directors' Guild, advised parents in the audience that 'if the producers don't make good films, keep your children out of the theatres'.[28] Well-known exhibitor Arthur Mayer, meanwhile, was typically blunt, observing that:

In my experience of over 30 years in the motion-picture industry, the American people have had plenty of opportunities to support [good]

> pictures and almost invariably have failed to do so. Although I have helped to import many of the finest pictures ever brought into this country, I was able to [...] only because I was simultaneously operating [Manhattan's] Rialto Theatre, which consistently showed the worst. The profits on the bad pictures enabled me to stand the losses on the good ones. Most of the critics of the industry are optimists, because they only write and speak about the demand for superior films. I am a pessimist, because I have invested money in them.[29]

Mayer concluded, resignedly, that 'no-one ever went broke underestimating the tastes of the American public'.[30]

Mayer's comments may have been inspired, in part, by the relatively lowbrow family fare churned out by Universal during the late 1940s and early 1950s. For much of the studio era, Universal had barely managed to remain afloat, and in lieu of the greater resources of its more illustrious competitors, relied heavily on the box office pull of a handful of contracted stars – notably Deanna Durbin during the Depression years, and Bud

Abbott and Costello Meet Frankenstein (1948)

Abbott and Lou Costello throughout the 1940s and early 1950s. The low-cost formula pictures starring Abbott and Costello, and Francis the Talking Mule (as voiced by husky Texan Chill Wills), traded on the cross-over appeal on these personalities, rather than the stories, which were often flimsy, derivative and repetitive. This also meant that profitable (if critically-derided) family films could be cranked out without recourse to enormous budgets or strong storylines, while also neatly bypassing the often staid, wholesome respectability of the top family films of the period. Like Laurel and Hardy, Abbott and Costello were figures of safety and fun for juvenile audiences, with Bud assuming the guise of an exasperated but ineffectual parent, and Lou a mischievous, but dim, symbolic child. Their early films were comparatively adult-orientated, but their once-formidable popularity began to wane in the post-war period. The studio responded by positioning its star attractions in a series of genre parodies, the most notable of which remains *Abbott and Costello Meet Frankenstein* (Charles Barton, 1948), which features not only Frankenstein's monster (Glenn Strange), but also Dracula (Bela Lugosi), the Wolf Man (Lon Chaney, Jr.) and, briefly, the Invisible Man (Vincent Price).

Universal's horror films had been popular fare for children even in the early 1930s, but here the monsters are reduced to mere caricature (as might be inferred from the title, which mirrors a popular conflation between Frankenstein the creator and his monster). The Wolf Man's metamorphosis – originally intended to be horrific – is even the subject of various gags, as when Talbot admits that 'in half an hour the moon will rise and I'll turn into a wolf', to which Lou replies, 'you and twenty million other guys' – an obviously doubly-coded allusion to male prurience. By this point, horror films were no longer widely considered commercially viable, but the marquee value of the monsters themselves remained. The juxtaposition of comedy with horror iconography, as well as the film's positioning of its stars as objects of family amusement, made commercial sense, and despite poor reviews, it did good business in theatres. The 'Francis' pictures, as well as a parodic family series based on the exploits of Ma and Pa Kettle (1949–57), were founded on a similar formula of semi-ironic escapism, reiterating that broadly-appealing entertainment could be produced without big stars, strong scripts or glossy production values.

By this point, the small-town family film was beginning to lose popularity with critics and audiences alike. It was not merely the over-familiarity of the milieu (for all their charm, it is hard to see *Cheaper by the Dozen* and *On Moonlight Bay* as anything more than pastiches of *Life with Father* and *Meet Me in St. Louis*) that led to this decline, but also comprehensive changes in North American living habits. The mass-migration from the small towns and cities to the suburbs – which began in the late 1940s – and the rapid entrance of television into North American homes were equally powerful factors. I will discuss the impact of television in more depth in the following chapter, but 'suburbia' – as both a concept and a social reality – deserves some analysis in relation to its immediate impact on the family film. From a purely practical level, movie theatres were less accessible in the suburbs than they had been in the cities or the sticks. Furthermore, television removed some of the necessity, or at least the desire, to attend movie theatres as regularly, and slowly replaced the cinema as the family recreational habit of choice. However, it runs deeper than that. Arguably one of the defining features of the suburban social model is its self-sufficiency, which almost directly contravenes the small-town model of community and social awareness. As Kenneth Jackson points out:

> Suburbia symbolises the fullest, most unadulterated embodiment of contemporary culture; it is a manifestation of such fundamental characteristics of American society as conspicuous consumption, a reliance upon the private automobile, upward mobility, the separation of the family into nuclear units, the widening distinction between work and leisure, and a tendency toward racial and economic exclusiveness.[31]

The avowed self-sufficiency of suburban living precludes the community-orientation regarded as the bedrock of the small-town lifestyle. People who choose to live in small-town and suburban communities in the post-industrial age are often motivated by a rejection of social change, and suburbia is the ultimate physical manifestation of the resistance to urban culture and its influences. With a miniature pastoral retreat in every suburban backyard, as Jackson wryly notes, 'there are few places as desolate and lonely as a suburban street on a hot afternoon'.[32] Indeed, the decline of the extended family, and increasing prominence of what Talcott Parsons called the 'structurally isolated nuclear family', points to the development of a social pattern that seems deliberately to exclude 'outsiders' in any form. The self-contained, self-sustaining realm of the suburban home, allied to increasing ideologies of privatism, becomes the perfect domain of the family, the institutionalised system determinately free from outside interference.

The small-town family film had been predicated on its appeal both to rural and urban audiences, but while naturalism had long been abandoned by this point, the genre still relied on the implicit assertion of authenticity, and the evocation of values which remained deeply-embedded within the national psyche. Suddenly, it was no longer the small town but the suburbs which seemed to exemplify post-war North America. As such, the same critics that had celebrated the genre several years earlier could now attack its anachronisms and derivativeness with impunity, just as European director Douglas Sirk could satirise its delusionary and self-serving representation of the American heartland with his trio of early 1950s family comedies, *Weekend with Father* (1951), *Has Anybody Seen My Gal* (1952), and *Take me to Town* (1953). If small towns no longer seemed an appropriate crucible for the on-screen family, neither did the suburbs. While the suburban family is often figured as an ideal incubator for the young, suburbia seems to lack the authenticity of the small town. One of the key characteristics of the small town family movie had been the centrally-important, powerful father figure. Suburban fathers lose some of this authority, which is replaced by comparatively feeble white-collar overtones. Middle-class suburban families lack the pastoral associations of authority, continuity and wisdom affiliated with natural surroundings, and although suburban fathers are often presented as loving and attentive towards the needs of their children, this is something of a back-handed compliment in a society that valorises 'strong' parenthood. Such weak fathers may attract begrudging respect for their devotion, but scarcely the same levels of admiration afforded the powerful father-figures of the 1940s family features.

Unsurprisingly, early 1950s family films moving away from the small-town setting evidence a marked decline in the importance attributed to physical surroundings. *Weekend with Father* focuses upon two lone parents, Brad Stubbs (Van Heflin) and Jean Bowen (Patricia Neal). Both are widowed from their previous marriages, and are raising young children. They meet while dropping off their children at summer camp, and the early sections of the film focus largely upon their burgeoning mutual attraction. Problematically, Brad is involved in a casual relationship with

Phyllis Reynolds (Virginia Field), a woman preoccupied with her professional life ('once in a while I wish you could forget about that career of yours'). Brad's dithering reveals an internal conflict between the possibility of romantic fulfilment – or the lack thereof – and the desire for a complete family unit. Both Brad's housekeeper and Jean's maid repeatedly reinforce the idea that they need to remarry, but whilst the fulfilment of romantic union is preferable, it seems to pale into insignificance when compared to the need to raise a successful family.

By the time the children are introduced in the narrative, the parallel expectation for a loving but authoritative father has been repeatedly underlined. Like many studio-era family films, much of the intended juvenile audience appeal comes from the light mockery of the father-figure. However, the variety of satire here is more biting, arising as it does from Brad's only semi-comic inability to be the athletic, imposing father his adopted sons, Gary (Jimmy Hunt) and David (Tommy Rettig), want him to be. Brad and David are persistently defeated, humiliatingly, in the camp's father-and-son outdoor activities, invariably because of Brad's incompetence when facing any practical challenge. Although Brad appears to be the correct marital pairing for Jean, his credentials for assertive fatherhood are undermined by his haplessness, passivity and white-collar identity. This is ironically underlined by the fact that whereas Jean's dead husband was a marine, Brad is an office executive who lives by the mantra, 'when I feel like taking some exercise, I lay down until the feeling goes away'. He is eventually chosen over his rival for Jean's affections, the athletic, cocksure Don Adams (Richard Denning), but only when it becomes clear that Don is a health-food fanatic (an even more unpalatable marker of metropolitan artificiality). Brad, on the other hand, likes hamburgers and ice cream, demonstrating his kinship with the boys, and this goes some way to effacing his embarrassing lack of pragmatism and potency.

The relocation to the artificial wilderness of the summer camp in the second half of the film can be seen as an ironic comment on the rural/urban opposition. Indeed, the city is symbolically rejected in two significant ways. Firstly, the retreat to the summer camp and the subsequent camping adventure in the hills displays an aesthetic preference for the relative beauty of the countryside. Secondly, the corrupt spirit of the big city, as embodied in the character of Miss Reynolds, is rejected by Brad in favour of the more comfortable Jean, who represents the victory of his family's long-term security over his own carnal desires. Brad and Jean, for all intents and purposes, are a suburban couple. White, middle class, politically conservative and ill at ease in either wilderness or big city, they are yet to discover their natural habitat. Where 'the city' is presented in family films of the period without any apparent attempt to ruralise or suburbanise, its labyrinthine, dizzying and bustling qualities are exaggerated, and presented in overt counterpoint to the relative serenity of the country. When later family films deal with the issue of raising a family in urban conditions, as in *The Courtship of Eddie's Father* (Vincente Minnelli, 1963), the response is ambivalent, recognising its convenience, but distrusting its affective impact on social interaction.

Changing social mores and lifestyle patterns weakened the format, but the advent of television dealt a final hammer blow to the pastoral family film – at least as a consistent high grosser at the box office. Hollywood initially hoped to weather the storm of television in the post-war period, but gradually, it became apparent that it could hope to survive as a prosperous industry only by altering its production strategies to accommodate areas that television could not. The major studios cut down on production considerably, the second-feature movie was abolished, and the age of the blockbuster began. Television, though, was able to reach the highest number of viewers of all ages, and replaced the need for modest family-based dramas on the big screen. Viewers could watch material of similar thematic content and artistic standard from the comfort of their own homes. Television was in a position to achieve what Hollywood had long sought – cross-demographic audience saturation. The film industry was forced to seek alternatives, and the popular emergence of teenage culture in the mid-1950s prompted the proliferation of the teen pic, which simultaneously divided the audience, broadened the potential subject matter and permanently altered the style of the Hollywood cinema. It confirmed what various polls and marketers had been telling industry leaders for over a decade: the largest audience for movies were pre-teens, teenagers and young adults, not some universalised, archetypal nuclear family.

THE TRADITIONAL FAMILY FILM IN DECLINE, 1953–68

A new paradigm was rapidly emerging in Hollywood cinema by the early 1950s, which manifested itself in seismic industrial developments, and equally profound changes in film style. The emergence of television as a mass entertainment medium, coupled with vast swathes of the US population moving from the cities and small towns to the suburbs, fundamentally changed recreational habits. As nebulous as it may sound, it is difficult to overestimate the impact of this great wave of suburbanisation, which Douglas Gomery has called 'one of the great postwar historical phenomena'.[1] The emergence of television was similarly swift:

> By 1948, there were 250,000 [television] sets in use; a year later, a million. In 1951 televisions outsold radios for the first time, and by 1952, 15 million television sets were in use.[2]

Other historians have variously pointed towards the 1948 Paramount Consent decree, whereby the major studios were ordered to divest themselves of their vertically-integrated theatre chains, and the 1952 reversal of the 1915 Supreme Court First Amendment ruling, as the predominant causes of a precipitous decline in theatre audiences.[3]

Hollywood was forced to adapt in radical ways, both creatively and technically, to survive. As Gordon Gow observes, the decade saw two critical developments in Hollywood's internal policy:

On the one hand, a last big stand was mounted to overwhelm the public with demonstrations of the cinema's superiority as a medium, by complex technical devices aligned with a subject matter of a primarily simplistic kind. At the other extreme, more interestingly, the outdated formulae of the big companies began to give place to independent producers, while the companies served as financial backers and distributors.[4]

The latter development was more significant in terms of the wider history of Hollywood production. Hitherto, under what Bordwell, Staiger and Thompson have called the 'producer-unit' system, films had been made in-house by producers in charge of units specialising in specific areas, a system which allowed for a quick turnover of standard 'programme' films.[5] The gradual introduction of this new 'package-unit' system ceded creative control to independent producers, and this system has remained in operation ever since, with various modifications.[6] However, it was the attempt to compete with the growing threat of television that underpinned Hollywood's creative endeavours in the short-term. The major studios invested heavily in 'prestige' or 'epic' productions, often Biblical in theme and setting. Although the blockbuster is commonly thought to be a mid-1970s invention, Steve Neale has more accurately traced its introduction to the early 1950s, a period which saw the increasing abandonment of small-scale productions in favour of the extraordinary.[7] The three top earners at the US box office during the 1950s were all 'epic' films: *Ben-Hur* (William Wyler, 1959), *The Ten Commandments* (Cecil B. DeMille, 1956) and *The Bridge on the River Kwai* (David Lean, 1957).[8] These productions were designed to curb the decline in admissions, which had seen movie attendance as a percentage of US recreation expenditure drop from around 25 per cent in the mid-1940s to just 5.2 per cent by 1960.[9] With television providing more modest, everyday material, these epics 'carried significance in excess of box office as the loci of quintessential Hollywood spectacle'.[10] The pre-eminence of the epic form in the mid-late 1950s provided a suitably grandiose showcase for such technological gimmicks as Cinerama and 3D.

The 1950s was also the decade in which the requirements of foreign audiences began guiding production strategy. Between the mid-1910s and late 1940s, as Kristin Thompson suggests, Hollywood commanded a hugely powerful domestic theatre-going audience which often allowed production costs to be paid off during the North American release; many films, she notes, 'might begin earning profits apart from revenues coming in from other countries'.[11] The turning point, as Thomas Guback has argued, was the Paramount anti-trust case, which ruled in 1948 that the major Hollywood studios must divest themselves of their theatre chains, removing the 'sure outlet' that had been supplied by block-booking practices and their hegemonic control of the domestic exhibition sector. In conjunction with the decline in attendances, these factors forced producers to consider international requirements, albeit on a limited scale. For the first time, exhibitors were encouraged to open theatres offering 'art and foreign pictures in a small way'.[12] More significantly, in 1956, a United Artists representative informed a US Senate Committee that without foreign revenues, 'the industry would soon face insolvency and bankruptcy, or would have to change its method of production in such a way that the type and nature of its films would radically change'.[13] A Columbia executive noted that 'it has become necessary to produce pictures palatable to tastes in England, Italy and Japan as well as here at home'.[14] Initially, the influence of foreign audiences upon film content was rather modest. One executive admitted that 'if in making an American story [...] we could insert some incident that might take place in Paris, we would be glad to do it, because it would add flavour for the foreign market'.[15] Although this incremental interest in foreign audience tastes was crude and transparent, it no doubt dissuaded producers from making big-budget films appealing predominantly to domestic audiences, such as traditional family fare – often the very definition of self-absorbed Americana.

Cultural Change, the Teen Film and the Popularisation of Television

Although most of the Hollywood studios began to turn away from wholesome family entertainment during this period, the impact upon audiences was cushioned, to some degree, by Disney's sudden resurgence. April 1950 saw the release of *Cinderella*, the studio's most successful animated feature since the early 1940s. Even more significant was the subsequent popularity of *Treasure Island* (Byron Haskin), its first totally live-action production. Disney's diversification into live-action filmmaking occurred solely because of post-war trade restrictions in Britain. Foreign companies were prevented from exporting 100 per cent of earned capital, and the only viable recourse for Hollywood studios was to reinvest the frozen capital in locally-produced films. The result was a series of relatively low-budget but colourful family movies filmed in Britain, with mainly local talent. *Treasure Island* benefits from a fast-paced narrative and larger-than-life performance from Robert Newton as Long John Silver, but as *Boxoffice* reported (when awarding the film its Blue Ribbon award), the proportion of adult audiences were greater 'than is usual for cartoon features'.[16] The popularity of these two Disney films – as well as MGM's *Father of the Bride* (Vincente Minnelli) and Universal's *Louisa* (Alexander Hall) released the same year – led *Variety* optimistically to observe that 'family pix' were the box office 'backbone':

> Family type product has provided the backbone of the improvement in grosses which has been felt by most theatres this summer. This gives strength to the argument recently put forth by many exhibs that studios should lean more heavily to films for the family trade. It's the kiddies and the old folks attracted by these pix that make the difference in grosses, exhibs say. The teenagers and early 20s group can be counted on pretty much in any case, so the family pix get some of that 'lost audience' that has become an industry maxim. Most seasoned trade observers, however, are of the opinion that too much emphasis on the family pix could be as deadly, as other cycles have proved.[17]

This boom was temporary. As television began to colonise the areas in which Hollywood had previously depended, studios re-orientated towards more sensational, adult-orientated material.

Until the early 1950s, Disney was not widely considered to be the leading purveyor of family entertainment in Hollywood. It is significant, but nonetheless unsurprising, that when *Parents' Magazine* honoured a famous studio head in 1949 with a special award for the company that had produced the 'greatest list of family pix', the recipient was not Walt Disney, but MGM's Louis B. Mayer.[18] In 1953, MGM was also awarded a citation by *Boxoffice* for having produced the greatest quantity of Blue Ribbon award-winning films since 1932.[19] The key factors in Disney's ascendance to its almost monolithic status in the 'family' business during the late 1950s and 1960s were the unexpected popularity of its live-action productions;

the creation of its own distribution arm, Buena Vista, in 1953 (removing its prior dependence on RKO); a pioneering partnership with television network ABC in 1954, in which the network would offer investment in return for an exclusive television show and other original material; the release of live-action spectacular *20,000 Leagues under the Sea* (Richard Fleischer) later the same year; and the opening of theme park Disneyland in 1955, which was partly funded by the ABC deal. Disneyland was immediately successful. In 1956, the park's first year of business, it received about 3 million visitors; over the next decade, this figure had risen to nearly 7 million.[20] Furthermore, reportedly more than three-quarters of park attendees were teenagers or adults.[21] Disney's success during this period can be attributed to its expansion into alternative revenue streams; the firm transcended its earlier limitations as a producer of eccentric film fare and became a diversified conglomerate, targeting mass audiences of all ages and backgrounds.

20,000 Leagues under the Sea marked a new creative direction for Disney. Previously, its films had not explicitly differentiated between audience demographics. The focus was always the 'child of all ages' – what some marketers call the 'kidult' consumer – as Disney explained in 1938:

> Over at our place, we're sure of just one thing. Everybody in the world was once a child. We grow up. Our personalities change, but in every

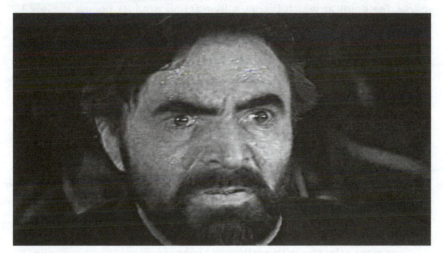

20,000 Leagues under the Sea (1954)

one of us something remains of our childhood [...] in planning our picture, we don't think of grown-ups and we don't think of children, but just that fine, clean, unspoiled spot down deep in every one of us that maybe the world has made us forget and that maybe our pictures can help recall.[22]

Although this comparatively undifferentiated address continued to characterise Disney's animated films, a more adult, middlebrow address henceforth announced itself in its live-action fare. *20,000 Leagues under the Sea* is talky and relatively cerebral, with some interesting moral discussions between the crazed Captain Nemo (James Mason) and the sympathetic Professor Aronnax (Paul Lukas). In one powerful sequence, Nemo, having given the order for the Nautilus, his nuclear submarine, to destroy a British warship carrying a hold of gunpowder, is seen wracked with guilt and anguish as the deed is carried out. He later explains to Aronnax 'the power of hate'. There is surprisingly little dramatic action. Advance publicity – including a promotional feature on Disney's weekly children's television show entitled 'Monsters of the Deep' – focused on the giant squid which attacks the Nautilus, yet this scene barely lasts five minutes in the completed film. Although there had been earlier signs of Disney's absorption of the production methods of rival studios – particularly when it began to replace technical innovation with ideological conventionality after its early 1940s artistic heyday – *20,000 Leagues* marks the point at which Disney's live-action product begins closely to resemble the family entertainments of its competitors.

The film's clear interest in appealing explicitly (rather than implicitly) to an older demographic no doubt reflects the ongoing emergence of the teenager as a social entity and consumer group. The idea of the teenager, which lies at the heart of 'youth culture', was, at this point, relatively new. As Thomas Hine explains:

Standard references cite a 1941 article in *Popular Science* magazine as the first published use of the word 'teenager'. The term came into use during World War II and first turned up in a book title in 1945. It seems to have leaked into the language from the world of advertising and marketing, where demographic information was becoming an increasingly important part of predicting which sales approaches are most effective with particular buyers.[23]

Unsurprisingly, the concepts of the 'teenager' and of a burgeoning 'youth culture' – which seemed to place themselves in opposition to the dominant 'adult' aesthetic – were matters of concern to social scientists and the general public alike. Nevertheless, the concept is expressly North American in origin, and as Hine argues: 'America created the teenager in its own image – brash, unfinished, ebullient, idealistic, crude, energetic, innocent, greedy, changing in all sorts of unsettling ways.'[24]

Within a climate of distrust and discontent towards youth culture fostered by politicians and the popular press, teenage delinquency swiftly became a moral panic in the United States. As Jon Lewis notes:

> The adult public's morbid interest in the delinquent juvenile [was] fanned by [newspaper] headlines like 'Two Teen Thrill Killings Climax Park Orgies', 'Teen Age Killers Pose A Mystery – Why Did They Do It?' and 'Twenty-Two Juveniles Killed in Gang War'.[25]

Public anxiety concerning this supposed moral problem prompted, and was in turn exacerbated by, Estes Kefauver's notorious Senate Committee Investigation into juvenile delinquency. The social science community, meanwhile, was attempting more temperate investigations into juvenile behaviour and youth culture, but its liberal humanistic conclusions were arguably no more attuned to the realities of teenage culture than conservative, reactionary responses.[26] Despite this fact, what is now referred to as the 'teen film' has its origins in what were explicitly *adult* reactions to social stimuli. *Rebel without a Cause* (Nicholas Ray, 1955) is now regarded as a watermark in the development of the teen film. Although its theatrical poster describes 'Teenage Terror Torn from Today's Headlines', explicitly highlighting the movie's sensationalist, exploitative qualities, the movie was codedly sympathetic to the teenage protagonists, and remains a colossal influence upon 1950s youth culture. However, youth culture was not simply innate and self-supporting; it was a commodity, directed towards a large, increasingly solvent exploitable group. The nostalgic allusions Pomerance makes to

> the icons of James Dean, Montgomery Clift, and Marlon Brando [and] the sounds of Elvis Presley, Little Richard, the Platters, and starchy Paul Anka

are apposite, with each of these individuals having originated through adult marketing and exposure strategies.[27] What emerged as the teen film was born from a wider interest in the teenager consumer, which transcended cinema and infiltrated all US consumer markets. As Thomas Hine explains:

> The man who had the facts on how powerful [teenage culture] could be, and who is frequently credited with shaping it, was Eugene Gilbert [...] By the time mainstream manufacturers and retailers were willing to pay attention to the young market, Gilbert had 5,000 teenage pollsters throughout the country, gathering information for his corporate clients and providing data for his syndicated column, 'What Young People Are Thinking', which ran in more than 300 newspapers.[28]

By 1958, Gilbert estimated that the purchasing power of teens was '$9.5 billion – ten times the total receipts of the movie industry – two thirds of which came from their parents, and the other third from their own earnings'.[29] As audience research began – in limited form – to be adopted by the studios in the 1940s, reports by Leo Handel (founder of the Motion Picture Research Bureau) and Paul F. Lazarsfeld confirmed that audiences were dominated by young people. The teenage demographic was a vast, exploitable audience which Hollywood hitherto had failed to address directly.

Given the industry's innate conservatism, it is unsurprising that the first big hit specifically targeting teenage audiences was produced independently. Doherty argues that *Rock Around the Clock* (Fred F. Sears, 1956) '[showed] that teenagers alone could sustain a box-office hit' and 'pushed Motion Picture Production strategy toward the teenpic'.[30] The producer in question was Sam Katzman, who had

> [Worked] at Monogram in the 1940s, and later with Columbia [...] He specialised in B-movie matinee fare pitched alternately to the preteen 'cap pistol set' (the serials *Atom Man vs. Superman* [1950] and *Captain Video* [1951]) or to a slightly older group comprising mostly adolescent males (the Bowery Boys and Jungle Jim series). As early as 1946, he had become especially attuned to the latter group, billing himself in Monogram trade ads as a producer for 'Teen Agers'.[31]

Rock Around the Clock was the first in a series of semi-fictional movies starring DJ Alan Freed and featuring a selection of popular contemporary rock 'n' roll stars. *Don't Knock the Rock* (Fred F. Sears, 1956), *Rock, Rock, Rock* (Will Price, 1956), *Mister Rock and Roll* (Charles S. Dubin, 1957) and *Go, Johnny, Go!* (Paul Landres, 1959) followed the blueprint. The films are dominated by live musical performances, but the pretence of narrative is maintained. Lightweight, soapy teenage storylines are used as connecting material between performances, and with the exception of Freed, all the leading characters are teenagers. As the benevolent benefactor of teen culture, Freed operates as a mediator between the worlds of youth and adulthood. Although replete with blatant self-publicising, these otherwise inoffensive films correspond with the general tone of the rock 'n' roll music: energetic, youthful and predominantly carefree.

Doherty has identified various different strains of teen pic in addition to the 'rock 'n' roll pic', including 'the delinquent movie', the 'drag-strip cycle', 'weirdies' and 'clean teenpics'.[32] In spite of generic differences, of course, they were all essentially doing the same job; they were exploitation films, cashing-in on the cultural Zeitgeist. The movement towards demographic targeting on a mass scale (as opposed to the limited confines of child-orientated B movies in the 1930s) was undeniably facilitated by the rise of independent production. In 1958, United Artists executive Max E. Youngstein estimated that the proportion of independently-produced Hollywood films had risen from approximately 1 per cent at the start of the decade to over 50 per cent.[33] Companies such as American International Pictures (AIP) directed their attention towards low-budget teen films (specifically horror films in this case), and thrived. AIP's owners, James J. Nicholson and Samuel Z. Arkoff, believed that 'teenagers made up the only market that could sustain the modern Motion Picture business'.[34] With the meteoric rise in independent production, it is unsurprising that many of the formal and ideological practices of studio-era Hollywood were subject to radical change.

Hollywood production strategy became increasingly fragmentary and polarised. Although most movies still conformed to studio-era norms, the divergence between the adult-orientated epic form and the youth-oriented teen film underlined the industry's weakening grip on the pluralistic 'family audience'. Television was now catering to this market with the sort of modest, homey fare that had characterised family films throughout the 1930s and 1940s. Television strategy – unlike that of cinema – was innately geared to tapping the family audience. Networks also believed that women, specifically housewives, were the key to unlocking the profit potential of the family as a whole. Lynn Spigel argues that NBC's *Today* programme (1952–), broadcast daily between 7.00am and 9.00am on weekdays, emerged as one of the first network TV shows calculatedly targeting families.[35] It 'attempted to lure men, women and children with discrete programme segments that addressed their different interests and meshed with their separate schedules'.[36] A network poll calculated that television audiences comprised 52 per cent women, 26 per cent men and 22 per cent children.[37] With advertising space on major network television at a premium, programming was designed with maximum possible demographic broadness.

The two most popular television forms in the late 1950s were soap operas and sitcoms. Soap operas were produced by commercial radio as early as the 1930s, aggressively targeting housewives and, by association, young children.[38] In the 1950s, television colonised this market. During the late 1940s – television's formative years – family sitcoms were a marginal genre, but as Spigel notes, the success of *I Love Lucy* (1951–7) changed this:

> When *I Love Lucy* came to the CBS network in 1951, it was a huge popular success, soaring to number 1 in the Nielsen ratings. CBS aggressively developed the genre over the course of the early 1950s, and its successes did not go unnoticed by the other networks, which also increasingly turned to sitcoms and other film formats. By 1960, there were about twice as many sitcoms as there were variety shows.[39]

The family sitcom did not merely reproduce the low-key formula of the movies. Instead, early television was much closer to radio, in that the tone was often self-aware and, in spite of the prosaic subject-matter, inherently unrealistic. As Spigel argues, 'some early family comedies used studio audiences in order to provide the sense of spontaneity that spectators enjoy at the theatre'.[40] Furthermore, Spigel does not believe that shows like *I Love Lucy* and *Make Room for Daddy* (1953–64) were 'realistic'. Instead, 'Lucy's slapstick clowning, trick costumes, and wild antics made for highly unrealistic depictions of domesticity'.[41]

In spite – or perhaps because – of the extreme, exaggerated depictions of domesticity in such massively popular, long-running shows as *I Love*

Lucy, *The Adventures of Ozzie and Harriet* (1952–66) and *Father Knows Best* (1954–60), they outstripped the popularity of Hollywood's family features. Pitched very broadly, both thematically and comedically, they relied heavily on pratfalls and visual gags that offered multiple avenues of access to cross-demographic audiences. Their popularity also derived from their longevity. Long-running family sitcoms were unfolding texts in which events and characters were given time to grow and develop their fan-bases – assuming, that is, that they attained high enough ratings to avoid cancellation. Because of its transparent populism, the family sitcom has, like the soap opera, been persistently denigrated. Whilst Gerard Jones contends that 'the most successful [sitcoms] usually display a particularly shrewd insight into the concerns of the vast American public and a special kind of integrity of their own', he concedes that 'the bulk of sitcoms [...] rarely display either, and that was never truer than in the flood of '52, '53 and '54'.[42] Most were devoid of genuine conflict, and hence 'characters were allowed to tease each other in an authentic-feeling but completely safe manner'.[43] Because of this, Jones views *The Adventures of Ozzie and Harriet* as 'one of the most determinedly bland programs ever broadcast'.[44]

Nevertheless, this lack of conflict and essential 'blandness' was entirely deliberate, rendering these shows broadly suitable, and also comfortingly escapist. Inoffensive productions are better-suited to television than commercial cinema. One may passively watch a prosaic, sentimental television show if one is bored, has nothing better to do, or desires comfort, but is far less likely to visit a cinema and pay money upfront for the same low-key amusement.

This is not to say that the relationship between television and cinema was *entirely* one-sided. The major studios recouped considerable revenues from selling their film libraries to the networks. Unsurprisingly, given television's natural identity as a 'family' medium, there was particular demand for cross-demographic film entertainment – particularly of a kind that television studios found impossible to produce themselves; for example, spectaculars (such as *King Kong*) and prestige pictures, especially those made in Technicolor. Films suitable for showing over the Christmas period became desirable targets for acquisition, and this led to several films which had fared only moderately when released theatrically – notably *Babes in Toyland*, *The Wizard of Oz* and *It's a Wonderful Life* – enjoying considerable renewed popularity. The latter two films, in particular, have attained an exalted status in the Christmas schedule that borders on the ritualistic. *It's a Wonderful Life* is perhaps the quintessential example of how television can manufacture family entertainment through judicious editing, astute programming and basic repetition. As Jonathan Munby has observed, it has 'assumed the status of *the* Christmas movie', yet was viewed upon release essentially as an adult drama.[45] This process of manufacturing has subjected the film to considerable mythologisation. Today, as we watch George Bailey (James Stewart) fall deeper into despair as his business and then family life seem to fall apart, thereby threatening to leave the town at the mercy of the wicked industrialist Potter (Lionel Barrymore), we do so in the knowledge that an angel (Henry Travers) will prove to George the value of his life, and that the townsfolk will ultimately rally round to save his business, ending the film on the pleasurable image of utopian family and community spirit. The *noirish* despair of the mid-point in the film is effaced by the surety – borne through familiarity – of a happy ending. This knowledge was not available to audiences upon initial theatrical release, when the film flopped badly and virtually ruined Capra as an artistic and commercial force. Indeed, unless one believes in angels or in divine intervention, the second half of the movie might very well be interpreted as the impossible fantasy of a dying man (when George attempts suicide by throwing himself into the river). The *deus ex machina* ending does little to refute that interpretative possibility.

The Decline of the Traditional Family Film

During the mid-1950s, family films were conspicuous by their absence in movie theatres, just as children largely disappeared from the big screen. By 1954, only one child performer – MGM's Sandy Descher – was under studio contract.[46] The trend towards adult-orientated programming, which begun in the late 1940s, accelerated with the release of Otto Preminger's *The Moon is Blue* (1953) – the first major studio production released without a Code Administration seal of approval. Preminger's *The Man with the Golden Arm* (1955) and Elia Kazan's *Baby Doll* (1956) were similarly controversial, receiving 'Condemned' ratings from the Catholic Legion of Decency. However, it is clear that social standards of cultural acceptability had relaxed since the 1930s, as these films still did good business in Catholic strongholds.[47] In May 1955, *Variety* identified an uncomfortable squeeze between [the industry's] public relations sense and its pocketbook. Observers feel that the dilemma is inevitably the result of producers moving to satisfy what they conceive to be the public's slowly developing but very real yen for challenging, more adult entertainment. At the same time, there has been a diminishing flow of the type of 'family' pix on which Hollywood used to thrive. First, there is less room now for 'family' type of pix on studio's production skeds; secondly, it's been found that the popularity of this sort of film is no longer what it used to be.[48]

Clearly, a slow but perceptible period of cultural transition was taking place in the United States, in which more liberal attitudes were gradually subsuming the older, typically-middlebrow consensus. Although Eric Johnston publicly defended the Production Code in May 1955, arguing that the movies provided more family entertainment than any other media, 'including the newspapers, magazines, theatre, radio and television', the MPAA bowed to pressure and a slightly revised Code was introduced in December 1956.[49] By 1966, however, only 59 per cent of films released in the United States carried the Code seal of approval.[50] The typical industry response, when challenged, was to state its ongoing support for family entertainment whilst continuing to supply more violent, sexually-themed and youth-orientated products in line with demand.[51] On the whole, exhibitors blamed producers for failing to produce sufficient family fare, whilst producers accused exhibitors of failing to adequately exploit those films that *were* released. Television networks were the main beneficiary. An ever-increasing proportion of young people had access to television (a 1957 audience report found that 77 per cent of children between the ages of six and 11 watched it regularly) and, increasingly, networks programmed specifically for children, differentiating by age and gender, rather than targeting all-encompassing 'family' audiences.[52]

By this point, the Children's Film Library was virtually defunct. The Library had always been a cooperative initiative between the MPAA and the leading studios. Theoretically, the process worked like this: the major studios selected their most notable family films dating back to the early sound era, and donated a number of prints of each film to a central exchange. Theatre owners who wished to stage children's matinees would request prints of the desired films before returning them to the exchange, and gradually the studios' expenses would be amortised by participating exhibitors. By the mid-1950s, this system was no longer economical. The primary reason was the industry-wide transition from the dangerous nitrate to the safer acetate film base, from 1952 onwards. Faced with the option of creating a whole new set of prints based on the more expensive acetate system, distributors opted simply to withdraw their old films from circulation. The remaining nitrate prints were, in any event, deteriorating with age, and colour prints were markedly more expensive than black-and-white.[53] The MPAA attempted to revitalise the Library in early 1956 with the aid of affiliated civic organisations, but by 1960 it had ceased operations entirely.[54] By this point, Disney had largely cornered the market on family films, largely by virtue of its successful programmes of expansion and diversification. A Disney-produced animal film, *Old Yeller* (Robert Stevenson, 1957), was one of the biggest hits of the decade, but although well-made, it certainly offered nothing new. Most independent producers, meanwhile, were more interested in attracting teenagers, which carried with them a sense of edginess patently lacking in the unfashionable 'family' market. In 1958, MGM made an extraordinary attempt to resurrect the Andy Hardy series with *Andy Hardy Comes Home* (Howard W. Koch). Predictably, it was a resounding critical and commercial failure.

In February 1960, *Variety* observed that the film industry had 'practically forfeited the children's market to television', pointing out that no studio except Disney

> is bold enough to state frankly that a particular film is 'aimed at the moppet trade', preferring to employ the description 'family picture'. At the same time, the majority of the film companies, in offering films that have a children's appeal, are careful to leave the impression that there are elements of interest in these pix that will attract teenagers and adults as well. It is considered sacrilegious to claim unabashedly that a specific entry will appeal to children between the ages of 7 and 14.[55]

The same article argued that 'despite the constant exhibitor wail for so-called "family-type pictures", most theatremen are secretly afraid of these entries, especially if they are of the type that will not attract adults during the evening hours'.[56] Some of the biggest Hollywood-produced hits in 1960 were marketed as adult-orientated entertainment, most notably

The Apartment (Billy Wilder), *Psycho* (Alfred Hitchcock) and *Elmer Gantry* (Richard Brooks). United Artists explicitly advised patrons that the latter film was not suitable for children – a direct contravention of Hollywood's supposed ethos of universal suitability.[57]

The increasing regularity of Code violations, coupled with persistent criticism from the Legion of Decency and other civic groups, inevitably led to a renewed threat of Federal censorship. Glenn Norris, Fox's general sales manager, suggested that exhibitors complaining about the proliferation of adult films should afford family pictures 'the same preferential and sympathetic treatment' they gave a film like *Psycho*.[58] Again, widespread criticism and the threats of censorship were enough to temporarily stimulate the family market. Among the non-Disney family films released during 1960 were MGM's *The Adventures of Huckleberry Finn* (Michael Curtiz), Universal's *The Snow Queen* (Phil Patton) and Columbia's *My Dog, Buddy* (Ray Kellog), with an expanded roster for the following season. On this occasion, however, there was no commensurate cutting-back of controversial content, as there had been during the backlash of 1933/34. The Theater Owners of America admitted that 'many current films are controversial' but insisted that 'our industry has done a job on family and child fare'.[59]

Universal advertising executive Philip Gerard argued that with aggressive publicity and creative merchandising, the public would accept family films 'as readily as raw realism, sophisticated sex, and savage sadism'.[60] Nevertheless, there were reports of studios failing to cooperate with exhibitors attempting to stage children's shows (exacerbated by Disney's alleged refusal to supply prints of old films in order to maximise revenues for future re-releases), and by 1963, television network NBC was complaining that Hollywood features were becoming too adult-themed to broadcast to general audiences.[61]

Concurrently, for the first time, teenagers were being offered films directly tailored to their entertainment needs. Successful independents, such as AIP, although limited by modest resources, often had a closer understanding of demographic targeting than more established studios. By the 1960s, television and independent film producers alike had grasped the value of the male teenager, both as consumer and opinion leader. AIP developed a useful syllogism (dubbed the 'Peter Pan Syndrome') which they applied to teenage audience tastes when deciding upon film content:

a) a younger child will watch anything an older child will watch;
b) an older child will not watch anything a younger child will watch;
c) a girl will watch anything a boy will watch;
d) a boy will not watch anything a girl will watch; therefore,
e) to catch your greatest audience you zero in on the 19-year-old male.[62]

By the mid-1960s, the music and television industries had adopted this philosophy on a grand scale, resulting not only in the massive proliferation of rock 'n' roll, but such cross-over hits as *The Monkees* (1966–8). In comparison, Walt Disney's quaint insistence that he made movies 'to suit myself, hoping they will also suit the audience' seems positively prehistoric.[63]

Nevertheless, with its ever-tightening hold on the theatrical 'family' entertainment market, Disney profited considerably from the controversies surrounding both 'adult' and 'teen' films. By this point, the studio had evidently grasped that it was impossible to dominate the family market solely with animated features. It required a constant, year-round supply of screen entertainment to maintain its near-hegemony. Live-action features could be rapidly produced, and designed to fit the company 'house style'. As Schickel observes, 'the Disney [live-action] films tended to look alike' – they adhered to a finely-honed formula.[64] Between 1953 and 1968, Disney produced a mere five feature animations, but over 50 live-action films.[65] The quantity of live-action films accelerated after 1959, when they were released roughly at the rate of one every two months. With the success of *Pollyanna* (David Swift, 1960), the studio 'discovered' its first bona-fide child-star, Hayley Mills. Walt Disney, who reportedly was enraptured by Mills, fancifully described her as 'the finest young talent to come into the motion picture industry in the past twenty-five years'.[66] Nonetheless, he felt that *Pollyanna*'s title damaged revenues: 'girls and women went to it, but men tended to stay away because it sounded sweet and sticky'.[67] Later films stressed a more equal balance between boys and girls, parents and children. *The Parent Trap* (David Swift, 1961) centres on twin girls – both played by Mills – who attempt to bring their estranged parents back together, thereby restoring a broken nuclear family unit. *Swiss Family Robinson* (Ken Annakin, 1960) centres on a family marooned on a desert island during the Napoleonic era. Faced with the likelihood of a long stay, the family determines to tame the wilderness and build a new, happy life on the island. The first half of the movie plays like a wish-fulfilment fantasy, as the family, in exaggerated Robinson Crusoe style, manufactures a huge, resplendent tree house, more than large enough for the family of five (and two dogs). The tree house even features a retractable staircase – 'to keep out the neighbours', as Father (John Mills) puts it, recapitulating the adult suburban fantasy of the self-contained, self-sustaining family unit. It is a pastoral idyll, a wilderness truly tamed by human ingenuity, where even the fierce animals that threaten the family upon their arrival later mysteriously disappear; a private sphere insulated from the unwanted intrusion of society.

The function of the parents is universalised and familial, rather than sexual. As highlighted by the fact that they only ever refer to each other as 'Mother' and 'Father', their position is not that of lovers, but generic parents, projecting authority but benevolence. The casting of English actor John Mills – scarcely the most sexually-potent or charismatic leading man – seems designed to impose a level of benign, unthreatening masculinity. This was typical of the Disney studio's overall casting strat-egy, in which performers were hired for basic competence, rather than force of personality. As Schickel argues, 'the stars of a Disney movie are utterly interchangeable with others of their type'.[68] Just as the teenage boys are predictably brave and resourceful, displaying stereotypical adventure-story hunger for daring-do, the parents are archetypes of traditional North American ideology surrounding the required roles of parents. The only moment in the film where Mother (Dorothy McGuire) and Father seem to possess any degree of intimacy comes shortly after the family complete the tree house. Father shows Mother to the highest room in the tree house, their bedroom, which is open to the night sky:

> Don't you remember? That summer we went to Interlaken? You said that some day, if you could have your wish, you'd sleep each night so you could see the stars.

The scene is a curious, but isolated, allusion to a deeper, more romantic relationship, in a film generally uninterested in the intricacies of adult concerns.

Although Father appears totally naive concerning the adolescent needs of his three sons, Mother becomes concerned at the lack of a young woman. As with the small-town family comedies of the 1930s and 1940s, women satisfy the need for generational continuity; for the procreative, rather than recreational, aspect of sexual intercourse. A brief allusion to teenage hormones occurs in a scene where the two teenage boys – Fritz (James MacArthur) and Ernst (Tommy Kirk) – begin exploring the island. They are seen reclining on the shores of the desert island, both topless:

> **Ernst:** Fritz, listen: do you think if we get to New Guinea, if we ever do, there'll be any girls our age?
> **Fritz:** By the time we get to New Guinea, we won't care what age they are!

The boys are behaving within the bounds of adult expectation, a fact made explicit by Mother's earlier concerns regarding the lack of a woman on the island. Their sexual drive is heavily mediated by the bounds of decorum, hence its complete absence in the family sections. Their relatively short passage into manhood, framed by a brief discussion between the teenagers in which they allude to their greater physical strength and bravery, is heavily sanitised and unproblematic; ideal youth into ideal manhood. Like the island, their burgeoning sexuality is shown to be unaffected and natural.

As teen films became more established, catering to teenage audiences in family films no longer made logical or financial sense. As a result, family films refocused to accommodate the surviving pre-teen and adult middle-class demographics. Previously, in spite of the concentration upon the entire family, narratives had relied heavily upon the central teenage figure(s) (such as the pairing of Mickey Rooney and Judy Garland in MGM's early 1940s productions), but without this mediatory influence, 1960s family films became polarised; either strongly child-centred, or adult-dominated family 'epics'. Therefore, the 'juvenilisation' of Hollywood films in the late 1950s (as Thomas Doherty has it) was paralleled by a similarly potent trend of 'adultification' in mainstream family movies. While Disney persisted with child-orientated live-action productions, the other major studios embraced more middlebrow 'family' blockbusters, such as *My Fair Lady* (George Cukor, 1964), *The Sound of Music* (Robert Wise, 1965), *Chitty Chitty Bang Bang* (Ken Hughes, 1968) and *Oliver!* (Carol Reed, 1968). Like the small-town family films of the 1940s, they were primarily aimed at adults, but calculatedly avoided contentious thematic content. Unsurprisingly, the more adult-orientated family blockbusters found considerable favour with the Academy Awards – a useful register of industry approval.

Although *My Fair Lady* and *The Sound of Music* echo such mid-1950s productions as *The King and I* (Walter Lang, 1956) in their broadly suitable but resolutely middlebrow approach, arguably an even greater influence was *Around the World in 80 Days* (Michael Anderson, 1956). Like those later films, it received rave reviews from mainstream critics who lauded it as a wonderful family film with universal appeal.[69] Although distributed and part-funded by United Artists, it is less a product of studio excess than the chutzpah of a single producer, Michael Todd, who determined to make the biggest film in the history of commercial cinema. The all-star (and all-adult) cast includes David Niven (as Phileas Fogg), Cantinflas, Robert Newton, Shirley Maclaine, Marlene Dietrich, Red Skelton, Noel Coward, Frank Sinatra, Ronald Colman and Buster Keaton. Mature, middlebrow, urbane, witty in an ostentatiously aristocratic sort of way, and impressive visually and sonically, the film is also very long, at just over three hours (with an intermission). Whether or not its success stemmed more from its absurdly starry cast or from the immense amount of pre-release hype, North American rentals in the region of $25 million (from a $6 million outlay) – as well as considerable Academy Award recognition – testify to its immense impact upon release. As an example of fiscal impropriety at least as much as showmanship, the film is a landmark in the history of mass-audience filmmaking, partly because its affirmation of the traditional Hollywood values of stardom and spectacle underlined the potentialities of cinema in the age of television, and, indeed, of 'family'-suitable entertainment in an era of surging 'youth' culture.

In a sense, its grotesquery signifies both the endurance and the irreversible decline of classical Hollywood cinema. *Around the World in 80 Days* can be interpreted alternately as a celebration and as a parody of Hollywood generic norms and production practices. Whilst stardom has been a central attraction in mainstream cinema almost from its very beginnings, here it is taken to farcical, yet intriguing, extremes. On the one hand, the relegation of literally dozens of talented performers to brief cameos is a monumental waste of talent and resources. Yet one of the primary points of interest – indeed, arguably its most enduring quality – is the presence of a seemingly endless array of stars and personalities dating across Hollywood's history. Its generic identity is similarly loaded, with adventure, mystery, comedy, musical, romantic and western tropes all clearly evident. Like many of Hollywood's epic films of the period, it addresses a vaguely-defined mass audience of indeterminate composition. Although there is nothing that would make it morally or aesthetically damaging for juvenile audiences, a variety of factors – ranging from its considerable length, sophisticated tone and extreme allusiveness – delineates it as adult entertainment. In fact, the movie depends for much of its impact on audience awareness of the genres to which it alludes, the industrial and formal codes it subverts, and the range of talent it showcases. The tone, dialogue, humour and referentiality all imply an educated, cine-literate adult audience-base; it is little wonder it was so popular with critics. Although the focus on the family and obvious sentimentality strikingly evident in 1960s mainstream family movies are absent in this film, the same atmosphere of exaggerated, faux-aristocratic gentility is unmistakeable.

With its sense of ironic detachment coupled with unsurpassable excess, *Around the World in 80 Days* announces the impending end of a period in North American cultural history where a middlebrow, adult-inflected aesthetic dominated. While these qualities bring into sharper focus the rapid changes in teenage and adult filmmaking then taking place, they also articulate the ongoing desire for continuity – both ideological and formal – among the North American public. With an ever-deepening divide between liberal youth and the conservative establishment, the 'family' musical, with its bloated, anachronistic style, could no longer legitimately claim to represent the interests of all audience sections. Yet the popularity of the format – at least until the late 1960s – hints at a silent majority who still desired such entertainment because of its attendant associations of comfort and familiarity. Even Disney shifted its attention during the mid-1960s towards this amorphous audience section, resulting in a more traditional, adult-orientated and ideologically-conservative style. Indeed, *Mary Poppins* signals a new direction for Disney. It centres upon a 'practically perfect' but eccentric nanny, Mary Poppins (Julie Andrews), reluctantly enlisted by the rigid patriarch of a slightly troubled Edwardian family. Most of the family's problems appear to originate with stuffy, autocratic father Mr. Banks (David Tomlinson), an executive who philosophises that since 'a British bank is run on efficiency, a British home requires nothing less'. Mary has a firm grasp of magic, and promises to re-instil order in the family through a mixture of kindness and firmness. Aided by chimney-sweep Bert (Dick Van Dyke), she finally manages to convince Mr. Banks of the error of his ways. It is therefore significant that, like the small-town comedies of the 1940s (which were also produced during a period of social anxiety regarding the family unit), *Mary Poppins* is set in the distant past. The action is relocated to Edwardian England, a supposed bastion of etiquette, high society and family unity. To borrow Fredric Jameson's term, *Mary Poppins* shares much of the 'feeling tone' of such 1940s Hollywood productions as *Life with Father*.[70] In both cases, the overtly nostalgic mood is heightened by tokenistic period detail, such as family servants, gaslights and horse-drawn carriages.

However, although the similarities between the two forms are clear, closer examination reveals an important difference: in the 1940s pastoral family drama, the family unit operated as a bulwark against external pressures. The genre focused upon individuals about to enter the adult social sphere and in need of guidance, assisted by wise, benevolent fathers who helped them overcome their anxieties in preparation for adulthood. The family was the locus of kindly wisdom and support, capable of overcoming all problems if its members pulled together in a common cause. In

Mary Poppins (1964)

Mary Poppins, problems do not reside with individual family members. Instead, it is the family as an institutional system which must be rehabilitated. The rehabilitative process is twofold: the on-screen salvation of an unhappy, malfunctioning family; and, more importantly, the broader cultural mission to restore 'the family' to its prior, exalted position in the national consciousness. The very thrust of the film, and specifically the character of Mary, can be seen as projections of order and ideological normality upon an institution widely regarded as disintegrating. Indeed, the radical conclusions of such social scientists as R. D. Laing, who posited that self-interest was the governing force behind the family, were disquieting for a society that has long valorised the nurturing qualities of the family as the fulcrum of the socialisation process.[71] Previous Hollywood films had positioned the family as the solution to life's problems. Here, family is the problem.

With its greater focus upon the family unit, Disney was now displaying a more pronounced ideological populism.[72] *Mary Poppins* still attempts to tap a juvenile mode of appeal with the special-effects-heavy fantasy sequences, the musical numbers and elaborate dance choreography, the man-boy figure of Bert, and the presence of the child protagonists (Karen Dotrice and Matthew Garber). However, the scene in which Bert chastises Mr. Banks for the neglect of his children, pointing out that 'childhood slips like sand through a sieve', merely reflects familiar adult wistfulness regarding the transience of childhood and a broader preoccupation with ageing and mortality. The immutably 'teacherly, gentle, solicitous, candid, occasionally commanding' persona of Julie Andrews (as Bruce Babington describes it) adds a further level of didacticism to proceedings.[73] Although Disney's films retained a more obvious child emphasis than those of its competitors, the success of *Mary Poppins* appeared to convince Disney that the biggest profits were to be captured replicating the basic structure of their most adult-inflected film to date.

Walt Disney may have protested that he never made a film 'that did not have, as its primary criterion of success, its ability to please him', but the creative direction of his studio in the 1960s casts that statement into doubt.[74] In attempting to reproduce the successful formula of *Mary Poppins* – the decade's second most successful film at the domestic box office behind *The Sound of Music* – the studio manoeuvred itself even further towards a middlebrow orthodoxy.[75] Admittedly, its products were always *aesthetically* attuned to mainstream audience taste; as Schickel has observed, Walt Disney appeared to possess 'some almost mystic bond between himself and the moods and attitudes and styles' of the public.[76] However, by positioning itself within the creative confines of the belea-guered nuclear family unit, the studio was almost bound to articulate the anxieties surrounding that institution, thereby reflecting the ideological concerns of the adult establishment as never before.

Not helped by the death of its founder in 1966, Disney entered a period of commercial and artistic anomie that lasted until the mid-1980s. Douglas Gomery suggests that a major factor in the studio's decline lay in the fact that Roy Disney never possessed the intuitive insight of his brother Walt:

> Roy never learned from the success of his brother's risk-taking; he remained always the fiscal realist. He and Walt complemented each other. Now only one side of that balance was left. And it was not the side that had pushed the company forward.[77]

Disney's problems stemmed largely from its refusal to engage with the teenage and young adult audiences. Partly, the company's booming theme park operations were to blame; Disney executives were fearful of damag-ing its brand identity as the quintessential purveyor of multimedia family entertainment by abandoning its traditional consumer-base of parents and children. Because 'youth culture' identified itself partly in *opposition* to the traditionally-conservative social institution of the family, Disney resisted embracing this new cultural paradigm. Admittedly, the prospect of unifying 'family' and 'youth' audiences – as George Lucas and Steven Spielberg would ultimately succeed in accomplishing a decade later – seemed impossible, at the time. Consequently, *The Jungle Book* (Wolfgang Reitherman, 1967) – one of the studio's lightest animated features – and *The Love Bug* (Robert Stevenson, 1968) – the first in a long-running series of live-action comedies based around a sentient racing car called Herbie – were Disney's last major box office hits until the late 1980s.

The Sound of Music and the 1960s Adult-Orientated Family Blockbuster

In the short term, during the mid-1960s, pitching films more towards the adult elements of the 'family audience' was a sound financial strategy

The Sound of Music (1965)

which paid dividends. The window of opportunity for these films achieving sizable box office success lasted just over four years: the period between the release of *Mary Poppins* in 1964 and the implementation of the MPAA's movie rating system in November 1968. Following the release of *Mary Poppins*, and Warner Bros.' success with *My Fair Lady*, Twentieth Century Fox scored massively with its production of *The Sound of Music*.[78] The 'epic' treatment, song-and-dance numbers and broad comedy evidenced in these films showed a prevailing faith in the studio-era belief that broad suitability will inevitably capture a broad range of viewers. In most respects, these films were adult in their ideological content. It is surely significant that *Chitty Chitty Bang Bang* – comfortably the most juvenile of these films in theme and approach – received poor reviews, weaker returns and far less attention from the Academy Awards than the others.

The high esteem with which these movies were received stemmed as much from their inherent conservatism in a time of social and industry upheaval than their intrinsic merits as popular entertainment. *The Sound of Music* was a massive critical and commercial smash, providing ballast to the floundering major studios. It won Academy Awards for 'Best

Picture', 'Best Director' (Robert Wise), 'Best film editing', 'Best Music' and 'Best Sound'. Its domestic rental figure has been placed at $72 million, making it the highest-grossing movie of the decade by a considerable margin.[79] Julie Andrews was nominated for the second consecutive year for 'Best Actress in a Leading Role'. The US Library of Congress selected the film for preservation to the National Film Registry in 2001, another noted measure of establishment approval.[80] *Oliver!*, meanwhile, received six Oscars, including 'Best Picture' and 'Best Director' for Carol Reed, and was nominated for a further six awards. In contrast, *Meet Me in St. Louis*, perhaps the most famous and well-regarded family film of the 1940s, only received four minor Oscar nominations. The divergence is easily explained: the 1960s prestige family musical served to affirm middlebrow cultural values in an era in which mainstream Hollywood was heading into uncertain territory. Inoffensive films still ascribing to the prescriptions of the Production Code were promoted in favour of more challenging fare, which disregarded industry conventions by *only* addressing the 'adult' and ignoring the 'family'.

Such productions are characterised by an inescapably reflexive, reactionary quality. The industry had always attempted to accommodate the dominant social and cultural expectations regarding family films. Although industry leaders purposely aligned themselves and their products with the dominant ideology, they made middlebrow family entertainment because opinion leaders demanded it and audiences appreciated it, just as juvenile entertainment was marginalised and rejected by mainstream audiences time and again. By this point, however, opinion leaders were teenagers, rather than adults in their 30s and 40s. Films such as *My Fair Lady* and *The Sound of Music* were a bulwark against the new threats to the long-standing dominance of middlebrow culture: young, independent filmmakers, and childish adults. The decision to give the directorial responsibility for such projects to aging directors such as George Cukor, Robert Wise and Carol Reed could simply be interpreted as a natural desire to see expensive prestige productions handled by competent, experienced craftsmen. However, it also evidences the obvious lack of trusted young filmmakers in Hollywood. The studio system had traditionally nurtured emerging directorial talent, but the post-studio system was actively constraining it. Kubrick aside, most of the prominent young auteurs of the period were operating in the European art-house industries. Having entrusted its survival to surviving adherents of the studio system who collectively represented the old ways, the industry had lost its long-standing claim to represent popular tastes. Although we can certainly ascribe this trend to professional resistance to radically altering Hollywood's established entertainment ethos, there was surely also personal resistance as well. Hollywood executives like Daryl F. Zanuck, Barney Balaban, Jack Warner and even Walt Disney belonged to the old generation whose control was rapidly diminishing. If – in the midst of a cultural and political revolution apparently inimical to these ideals – they dug their heels and defended themselves against perceived insurgency, it is hardly surprising.

Youth culture – as commonly represented by the emergence of rock 'n' roll and a large stratum of independent cinema – was a phenomenon still dimly understood and often misrepresented. It was particularly apt to be conflated with liberalism and the counter-cultural movement. In what Maurice Isserman and Michael Kazin have described as a second American civil war, the 1960s were marked by a number of political and cultural oppositions, in which

> many Americans came to regard groups of fellow countrymen as enemies with whom they were engaged in a struggle for the nation's very soul. Whites versus blacks, liberals versus conservatives (as well as liberals versus radicals), young versus old, men versus women, hawks versus doves, rich versus poor, taxpayers versus welfare recipients, the religious versus the secular, the hip versus the straight, the gay versus the straight – everywhere one looked, new battalions took to the field, in a spirit ranging from that of redemptive sacrifice to vengeful defiance.[81]

In addition to these social divisions was the dilemma faced by exhibitors as to whether to try and attract respectable, middle-class adult patrons, or an edgier, less reputable but potentially more profitable youth clientele. For one drive-in theatre owner in Charlotte, North Carolina, it was a straight choice between 'family' and 'nudie' films:

> During the summer I did have some very nice people in here. They were very much interested in family pictures. But they were few and far between. And I played the best pictures all summer [...] In wintertime you can't survive on family business. You have to pick up what

you can get. For nudies, my audience is mostly salesmen, professional men. My customers are not a bunch of bums at all. They're just good people. They support me, which is something the family people don't do [...] I sure did want to run the family pictures for the people. I really did want to put 'em on the screen. But, if you have a rainy Saturday night on a family picture, nobody will be there. For a nudie they come out in rain, snow, sleet, or whatever it is.[82]

Many exhibitors doubtless felt a moral compunction to at least *try* to privilege family movies; such was the overriding propaganda that they had a duty to a higher cause of public betterment.

Inevitably, though, exhibitors were motivated by the bottom line. In 1970, when Disney re-released *Fantasia*, National General Theaters caused a minor scandal when a top-down directive suggested that theatre managers should avoid trying to attract families and instead target 'nice, unwashed, pot-smoking citizens' in search of a visually-augmented psychedelic trip.[83] 'To offer it as you would ordinarily sell a normal Disney film is to invite box office disaster', argued the leaked memo, which exhorted managers to sell the film to teenagers, as they would *Easy Rider* (Dennis Hopper, 1969).[84] While this may be a somewhat extreme and colourful example of exhibitor behaviour, it nonetheless illustrates the difficulties in selling family films by appealing to conventional artistic virtues. Producers, on the other hand, were guided more by the overall performance of a given film, thereby remaining insulated from the clear demographic and ethnographic divisions witnessed by theatre owners.

This insularity can be seen in the development of the family blockbuster, which, at this stage in Hollywood's development, was still closely-identified with a primarily adult-orientated aesthetic. As Thomas Schatz argues:

The biopics, historical and biblical epics, literary adaptations and transplanted stage musicals of the 1950s and 1960s differed from the prestige pictures of the classical era only in their oversized budgets, casts, running times and screen width.[85]

During the 1960s, particularly lengthy films were heavily associated with high-minded 'event movies' – *Birth of a Nation* (D. W. Griffith, 1915), *Gone with the Wind* and *Ben-Hur* are notable examples. Such films neglect the entertainment needs of children in two important respects. Firstly, the narratives themselves are emphatically 'adult' in orientation. Just as significantly, it had long been acknowledged in Hollywood that particularly long films disengage children, whose attention spans tend to be shorter. The series and serials of the 1920s and 1930s – many of which were made specifically for children – were usually less than one hour in length. Even the more mainstream family films of Rooney and Temple were relatively short. Although the average length of features had increased considerably by the 1960s (emphasising the motion picture's grander design over television), a running time of three hours tended to be reserved for large-scale prestige productions targeting the adult audience demographics.

The Sound of Music builds on the emerging formula of the middle-brow blockbuster. Such prestigious source material – a Rodgers and Hammerstein stage musical, which premiered in 1959 – is a rarity, demanding lavish screen treatment. In this case, hiring high-profile director Robert Wise and leading lady Julie Andrews – fresh from her box office success in *Mary Poppins* – were financially-astute moves, as were retaining the songs from the stage version. Although its defining qualities – crystalline photography, didactic songs, Julie Andrews, sweet sentiment – are all broadly suitable, they are hardly specifically appealing to young children or teenagers. Like the domestic comedies of the 1940s, *The Sound of Music* may have been imposed upon children by misty-eyed adults. Relatively few children, surely, would have independently chosen to see a three-hour musical, heavily foregrounding an adult romance, with a roster of virtually undifferentiated children. Indeed, rather than identifying with youth culture on level terms, it imposes a nostalgic, mythologised view of children as a homogenous entity. One scene shows the children enacting a complex song-and-dance routine for the benefit of a group of adult party guests, one of which eulogises: 'is there a more beautiful expression of what is good in this country of ours than the innocent voices of our children?'.

The European settings in *Mary Poppins*, *The Sound of Music* and *Oliver!* could be viewed as attempts to appeal to foreign audiences by transcending the North American cultural idiom. In reality, however, their old-timey, bourgeois respectability constitutes a continuation, rather than disruption, of the cultural imperialism Hollywood was supposedly abandoning in response to economic and cultural globalisation. In 1956, a prominent exhibitioner argued that 'American producers now rarely make pictures especially adapted to American audiences' and that this policy 'has virtually eliminated the American family-type pictures and those featuring familiar American sports and customs'.[86] In actuality, though, the supposedly radical shift towards movies featuring a 'continental' tone – evident in such 1950s musicals as *An American in Paris* (Vincente Minnelli, 1951) and *Gigi* (Minnelli, 1958), and continuing in these 1960s family blockbusters – was almost entirely cosmetic. The real concessions to overseas markets were industrial, rather than thematic; the emergence of the blockbuster was far more significant. Schatz sees *The Sound of Music* as a crucial step in the development of what he calls the 'New Hollywood':

> the movie industry underwent three fairly distinct decade-long phases after the war – from 1946 to 1955, from 1956 to 1965, and from 1966 to 1975. These phases were distinguished by various developments both inside and outside the industry [...] The key markers in these phases were huge hits like *The Ten Commandments* in 1956, *The Sound of Music* in 1965, and *Jaws* in 1975, which redefined the nature, scope, and profit potential of the Blockbuster movie.[87]

Moreover, there is reason to consider *The Sound of Music* as one of the first hybrids between 'epic film' and 'family film', a combination constitutive of most modern Hollywood blockbusters. While recalling the stylistic and ideological modes of classical Hollywood, it simultaneously anticipates the emergence of the mainstream family blockbuster.

Chitty Chitty Bang Bang and *Oliver!* imply an industry caught between opposing styles of filmmaking. Both were released shortly before the establishment of the rating system, which, in conjunction with the emergence of a new generation of challenging independent films and filmmakers, dealt a hammer blow to the old-style family musical. *Chitty Chitty Bang Bang*'s credentials as an early family blockbuster are apparent not only from the on-screen treatment, which foregrounds fantastical special effects, but from the personae involved in its production. It was overseen by James Bond producer Albert R. Broccoli, designed by Bond designer Ken Adam, and adapted for the screen by Bond scriptwriter Roald Dahl from a novel by Bond creator Ian Fleming. The composition of the production crew demonstrates the movement away from the studio-era model of creative personnel having particular generic specialisations, towards the increasing generic irrelevance of the blockbuster – a phenomenon I will examine in more depth in later chapters.

In November 1968, new MPPA president Jack Valenti introduced a movie rating system to replace the now-defunct Production Code. The rating system initially comprised four categories of supposed audience suitability: G (all ages admitted; general audiences), M (suggested for mature audiences – adults and mature young people; later amended to GP and finally PG), R (restricted; under 16 requires accompanying parent or adult guardian) and X (no one under 16 admitted). As Geoff King notes, the rating system 'heightened and institutionalised' the 'targeting of different films to different audiences'.[88] In a sense, it had precisely the opposite intended effect as the Production Code, which symbolised the unity of Hollywood's 'great audience' and underlined the industry's credentials as a democratic system. In contrast, the rating system constituted an open manifesto of Hollywood's new democratic selectivity, and was designed to regulate the already-immutably deep divisions in Hollywood's audiences. As the nihilistic, independently-produced road movie *Easy Rider* achieved record grosses at the box office, the Hollywood establishment finally relinquished its long-since spurious identity as a 'family' institution. The industry entered a period in which the entertainment requirements of teenagers and young adults drove studio production policy, and, indeed, the broader sphere of popular culture in the United States.

THE INDEPENDENTS: PAL, HARRYHAUSEN AND RADNITZ

Although the 1950s was the decade in which the independent filmmaker came to the fore within the Hollywood system, for various reasons few of them pursued the 'family audience'. Firstly, after the emergence of television, the kinds of family movie capable of enticing mass audiences to theatres were generally prohibitively expensive and complicated to produce. Secondly, such producers naturally sought to position themselves as cutting-edge, and family films had come to be regarded as stultifyingly bland. Thirdly, and most importantly, most independents focused their energies on audiences and niches hitherto neglected by the major studios, such as teenagers and exploitation films. Perhaps they were also wary of repeating the mistakes made by Stanley Kramer with *The 5,000 Fingers of Dr. T* (Roy Rowland, 1953) – which lost over a million dollars from a $2 million budget. Although technically the product of a producer-unit setup, it was one of the projects independent filmmaker Kramer produced under his disastrous tenure at Columbia during the early 1950s. Unwisely given money, resources and creative authority by Columbia studio head Harry Cohn, Kramer proceeded to turn out a series of box office flops of which *The 5,000 Fingers of Dr. T* was the most catastrophic.[1] Surely the most aberrant family film ever released by a major studio (from a script by Dr. Seuss), audiences at the film's Hollywood premiere allegedly walked out in disgust 15 minutes into the film in protest against its wilfully weird, nonsensical script.[2] Such endeavours hardly provided a solid foundation for a strong, independent family film movement. In the event, a mere handful of independent producers – most notably George Pal, Ray Harryhausen and Charles H. Schneer, and Robert B. Radnitz – showed a sustained commitment to family entertainment during the late 1950s and 1960s.

George Pal, a Hungarian, worked as an animator in Budapest, Berlin and Paris before moving to the United States.[3] Between 1941 and 1947, he created and oversaw a long-running series of three-dimensional animated shorts for Paramount called *The Puppetoons*, which received wide acclaim. When the series was cancelled, Pal tried to break into feature filmmaking, but his story proposals did not find favour with the studios. However, Peter Rathvon, the former president of RKO, formed his own production company and remembered Pal's idea of a comedy film based on the exploits of an intelligent squirrel.[4] Rathvon contracted Pal for a two-picture deal, and *The Great Rupert* (Irving Pichel), a relatively low-budget black-and-white production, was released in March 1950. Interviewed by the *Motion Picture Herald*, Pal explained:

> It is not whimsical, as the Puppetoons were, but it is like them in that it is a clear, round story, a wholesome subject which the whole family can enjoy. I have always regarded the film audience as being composed of family units, and have tried to give it subjects that would prove interesting and amusing to the youngest and eldest member of each unit. The family audience regarded my Puppetoons with their favour, and I am hopeful that by following the same principles I may experience the same result with my feature pictures.[5]

Although good-natured, *The Great Rupert* was not a commercial success. Pal achieved far greater plaudits with the documentary-style sci-fi film *Destination Moon* (Irving Pichel, 1950). Astutely exploiting the sense of national anticipation surrounding the space programme, the film depicts the first manned moon landing, and became one of the box office hits of the year. Pal's later adaptation of H. G. Wells's *The War of the Worlds* (Byron Haskin, 1953), which was distributed by Paramount, was similarly successful, and has come to be regarded as a sci-fi classic.

As an independent producer of family films, Pal's position within Hollywood was always precarious. His films remained subject to interference from distributors. For example, Paramount insisted on changing the married hero of Wells's novel into a more conventional romantic lead in the film. Furthermore, for much of his career, Pal seemed to lack the ability to gauge and to exploit current cultural trends, instead pursuing projects that appealed to him personally and which spanned a diverse generic range, such as the biopic *Houdini* (George Marshall, 1953) and action film *The Naked Jungle* (Byron Haskin, 1954). Pal's first overtly child-orientated film (and his directorial debut) was *tom thumb*, financed by MGM and released in December 1958. A lavish fantasy movie starring Russ Tamblyn, *tom thumb* was produced relatively cheaply at just under $1 million, and comfortably recouped its costs with a strong showing at the box office over the festive period. Reviews were similarly positive, with *Time* magazine calling it 'one of the nicest Christmas presents Hollywood ever gave the pigtail-and-popgun set', adding that Pal had 'succeeded where Walt Disney often fails: he has managed to play down to his audience and still play up to a standard'.[6]

Although Pal's next production – a sentimentalised adaptation of *The Time Machine* (1960) – was critically and commercially successful, *Atlantis, the Lost Continent* (1961) and *The Wonderful World of the Brothers Grimm* (1962) were both received less favourably. His final mainstream film, and arguably his most creative, was *The 7 Faces of Dr. Lao* (1964) – again distributed by MGM, based on the 1935 novella, *The Circus of Dr. Lao*, by Charles G. Finney, and adapted by Charles Beaumont (best known for his macabre, fantastic short stories and scripts for *The Twilight Zone*). The narrative centres on a small, fictional town in Arizona called Abalone, at the turn of the twentieth century. We see ruthless local businessman Clint Stark (Arthur O'Connell) attempting to persuade the townsfolk to sell him their homes and move away, the only one aware that a railroad will soon be built through the town, creating jobs and prosperity. The only people able to resist Stark's bullying are newspaper editor Ed Cunningham (John Ericson) – a recent arrival in town – and young, widowed librarian Angela Benedict (Barbara Eden). At this point, a circus, owned by a mysterious, elderly oriental man, Dr. Lao (Tony Randall), arrives in town to teach the townsfolk some salient truths and moral lessons. Ultimately, Stark is made to see the error of his ways.

Star Tony Randall plays all seven 'faces': the abominable snowman, Merlin the Magician, Apollonius of Tyana, Pan, a giant serpent, Medusa and Dr. Lao himself. Makeup artist William Tuttle's work on this film earned him a Special Achievement Academy Award, and there is some impressive stop-motion animation in evidence. In spite of the film's aesthetic qualities, however, much of the dialogue is strikingly mature. The script does not shy away from depicting the prejudices of the towns-folk; a Native American man is beaten-up by some local thugs, while Dr. Lao himself is subjected to various racial slurs. In one frenetic, tightly-edited scene dripping with suppressed sexuality, the seemingly cold, stiff Angela is seduced by the flute-playing Pan, and begins unbuttoning her tunic before regaining her composure, and walking out in embarrass-ment. This sequence marks Angela's sexual reawakening, and paves the way for her romantic union with suitor Ed Cunningham. Another memo-rably jarring scene sees a vain old woman (Argentina Brunetti) having her fortune told by Apollonius, only to be reduced to tears by his brutal assessment that her life will never amount to anything. There are clear distinctions, then, between the comedic, fantastical elements of the film, and its more sophisticated, satirical aspects. This willingness to inject elements conventionally regarded as unsuitable for 'family' viewing, and the insistence on not playing-down to juvenile audiences, was one of the primary characteristics of the filmmakers under discussion in this chapter. However, what now appears innovative and imaginative was construed at the time of release as eccentric and obtuse; the reaction among MGM executives was one of bemusement, and the film was poorly promoted, which contributed to its box office failure. Pal's career never recovered, and he later commented, ruefully, 'if *tom thumb* or *7 Faces of Dr. Lao* had been released by Disney, they would have made millions'.[7]

Pal's family films implicitly constructed a differentiated dual audience of parents and children, broadly ascribing to the long-standing socio-cultural conviction that juvenile and mature audiences require different forms of intellectual and emotional stimulation. Ray Harryhausen and Charles H. Schneer were the first mainstream Hollywood producers successfully to debunk this perception. Their fantasy spectaculars targeted a far less demographically-segmented mass audience. Although producer-director Irwin Allen was also releasing escapist family films at this point – notably *The Lost World* (1961) and *Voyage to the Bottom of the Sea* (1961) – they had less impact on adult audiences because of their technical inferiority, which left them vulnerable to ridicule. In contrast, Harryhausen's medium of stop-motion animation (a technique in which three-dimensional models are animated one frame at a time to provide the illusion of movement, and used historically to bring fantas-tic creatures to life) is highly arresting visually, and much harder to dismiss. Although stop-motion animation had been used intermittently in Hollywood since the 1920s – most prominently and brilliantly by Willis O'Brien, who created the model animation sequences in *King Kong* – it was an extremely complex, time-consuming process. Furthermore, the industry's deep-seated resistance to fantastic subjects restricted its potential usage. It was not until the early 1950s surge in teen exploitation films – specifically the 'creature feature' – that stop-motion animation found a natural outlet. Harryhausen's services were suddenly in demand, particularly after the acclaim which met his contributions to *The Beast from 20,000 Fathoms* (Eugene Lourie, 1953). Intrigued by the potential of stop-motion, independent producer Schneer – who worked in Sam Katzman's production unit at Columbia – conceived the idea of a giant killer octopus let loose in San Francisco, and Harryhausen was contracted to provide the visual effects. The resulting film, *It Came from Beneath the Sea* (Robert Gordon, 1955), was a commercial success. The following year, Schneer and Harryhausen again collaborated on *Earth vs. the Flying Saucers* (Fred F. Sears, 1956). Soon after, Schneer formed his own company, Morningside Productions, whilst retaining his partnership with Harryhausen and association with Columbia as financial backer and distributor. Their next film, *20 Million Miles to Earth* (Nathan Juran, 1957), was a watershed: it was their last 'creature feature', and also their last film aimed primarily at teenage and youth audiences. From then on, they focused their attentions on addressing 'general audiences'.

Schneer – who was motivated by 'visuals and locations that had not been photographed' – possessed, like Katzman, a sharp eye for subjects that were topical and hence easily and cheaply exploitable.[8] Harryhausen, meanwhile, was seeking to expand the under-developed narrative and technical potentialities of stop-motion animation. He felt that an action-adventure fantasy based around the character of Sinbad – whom he regarded as the 'personification of adventure' – would be able to manoeuvre them into the Hollywood mainstream, and it was on this basis that *The 7th Voyage of Sinbad* (Nathan Juan, 1958) was conceived.[9] However, both the production personnel and the aggressive, jargonistic marketing strategy used to sell the film betrayed their origins in teen exploitation. Schneer and Harryhausen conjured the term 'Dynamation' to describe Harryhausen's methods of three-dimensional stop-motion, and thereafter used it endlessly to promote their films – sometimes with variations such as 'Superdynamation' and 'Dynarama'. Equally, Columbia's press department marketed *The 7th Voyage of Sinbad* as a 'kidult' film, designed, in the words of *Boxoffice*, 'to convey the intelligence that here is a parcel of escapist entertainment that will assert a strong appeal to both kids and adults'.[10] The thrust of this marketing strategy was to position the film *between* the emergent 'teen' and the established – but increasingly dusty – 'family' markets.

'Kidult' was a word first used in the early 1950s television industry to describe a child-adult amalgam; a consumer of any age who enjoys products nominally associated with children.[11] Although 'kidult'-orientated entertainment can be seen to operate within the broader sphere of 'family' entertainment, the two forms are far from analogous. Traditionally, 'family' entertainment presupposes a mass audience comprised of families, and operates on *multiple levels of appeal* to offer something unique to each family member. In contrast, 'kidult' entertainment, *in extremis*, does not differentiate in its audience address, constructing pluralistic mass audiences as a *single entity*. Today, with our ever-deepening knowledge of cognitive neural processes, the notion that popular entertainment may be capable of engaging equally with all types of audiences – whether juvenile or mature – by tapping innate affective and cognitive responses to stimuli does not seem particularly provocative. Pop psychology concepts like the 'Peter Pan Syndrome' – which implies an inability to graduate from childhood mentality – have slipped into common discourse in the intervening years. The Freudian psychoanalytical theory of 'regression' is also pertinent, describing as it does the reversion of the conscious mind to an earlier stage of development. These concepts are hardly new; the *puer aeternus* ('eternal boy') archetype dates back to Ancient Rome.

If we accept that 'childhood' and 'adulthood' are social constructs rather than merely biological conditions, we can hardly be surprised when slippages between these seemingly immutable states occur. Nor is it surprising that transgressions of child/adult behavioural codes are widely disparaged. Sociologists such as Neil Postman have (contentiously) argued that social barriers between adults and children in Western societies are breaking down. That is a matter for considerable debate, but I do think it incontrovertible that the *cultural* boundaries between childhood and adulthood are increasingly tenuous. Whilst this trend can be traced back to the mass emergence of the teenage consumer in 1950s North America, it must be stressed that *social* boundaries between childhood and adulthood remained well-defined at this point. As a result, 'kidult'-inflected entertainment was widely regarded as excessively juvenile, and adult consumption of such products – especially for 'selfish' purposes; that is, solely for personal pleasure, rather than as part of the parental duty of accompanying young children to the cinema – was liable to be perceived as inappropriate, if not distasteful. The 'kidult' trend in mainstream Hollywood was kick-started by the success of *The 7th Voyage of Sinbad*, which can be seen, in retrospect, as the most important family film of the 1950s. That it should merit this standing is less down to its intrinsic merits than as an antecedent of subsequent 'kidult'-orientated movies. Indeed, various major Hollywood figures have acknowledged the influence of Harryhausen's aesthetic, including George Lucas, Peter Jackson, Tim Burton and James Cameron. In the intervening years, as attitudes towards so-called 'childish' entertainment have changed, *The 7th Voyage of Sinbad* has been comprehensively reappraised. In 2008, it was added to the US National Film Registry.[12]

No doubt the Arabian Nights milieu in which the film operates contributes to its escapist functions. Eastern narratives are freed from certain Western narrative conventions, commonly operating within a more escapist, fantastic firmament. For instance, in Tony Curtis's early 1950s star vehicles *The Prince Who Was a Thief* (Rudolph Maté, 1951) and *Son of Ali Baba* (Kurt Neumann, 1952), this setting signals the suspension of some of the more rigid Western social conventions surrounding (for example) decorum and courtship rituals. Given that *The 7th Voyage of Sinbad* positions itself equivocally between traditional family filmmaking, Eastern adventure narrative and teen exploitation, it is unsurprising that it provoked an ambivalent critical response. *Variety* adjudged it to be 'primarily entertainment for the eye', with Harryhausen 'the hero of the piece', whilst *Film Daily* deemed it to be 'a spectacular presentation of the Sinbad story'.[13] On the other hand, *The Hollywood Reporter* wrongly believed that the stop-motion effects were achieved electronically, and *The Christian Science Monitor* regarded it as 'largely an excuse for Hollywood to toy with its latest technical process, "Dynamation"'.[14] As these responses indicate, *The 7th Voyage of Sinbad* was not really viewed as a family film, a format that was still construed in terms of its social use value, reinforcing the sanctity of the family as: i) a socialising apparatus; ii) an agent of social stability; and iii) a microcosm of society-at-large. Nevertheless, the fact that the film grossed over $6 million (from a budget of $650,000) points to a widening gap between the cultural establishment and the requirements of mass audiences.

In Harryhausen films, the narrative exists only to frame the special-effects sequences that lay at the heart of their appeal. All include a romantic subplot, because romance was considered necessary to appeal to mainstream audiences, but in each case, the romance is anaemic and perfunctory to the extent that it is almost irrelevant to the overall movie experience. Furthermore, instead of the more familiar family film patterns of emotional fulfilment and moral or spiritual revelation, the dramatic climax invariably involves a spectacular adventure set-piece. In *Jason and the Argonauts* (Don Chaffey, 1963), the narrative function of Jason's (Todd Armstrong) voyage to the distant land of Colchis in search of the Golden Fleece is to give him the means of reclaiming his kingdom by overthrowing the tyrannical King Pelias (Douglas Wilmer), who had seized his crown by force-of-arms when Jason was a child. In practice, this plotline offers little more than basic heroic motivation; the substance of the movie experience lies within the various dangers Jason and his crew encounter during their voyage. Jason and his band of followers encounter and defeat the enormous bronze statue Talos, overcome a group of harpies who are tormenting a blind seer (Patrick Troughton), pass through the lethal Clashing Rocks and battle a multi-headed Hydra for possession of the Fleece. The centrepiece of the movie – and probably the most famous and influential sequence in Harryhausen's oeuvre – occurs at the very end, where the vengeful King Aeetes (Jack Gwillim), in retribution for the theft of the Fleece, animates seven sword-wielding skeletons to do battle with Jason and his followers. When Jason succeeds in 'killing' them (after a titanic struggle), he safely returns to the Argo, at which point the film abruptly ends. The viewer is merely left to assume that Jason returns to his homeland and comfortably reclaims his throne.

Such tension between story and spectacle rarely arises. *Jason and the Argonauts* is an extreme example because of its structure, which effectively demands two forms of closure: a spectacular special-effects finale for possession of the Fleece; and the logical battle between Jason and Pelias for the throne – which is, after all, the film's 'MacGuffin'. However, in terms of the film as a spectacle, it is entirely fitting that it should end with this dramatic, aesthetic highpoint; the fact that it does not resolve the story – and complete Jason's internal voyage from symbolic boyhood to symbolic manhood – is less important. Indeed, while the film received

Jason and the Argonauts (1963)

predictably mixed reviews upon initial release in the USA, the ending itself passed without comment. Presumably, it was simply viewed as part of an enjoyable, but ultimately disposable, piece of screen entertainment undeserving of serious critical analysis. Although *Variety* praised this 'choice hot weather attraction for the family trade – a sure delight for the kiddies and a diverting spectacle for adults with a taste for fantasy and adventure', *The New York Times* dismissed it as 'absurd' and 'no worse, but certainly no better, than most of its kind'.[15]

These reviews were written in a period in which poor plotting and characterisation were seen as standard weaknesses in juvenile-minded fantasy films, the assumption being, of course, that juvenile and adolescent audiences have not yet graduated to a higher plane of cultural awareness, borne through adult interpretative skills. It is only when such entertainment was also presented as suitable entertainment for *adults* that serious objections arose. Little wonder, then, that the film's special effects were overlooked for Academy Award recognition. Unsurprisingly (in view of the lingering influence of middlebrow culture), the film that *did* win the Visual Effects Oscar in 1964 was the comparatively staid historical epic *Cleopatra* (Joseph L. Mankiewicz, 1963). Indeed, this lack of recognition is indicative of a wider industry disregard for Harryhausen, who was always forced to struggle for studio backing. *Jason and the Argonauts* was a commercial failure, and effectively ended Harryhausen's and Schneer's flirtation with the Hollywood mainstream. Their next 'Dynamation' film, *First Men in the Moon* (Nathan Juran, 1964) – adapted from H. G. Wells's novel by respected British sci-fi writer Nigel Kneale – was one of their most intelligent productions, but it, too, was a flop. Harryhausen then made a profitable but critically-derided film for Hammer, *One Million Years BC* (Don Chaffey, 1966), while *The Valley of Gwangi* (Jim O'Connolly, 1969) languished in obscurity.

Of the three major independent producers of family films during the late 1950s and 1960s, Robert B. Radnitz is the least remembered and perhaps the most interesting analytically, because his rise to prominence was so remarkable, and his eventual critical and commercial decline so precipitous. A former English teacher, Radnitz became a story consultant at Twentieth Century Fox during the 1950s, and managed to persuade his boss, production chief Buddy Adler, to allow him to produce a 'straight', low-budget adaptation of Ouida's 1872 novel, *A Dog of Flanders* (James B. Clark, 1960). Like all of Radnitz's productions, it was shot on location (in the Netherlands) with local actors, rather than in the studio. Although it was reasonably successful commercially, its critical reception was extremely positive. Furthermore, it won the Gold Lion (first prize) in the Children's Film category at the Venice Film Festival – the first North American-produced recipient of the award. *Variety* observed:

> At first, [the] leisurely pace [and] emphasis on character and back-ground rather than the frantic action of today's films, seems slow. But it has a beguiling warmth and credibility that builds a mounting interest and a cumulative effect. The 20th-Fox release proves that Disney needn't have a monopoly on this sort of wholesome film fare.[16]

Radnitz produced a regular stream of simple but well-made family films along similar lines throughout the 1960s and early 1970s, all directed by Clark, including *Misty* (1961), *Island of the Blue Dolphins* (1964), *And Now Miguel* (1966), *My Side of the Mountain* (1969) and *The Little Ark* (1972). Over this period, Radnitz's reputation grew rapidly among critics who appreciated his wholesome, unpretentious style, and also among opponents of Hollywood's simultaneous embrace of youth- and adult-orientated entertainment. Qualities often identified in Radnitz's films included 'truthfulness', 'authenticity', 'naturalism', 'universalism' and 'humanity'.

Radnitz worked hard to promote himself and his films. In 1962, for instance, he presented a paper on the subject of children's films at the annual Claremont Graduate School conference, and in 1964 was a guest speaker at the Federation of Motion Picture Council's national convention.[17] Radnitz also succeeded in attracting a rare official endorsement for *Island of the Blue Dolphins* from the American Library Association.[18] He criticised Fox's marketing of his first two releases, arguing, 'when you believe in something you should do everything you can to sell it, and you need the help of centres of influence and opinion-makers. If they don't know about the film, how can they help?'[19] Radnitz was particularly outspoken concerning the industry's perceived intransigent disdain for family entertainment. In 1964, he insisted:

> A child will look at most anything you present to him on the screen. Therefore it behoves us to present him with exciting visual fare – fare that will stimulate his imagination creatively [...] It is a shocking indictment today that in our industry today there is not one motion picture company, with the exception of Disney, that has a definite, planned slate of films initially aimed at an audience of children.[20]

He also pointed out that:

> If a musical flops, it is a flop. If a western flops, it does so because it's a flop. If a family film falls on its face, it is because it is a family film. The practice of denigration should be abandoned.[21]

Radnitz nonetheless disliked the term 'family film', and despite his contempt for studio executives who refused to follow its profitable example, he also criticised Disney's reliance on sentimentality and portrayal of violence. Radnitz was also an outspoken critic of the MPAA's movie rating system:

> Originally, the rating system as I understood it was to concern itself with both sexuality and violence in films. In practice, however, it only seems to be used in dealing with films of sexuality. I'm far more concerned with the violence in films. I don't subscribe to the theory that witnessing violence on the screen will cause some child to go out and commit violence; I just think we're becoming inured to it.[22]

Nevertheless, by the end of the decade, his stock was never higher among industry observers. In 1969, he received a joint award from the National Catholic Office for Motion Pictures and the Broadcasting of Motion Pictures, and the Film Commission of the National Council of Churches, in recognition of his 'overall work in the production of children's films'.[23] The *Los Angeles Times*' influential critic, Charles Champlin, even dubbed him the 'apostle of family films'.[24] It is not hard to see why Radnitz was such a popular figure with critics during the 1960s. A thoughtful, articulate, well-educated liberal, he produced understated and naturalistic adaptations of children's literary classics, usually on a relatively low budget and with untrained actors. His films were sentimental without being corny, and did not offend moral or religious orthodoxy. Inevitably, Radnitz was cast as the hero in a David vs. Goliath battle against the forces of corporate greed, the commercialisation of children's culture, and the economic exploitation of young consumers (as personified by Disney).

Disney's near-monopoly of the family market forced several Hollywood producers to shift their attentions from cinema to television. In 1964, Irwin Allen created a television spin-off from his 1961 movie *Voyage to the Bottom of the Sea*, which aired on ABC until 1968. He subsequently produced the science fiction series *Lost in Space* (1965–8) for CBS and *Land of Giants* (1968–70) for ABC. All attempted to combine the escapist tone of his earlier films with the soap-opera style of earlier family series, such as *The Adventures of Ozzie and Harriet*. Another Hollywood filmmaker who moved into television during the early 1960s was Ivan Tors, a former producer of teen sci-fi who made his name with rather more anodyne family series centring on animals, such as *Flipper* (NBC, 1964–7), *Daktari* (CBS, 1966–9) and *Cowboy in Africa* (ABC, 1967–8). The relative uniformity of 1950s family television gave way in the 1960s to the wide generic diversity we see today. Other producers left the United States and based themselves in the United Kingdom. From the early 1960s, Harryhausen and Schneer made all of their films in England. Another American independent based in the UK was Milton Subotsky, who also began his filmmaking career as a producer of teen pics. Subotsky took advantage of the popularity of the BBC family-orientated science fiction serial *Doctor Who* (1963–89; 2005– ; now the longest-running science fiction show in the world, as well as probably the longest fictional 'family' programme) by releasing two cheap, colourful and modestly successful spin-off films in 1965 and 1966. In spite of its smaller size, the UK was arguably a more receptive market to family fare, partly because the British Board of Film Classification operated a rating system which acknowledged audience segmentation, and hence a clearer distinction between adult- and family-orientated products.

During the late 1960s and early 1970s, various prominent North American 'family' brands sought to diversify into motion picture production as a means of cross-promotion. The trend started in 1969, when Quaker Oats signed a contract with independent producer David L. Wolper to produce educational and entertainment films for family audiences, the most notable of which was *Willy Wonka and the Chocolate Factory* (1971).[25] *Variety* observed that 'showmen, ever imaginative, see a significant tie between kids, theatres tubes, or "wholesome" food and "wholesome" entertainment despite current stress on sexplicity'.[26] In 1972, the Readers' Digest collaborated with United Artists on a series of 'traditional' family movies. The producers explained:

> Millions of Americans do not currently go to the movies, or go far less frequently than they might. We are convinced that the majority of these people will attend intelligent and entertaining motion pictures that are designed to appeal to the whole family.[27]

Unsurprisingly, Radnitz was not far behind. In July 1971, he formed a production company jointly with toy manufacturer Mattel, with a view to release eight films over a three-year period, with budgets ranging from $760,000 to $1 million.[28] Although it eventually ended acrimoniously in a lawsuit, the Radnitz-Mattel partnership immediately struck gold with *Sounder* (Martin Ritt, 1972).

Centring on the struggles of a poverty-stricken rural black family during the Great Depression, *Sounder* was comfortably Radnitz's most successful production, and was received with great enthusiasm. Charles Champlin called it 'beautifully acted, honest, angering and inspiring', whilst *Variety* thought it 'a film which transcends space, race, age and time'.[29] It received far wider attention than the typical Hollywood release. Congressman Charles C. Diggs Jr., a member of the House from Michigan, was quoted as saying that *Sounder* 'marks a turning point in the art of the motion picture. This is a black film to take pride in'.[30] Undoubtedly, *Sounder* is a powerful film. The story is small-scale and clearly allegorical; the characterisation is rich and nuanced; the direction by Ritt is assured and understated;

the drama is sentimental, but not to extremity; the production values are high, with the period setting both convincing and evocative; and the acting is uniformly excellent. Inevitably, with the civil rights movement still extremely active in the USA at the time of release, *Sounder* came to be received and understood not merely as a family film, but as a black film. Strong as it is, it would not have received such attention had the central family been white. Ritt – desperately trying to unburden himself of the criticism he received as a white man having directed a 'black' film – argued that the colour of the central family could just as easily have been white, but Radnitz had long harboured the ambition to produce a family film starring a black family.[31] Indeed, he was quoted in 1966 by the magazine *Jet* saying he was actively seeking a filmable story 'with a good Negro theme'.[32] A cynical observer might suspect that Radnitz developed *Sounder* as a means of gaining respectability (and, perhaps, notoriety) in the hope of extending his career as a filmmaker. Yet such criticism would be misplaced: Radnitz's entire career as a producer testifies to his commitment to making family films centring on characters from different cultural and ethnic backgrounds. For example, *Island of the Blue Dolphins* focuses on a Native American girl; *And Now Miguel* a Mexican boy.

From this highpoint, Radnitz's Hollywood career declined relatively quickly. Today, he is barely remembered, for all his accomplishments. His fall from grace stemmed not from any precipitous decline in the quality of his films, which nonetheless depend for their appeal on a highly specific set of values. All of the qualities which distinguished Radnitz throughout the 1960s – his challenge to Disney's increasing hegemony in relation to the family market, his liberal agenda and his focus on child protagonists – appeared rather less remarkable by the late 1970s, by which point North American mass entertainment was moving rapidly away from the ideological and stylistic elements his films encapsulated. Whereas Pal's and Harryhausen's output can today be enjoyed for their spectacle and adventure, Radnitz's films – laudable and groundbreaking upon release – now appear, shorn of their contextual meanings, quaint and old-fashioned.

Rising costs and changing cultural values virtually destroyed smallscale family filmmaking. George Pal's attempted comeback, *Doc Savage: Man of Bronze* (Michael Anderson, 1975), was a box office flop. Irwin Allen fared better, but only because he embraced a less juvenile mode of address with disaster movies such as *The Poseidon Adventure* (Ronald Neame, 1972) and *The Towering Inferno* (John Guillermin, 1974). Harryhausen and

Schneer operated a low-cost, low-returns operation, although even this became difficult to sustain because of the prohibitive costs of mounting even modest fantasy films. Harryhausen's effects work was relatively inexpensive – he did almost all the animating himself – but remained extremely time-consuming, with even short sequences taking months to film. Furthermore, in spite of their proven track record, Harryhausen and Schneer found it increasingly difficult to sell their projects to studios. Interference from executives, who misguidedly believed that a harder edge was necessary to appeal to older audiences, led to a regression to an increasingly anachronistic 'family' style, at the expense of the 'kidult' aesthetic in evidence in their early films. This can be seen progressively in their three late period films – *The Golden Voyage of Sinbad* (Gordon Hessler, 1974), *Sinbad and the Eye of the Tiger* (Sam Wanamaker, 1977) and *Clash of the Titans* (Desmond Davis, 1981). *Sinbad and the Eye of the Tiger* was Harryhausen's first production to contain nudity. Although brief and inexplicit (mostly in long-shot or from the rear), its very presence encapsulates the prevailing belief that adults require completely different forms of stimulation. There was, as Harryhausen admits, 'a gradual realisation that these films needed more adult interest'.[33]

Harryhausen's final movie, *Clash of the Titans*, was released during the summer of 1981. Following the critical and commercial failure of *Sinbad and the Eye of the Tiger*, Harryhausen and Schneer – realising that they did not have the resources to adapt their filmmaking style to match current market trends – returned to classical mythology, namely the story of Perseus. MGM – which was attempting to re-establish its credentials as a top studio – was interested in the idea, as it embodied the kind of 'good, exciting family entertainment' it was eager to produce.[34] The film was given a budget of $16 million, which exceeded that of all the producers' previous releases put together. In the event, *Clash of the Titans* was a modest box office hit, although *Variety*'s assessment of it as 'an unbearable bore' no doubt reflected mainstream Hollywood's re-orientation towards a faster-paced narrative aesthetic.[35] It is the least 'kidult'-orientated of all Harryhausen's films, yet its 'family' elements are largely unsuccessful. The romance between the romantic leads – although perfunctory – is far more central than the entirely gratuitous romantic subplots in previous Harryhausen films. Most obviously, there are two scenes containing brief nudity, as well as a sequence in which a man is burned at the stake, which ensured that the film received an 'A' rating in the UK, thereby preventing children under the age of 14 from attending without adult supervision. According to Harryhausen, the inclusion of these elements was at the insistence of MGM, which – bizarrely, given its supposed status as 'family' entertainment – 'wanted [the film] to have some adult content to appeal to a wider audience'.[36] Ironically, such 'adult' content had become unattractive to many adults, who, no doubt, attended 'kidult'-inflected films to *escape* the social and interpretative constraints of adulthood.

The only independent producer of traditional family films during the mid-1970s who enjoyed notable success was Joe Camp – writer-producer-director of the *Benji* (1974–2004) series. *Benji* – a narrative about a stray dog's relationship with a suburban family, and shot from the dog's perspective – asserts its credentials via the opening credits as a 'Family Film'. In this way, viewers can infer that it will possess all the elements that had come to typify the format in the minds of the public – child protagonists; anthropomorphised animals; a reaffirmation of the nuclear family unit; an absence of sex or violence; avowed 'wholesomeness'. Given the recent track record of family films, it is unsurprising that potential distributors were apathetic, advising Camp to avoid direct competition with Disney. 'We were told by everybody, without exception, that we were crazy', Camp recalled.[37] Unimpressed, he rejected deals from three major distributors and handled the marketing of the film himself. The same lack of enthusiasm among distributors was regularly observed by Radnitz. The growing conviction that mass audiences wanted titillation – rather than comfort and escapism – tended to result in a fatalistic mindset, reflected in the lack of effective promotion, which in turn ensured poor box office performance. Camp believed that:

> People give lip service to wanting clean pictures, but they're not going to pay money and go out there to see them just because it's clean. But I think there's a super market out there because people will respond to good entertainment [...] We knew we would have to bang you on the head to get you to see a G-rated dog picture.[38]

In the event, *Benji* was a sizable hit, grossing more than $12 million from a very small initial outlay. Press reaction was extremely positive, and the *Christian Science Monitor* optimistically hoped that it might herald a 'new era in family films'.[39]

Such runaway hits were necessarily rare, because they made little allowance for the teenage and young adult demographics that now dominated North American cinema audiences. In 1977, Camp explained that:

> With the original 'Benji' project we basically took a kid's project and produced it in such a manner that it would be entertaining to any adult. But that only works to an extent and it's been working less and less. So what we'll likely be focusing on in the future is taking what would normally be construed as an adult project and producing it in a manner that kids can enjoy as well.[40]

Radnitz was unoptimistic. He suggested that 'all these alternatives compete for our time – TV and sports and special activities – they have broken up the old movie-going habit of the family unit out of the house for a group treat'.[41]

What few observers could have realised at this time was that the Hollywood family film was on the brink of an extraordinary resurgence. However, this new era signalled the end not only of the traditional family film, but also of low-budget, independently-produced family filmmaking. As the following chapter will show, the new trend in Hollywood family filmmaking was towards spectacle, with enormous budgets and vast promotional campaigns targeting teenagers and young adults, as well as parents and young children. Hollywood entered a period in which cross-cultural, cross-demographic 'family' filmmaking moved to the very centre of its artistic and industrial operations. Of course, this did not spell the end for the independent producer of family films. By the early 1980s, George Lucas and Steven Spielberg probably had even more leverage – and certainly far more popular fame – than studio-era independent moguls like Samuel Goldwyn and David O. Selznick. Today, the vast majority of major family films and franchises are produced independently, albeit with major studio distribution. However, low-budget operators such as Radnitz, Camp and Schneer found it impossible to compete in this new epoch.

THE MODERN FAMILY FILM AND THE NEW HOLLYWOOD, 1977–95

As the 1960s drew to a close, the traditional Hollywood family film no longer represented the interests and satisfied the requirements of the majority. The teenage demographic acquired its own cinematic space with the development and popularisation of the teen film, which in turn disrupted the supposed all-age, cross-demographic function of the family film. In cultural terms, the 1960s is best described as a decade of renegotiation, in which North America readjusted from an adult- to a youth-centric orientation. By the end of the decade, it seemed a very real possibility that securing a trans-demographic, trans-cultural mass audience – a dream embodied by the mainstream family film – had become absolutely unfeasible.

One of the contributing factors to the industry's movement towards youth films was the spectacular failure of several so-called 'family' blockbusters during the late 1960s. *Camelot* (Joshua Logan, 1967, Warner Bros.), *Star!* (Robert Wise, 1968, Fox), *Sweet Charity* (Bob Fosse, 1969, Universal) and *Hello, Dolly!* (Gene Kelly, 1969, Fox) contributed heavily to a precipitous industry-wide depression in 1969 which produced more than $200 million in losses and nearly bankrupted several studios.[1] The majors, as Tino Balio notes, learned a valuable lesson: the market could only support a limited number of blockbusters, even taking into account the demand for new products from television.[2] Picking up on the success of low-budget films such as *Bonnie and Clyde* (Arthur Penn, 1967) and *The Graduate* (Mike Nichols, 1967), the majors refocused their attention towards youth audiences. A 1968 Yankelovich and Associates survey commissioned by the MPAA revealed that 48 per cent of box office admissions in that year were in the 16–24 demographic, and concluded that 'being young and single is the overriding demographic pre-condition for being a frequent and enthusiastic movie-goer'.[3] An examination of movie ratings from the period allows us to see how quickly the studios abandoned the supposed Production Code ethos of suitability for everyone. Initially, it seemed that G-rated films would be most prevalent, at around 44 per cent.[4] However, by November 1969, this proportion had fallen to around 32 per cent and continued to decline rapidly into the early 1970s.[5] Whereas in 1969, G and GP films comprised 71 per cent of all film ratings, by 1970, the most frequently-imposed rating was R, with just under 40 per cent of all ratings assigned that year.[6] Even with the subsequent explosion in family film production from the late 1970s onwards, the overall proportion of films rated R by the MPAA between 1968 and 2007 was 59 per cent, with G-rated films barely registering at 6 per cent.[7] From these figures we can infer that even though family-orientated films now dominate the top end of the market, Hollywood remains a predominantly teenage-orientated institution in which 'adult' content widely circulates.

The youth-film movement in mainstream cinema was kick-started by the success of *Easy Rider* (Dennis Hopper, 1969), described by critic Ryan Gilbey as 'the film that helped liberate American cinema'.[8] Grossing over $19 million from a miniscule budget, *Easy Rider*'s position within US film history is perhaps more symbolic than real. The industry turned to a new generation of film school-educated writers, producers and directors to exploit the youth market, and in the process brought exploitation genres like sci-fi, horror, pornography and blaxploitation into the mainstream. However, *Easy Rider* and *Midnight Cowboy* (John Schlesinger, 1969) transcended the pejorative associations of mere exploitation, marking a notable convergence of critical and commercial approval. Although Balio traces the demise of the 'youthpix' cycle to 1971, the socially-critical slant of such pictures lived on in critically-acclaimed, adult-orientated films such as Robert Altman's *McCabe and Mrs. Miller* (1971) and *The Long Goodbye* (1973), Arthur Penn's *Night Moves* (1975), Hal Ashby's *Shampoo* (1975), Alan J. Pakula's *All the President's Men* (1976), Martin Scorsese's *Taxi Driver* (1976) and Michael Cimino's *The Deer Hunter* (1978).[9]

Motion picture taboos were being broken on various levels. Beyond the increasingly anti-authoritarian slant of a certain strata of mainstream movies, the ratings system allowed for rapid proliferation of screen violence, nudity, sexually-explicit material and profanity. MPAA president Jack Valenti – who oversaw the transition from the Production Code – insisted that there was no lack of family films, 'just a shortage of family audiences'.[10] He reiterated that the rating system was designed to protect children, aiming 'to give parents the information that will enable them to make decisions about their children's moviegoing'.[11] Some younger filmmakers, however, rejected the 'family' label outright. The fact that director Richard Sarafian protested when *Run Wild, Run Free* (1969) was labelled a 'family film' illustrates how damaged the 'family' brand had become.[12] Certainly, family movies were no longer regarded as significantly profitable, much less capable of galvanising mass audiences. The filmic representation of children and families also became markedly critical during this period, both in earnest comedy-dramas such as *Paper Moon* (Peter Bogdanovich, 1973), and controversial horrors such as *The Exorcist* (William Friedkin, 1973) and *The Omen* (Richard Donner, 1976). The days when Hollywood producers felt compelled to show restraint – much less adhere to sweet sentiment – in their representations of children and adolescents were long gone. Predictably, studio executives remained insistent that the 'family' market remained their long-term focus. A survey of industry leaders conducted by *Variety* in December 1971 led it to propose that 'bare bosoms on the screen may become as rare as pies in the face and violence extinct like slapstick'.[13] According to MGM's Doug Netter, 'it's very obvious from the reaction of the public and theatre owners that they are sick and tired of excessive violence, excessive sex, nudity, and profanity'.[14] Herb Jaffe of United Artists predicted that 'the major companies are going to get away from sex and violence. Those aren't the films of lasting value. I'm talking in terms of re-release, television and whatever forms pay TV may take'.[15] As ever, exhibitor responses were closer to the mark. In 1969, Ray Boriski, the owner of Houston art-house theatre, The Alray, switched from showing family to pornographic films. He told *Texas Monthly* in January, 1975:

> I suppose if I had started with adult films five years earlier I'd be so wealthy now I wouldn't ever need to work. But that's all right. I think I did something to make my community a little better back then, tried to give people something they wouldn't have gotten, and I worked hard doing it. I'm going to relax a little now.[16]

A 1970 survey found that 68 per cent of respondents were unhappy 'with available children's fare'.[17]

Disney's performance during this period is highly revealing. Although the 1970s was a decade of fiscal expansion for Disney with the success of its Walt Disney World and Disneyland operations, in terms of feature film production the company had declined dramatically since its heyday. Tellingly, perhaps, Disney releases were no longer receiving much Academy Award recognition. Both factors were a sure sign of its ever-loosening grip on mass audiences. Moreover, by this point, its position within the film industry had become more isolated than ever, as other studios harnessed the potential for artistic freedom offered by the new ratings system, producing edgier fare tailor-made for young adults. Even though Disney's profits rose from $21.8 million in 1970 to $135.1 million in 1980, it went the entire decade without a major box office hit.[18] By 1972, former MPAA Code and Rating Administration member Stephen Farber could confidently – if prematurely – claim that 'fewer and fewer movies have [the] mass appeal' to 'cut across all segments of society to reach a huge, undifferentiated audience'.[19]

Reactively, the studios attempted to re-engage 'traditional' small-town family audiences with movies thought to possess 'family/adventure elements', such as Warner Bros.' *Billy Jack* (T. C. Frank, 1971) and *Jeremiah Johnson* (Sydney Pollack, 1972).[20] The most interesting examples, however, were the Readers' Digest/United Artists' musical adaptations of Mark Twain's *Tom Sawyer* (Don Taylor, 1973) and *Huckleberry Finn* (J. Lee Thompson, 1974), starring Johnny Whitaker as Tom and Jeff East as Huck. Opening with the tagline 'The Great Family Musical', *Tom Sawyer* was a notable critical success, receiving Oscar nominations for 'Best Art Direction', 'Best Costume Design' and 'Best Music'. These nominations, it should be noted, are aesthetically-orientated, recognising the film's fine period atmosphere, rather than its value as mass entertainment. The musical emphasis and general style, in fact, are similar to the literary adaptations of the studio era, as is the pastoral setting. In movies of the 1930s and 1940s, when the majority of people lived in small towns and pre-industrialism was a fairly recent memory, such invocations did not enter into such a polarised conflict with the cultural present. By this point, with urban and suburban living having become the North American norm, *Tom Sawyer* can be seen as a nostalgic evocation of a bygone age, albeit notably free from self-consciousness or irony in its presentation, with the staunch resistance even to mildly adult elements appearing pregnant with defiance against the emerging status quo in Hollywood entertainment. However wholesome, engaging and tuneful (with screenplay and songs written by the Sherman brothers and incidental music from future blockbuster specialist John Williams) it may be, there is a world of difference between entertainment of this ilk and the family blockbuster titles which would come to dominate the market.

Perhaps the biggest catalyst leading to Hollywood's embrace of a less culturally-specific, 'kidult'-inflected blockbuster aesthetic was the emergence of the multiplex theatre. The multiplex was developed in conjunction with the 1970s US shopping mall, and arose from economic practicality. A larger number of smaller theatres, each showing different films, allowed for greater product differentiation, while their location was designed to increase accessibility and approachability. The multiplex created the economies of scale required to fully exploit blockbusters, but it took the revolutionary approach of Universal president Lew Wasserman to reinvent the Hollywood blockbuster for the so-called 'New Hollywood'. *Jaws* (Steven Spielberg, 1975) redefined the methods of blockbuster construction and economies of success. The keys to its success, beyond its perceived merits as a piece of action/horror filmmaking, were the marketing strategies employed before release in order to maximise audience awareness. As Cook explains, *Jaws* 'pioneered the practice of saturation booking, combined with massive television advertising'.[21] Although this pattern of distribution had long since been adopted by exploitation filmmakers, it was new to mainstream methodology.[22] The wider industry significance of *Jaws* is neatly summarised by Gomery:

> Suddenly one film, largely marketed through the 'rival' medium of television, could break box-office records, generate millions of dollars in ancillary sales, fashion a profitable year for its distributor studio, and generate a rise in stock price which made investors into instant millionaires. Studios initiated a new way of doing business, never 'killed' by TV, but aided by it. A new era for industry practice had begun as studios looked for that single film with which to convert a poor year into a record one.[23]

Films that had previously been regarded as substantial hits now appeared comparatively small-fry. Such enormous success – and from a relatively small budget – raised the ceiling of feature film profit potential several notches.

Yet there were still many variables in formulating hit blockbusters. Producers Dino De Laurentiis and Peter Guber, respectively, oversaw *King Kong* (John Guillermin, 1976) and *The Deep* (Peter Yates, 1977). Both were heavily orchestrated and calculatedly designed to exploit the success of *Jaws*. They also embody traits typical of what has become known as 'high concept', as Justin Wyatt explains:

> High concept can be understood as a form of differentiated product within the mainstream film industry. This differentiation occurs in two major ways: through an emphasis on style within the films, and through an integration with marketing and merchandising.[24]

More bluntly defined by Steven Spielberg as 'a striking, easily reducible narrative which also offers a high degree of profitability', 'high concept' is synonymous with high-end mainstream filmmaking since the mid-1970s.[25] In manufacturing *The Deep*, Guber 'raised the marketing of event movies to a level of perfection that all Hollywood admired [...] in the process, the film itself became largely irrelevant'.[26] In the event, both movies were sizable hits by previous standards, but scarcely approached the success of *Jaws*. Blockbuster hits still depended heavily upon the merits of the film itself, and the publicity created by favourable word-of-mouth. John Friedkin, former vice-president of Twentieth Century Fox's advertising department, once remarked:

> All that [exhibitor] guarantees and promotions can buy is a couple of weeks' business and after that it has to be word of mouth. If the picture is bad, you might as well shoot everybody coming out of a theatre – they will quickly enough kill any film.[27]

In this regard, the Holy Grail for studios is the film that cuts across boundaries, tapping into so-called 'all-age' appeal by attracting children, teenagers, young adults *and* parents. *Jaws* had illustrated the potential for galvanising audiences beyond the regular cinema-goers; now the marketing and promotional frameworks were in place to exploit a potential blockbuster as fully as possible. All a studio needed was the right film.

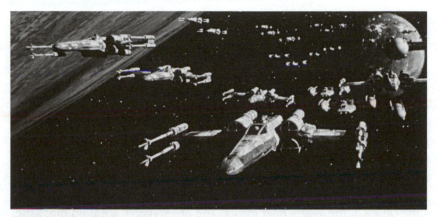

Star Wars (1977)

Reassembling the Family Audience for Contemporary Hollywood

Created on a $9 million budget and expected to recoup between $16 million and $25 million at the box office, *Star Wars* had an inauspicious production history.[28] Fresh from writing and directing his first feature, *THX 1138*, for Warner Bros. in 1971, Lucas pitched an early version of *Star Wars* to United Artists, which rejected it.[29] Two years later, in February 1973, following completion of his second feature, *American Graffiti*, Lucas approached Universal with the idea, and again the pitch was rejected.[30] When Twentieth Century Fox executive Alan Ladd Jr. finally gave Lucas the green light, it was allegedly on the strength of Lucas's obvious talent, rather than the believed merits of the film.[31] Lucas originally envisaged *Star Wars* as 'a modern myth', as well as an update on the children's serials of the 1940s and 1950s.[32] Indeed, he decided to develop *Star Wars* only after his failure to acquire the rights to Alex Raymond's *Flash Gordon*. After the enormous box office success of *American Graffiti*, Lucas declined the opportunity of a higher fee for writing and directing *Star Wars* on the condition that he retained ownership of the sequel, television, music, soundtrack and merchandising rights; this astute piece of bargaining was to cement his position in the upper echelons of the filmmaking industry. However, during the film's production, Lucas became concerned regarding its potential audience appeal. Fearing that its brash, pulp fiction, B-movie overtones, comic book villains, space battles and colourful

151

aliens would appeal *only* to children, Lucas lamented: 'I've made a Walt Disney movie [...] It's gonna do maybe eight, ten million.'[33] These concerns appeared justified when he showed a rough cut of the completed film to a group of friends and fellow filmmakers. Only Jay Cocks – a critic for *Time* magazine – and fellow filmmaker Spielberg liked the film, and Fox studio executives were similarly unimpressed.[34]

In the event, when it was released in May 1977, *Star Wars* became the biggest event movie of the decade. While a large part of its success was down to a colossal merchandising campaign, which effectively redefined the meaning of 'ancillary markets' and almost single-handedly inaugurated franchise cinema, it received almost universally strong reviews. *Time* called it 'the year's best movie' and observed: 'it's got no message, no sex and only the merest dollop of bloodshed here and there. It's aimed at kids – the kid in everybody'.[35] It was not marketed *explicitly* as a family film – hardly surprisingly, given that label's now-contaminating associations – but nevertheless won the *Boxoffice* Blue Ribbon award for that month. One ballot member enthused:

> Never have I had such an inoffensive, good time at a film. The crowds at the theatre I had the pleasure of attending shouted and applauded, even long after the credits had crawled off the screen. Probably the best recommendation and praise I can give 'Star Wars' is that in my field I seldom pay to go to movies. I was so overjoyed, enthralled and excited after the press screening that I paid the first-run prices – and didn't care![36]

Of course, not all reaction was positive. One of the few dissenters was the slightly left-field *New York* magazine, which argued:

> Strip the film of its often striking images and its highfalutin scientific jargon, and you get a story, characters, and dialogue of overwhelming banality without even a 'future' cast to them. Still, *Star Wars* will do very well for those lucky enough to be children or unlucky enough never to have grown up.[37]

It is not hard to see why *Star Wars* was embraced by mass audiences; nor is it hard to see why it was actively disliked by a relatively small but vocal contingent. In spite of its clichéd and simplistic scripting, *Star Wars* emerges almost unscathed as a fast-paced, spectacularly-presented live-action comic strip. Whilst the fannish assertion that it is the best film ever made will forever irritate purists, the fact that it repeatedly tops 'greatest film' audience polls testifies to its enormous and enduring impact.

Its modes of appeal are comparatively – perhaps misleadingly – straightforward. Essentially, *Star Wars* is an action-adventure film. The basic plot is simple enough – a young man, Luke Skywalker (Mark Hamill), with the assistance of a gang of fellow rebels, battles to overthrow a tyrannical galactic empire. In the process, he learns about his own abilities, specifically how to harness the power of 'the force', a pseudo-mystical energy field used by a powerful, ancient order of warriors, known as the Jedi. Ironically, the complexity of the back-story makes a mockery of the high-concept notion that a plot should be simple enough to articulate 'using a key phrase of ten or fewer words'.[38] Nevertheless, it is intellectually undemanding – an important quality for a film targeting mass audiences – whilst evoking well-established patterns of fantasy in its resurrection of the tone and pace of the studio-era serials.

Many of the action sequences, such as the climactic assault upon the Death Star, are standard action-adventure set pieces transposed to a deep-space setting. The fight sequences consciously invoke B-movie westerns, and, correspondingly, the violence, however frequent, is as 'clean' as mass-slaughter gets; the laser battles are bloodless and much of the fighting involves the mystical, invisible energy of 'the force'. The characters of Chewbacca (Peter Mayhew) and C-3PO (Anthony Daniels) are broadly comedic, counterpointing the heroic archetypes of Luke and Han Solo (Harrison Ford). The special effects are calculatedly designed to evoke exhilaration, rather than wonder. Like Lucas, it seems, the audience 'wanted to see this incredible aerial ballet in outer space'.[39] The Academy – always disproportionately inclined to reward the box office smash – shared the audience's approbation, awarding the film six Oscars from ten nominations.

If the manner of its extraordinary success seems almost childishly simple, then it is only because the conditions were exactly right. Five primary factors present themselves. Firstly, *Jaws* had opened up the possibility of reaching a genuine mass audience in contemporary cinema and demonstrated the necessity of strong, cross-media publicity. Secondly, the abandonment of the 'family' audience following the adoption of the rating system caused a product starvation in this sector.

Thirdly, Hollywood's audience base was becoming progressively younger. According to one source, by 1976, 62 per cent of the film audience were aged between 16 and 29.[40] Cook reports that between 1977 and 1979, 'the number of tickets sold to 12 to 20 year-olds increased by 8 percent, while those sold to 21 to 39 year-olds declined by the same number'.[41] Fourthly, *Star Wars* emerged at a point where Hollywood's technical capacities had just reached the point where the complex visual demands of the script could be realised. In fact, the movie pioneered various processes that later became standard industry practice.[42]

Finally, the increasing conglomeration of the Hollywood studios more easily enabled the creation of film franchises. The movement began in 1962 when MCA acquired Universal, initiating a gradual (and still on-going) process in which studios became just one section of diversified, verti-cally- and horizontally-integrated media conglomerates whose interests included broadcast media, publishing houses and merchandising. As Cook notes, before the release of *Star Wars*,

> it was not uncommon for studios to give merchandising rights away for free publicity [...] even when licensed for profit, as in the case of *Jaws* and *King Kong*, product tie-ins like T-shirts, jewellery, and candy had little life or value apart from the film once its run was completed. But with *Star Wars* – known to industry analysts as "the holy grail of licensing" – merchandising became an industry unto itself, and tie-in product marketing began to drive the conception and selling of motion picture products rather than vice versa.[43]

While it is easy to imagine the relationship between the film and its many ancillary products as a sprawling, incoherent web of related products, in fact the longevity of the franchise usually depends on audience response to the movie itself. *Star Wars* satisfied the initial criterion of being *suitable* for viewers of all ages, particularly children – the only audience demo-graphic automatically barred from certain films. It also satisfied the more problematic criterion of successfully *appealing* to a wide demographic cross-section. *Star Wars* can, in retrospect, be seen as the movie that reintegrated the teenage demographic into the so-called 'mass audience', bringing AIP's so-called 'Peter Pan Syndrome' and television's 'kidult' from the relative obscurity of the teen quickie and low-budget family movie to the very heart of mainstream Hollywood audience address.

From this point, nearly all family films have been constructed with this pivotal cross-demographic potential.

Later the same year, Steven Spielberg's *Close Encounters of the Third Kind* was released. Although markedly dissimilar to *Star Wars*, it was almost as successful, partially as a result of a hugely successful pre-release marketing campaign that itself cost $9 million.[44] Yet whilst both films provide higher-than-average quotients of spectacle, *Star Wars* is concerned with eliciting basic thrills and excitement from mass audiences, coupled with the fulfilment of its predictable narrative pattern, whereas *Close Encounters* is more nuanced in its modes of emotional stimulation. Thematically-speaking, the latter is a drama about the psychological impact of extraordinary events upon the human psyche. The narrative centres on a group of resolutely demographically-'average' residents of small-town Muncie, Indiana – the 'Middletown' of the Lynds' classic sociological texts of the 1920s and 1930s – each of whom experience a close-up UFO sighting. Spielberg presents an overwhelming amount of visual information to feed the senses, creating a heightened dialectic between the ordinariness of the geographical location and interpersonal relationships with the extraordinary context of alien visitation.

It is an oft-repeated piece of biographical trivia that Spielberg believes in UFOs and poltergeists. For a director who has built a career on reconciling technical virtuosity with a more intuitive aptitude, his contention that 'in every movie I've ever made I've essentially believed in what the films were about' is probably genuine.[45] Only during the post-production process, it seems, did Spielberg realise that audiences wanted the same thing:

> On *Close Encounters*, I had a very important decision to make: whether or not to use the Walt Disney song, 'When you Wish upon a Star' at the end of the movie, with Jiminy Cricket's actual voice performing it. And the only way I could tell was to have two different previews, on two different nights: one night with the song, and one night without it. I then analysed the preview cards very carefully, interviewed the people who left the theatre, and made a determination that the audience wanted to be transported into another world along with Richard Dreyfuss as he walked about the mothership. They didn't want to be told the film was a fantasy, and this song seemed to belie some of the authenticity and to bespeak fantasy and fairy tale.[46]

Spielberg's camera alternates between evocations of sweeping grandeur and intimate honing in on ordinary people. Roy Neary (Richard Dreyfuss), whose family life begins to fall apart as he obsesses over discovering the truth behind the UFO, is established as the viewer's emotional and sensory avatar. As one of the first people to spot the UFO, the camera tracks his emotional journey from uninterested family man, to introverted, agonised fanatic, and finally liberated symbolic child. The manner of this honing in suggests a creative desire to tap basic, universalised emotional responses. Roy's bedazzled, inarticulate responses to stimuli are not those of a mature, reasoning adult. They are more intuitive, reactive; Roy *feels* – and the audience feels with him – but he does not reason. Like many other Spielberg protagonists, Roy is a 'man-boy', an archetype described by Murray Pommerance as 'the man who never quite abandons his boyhood although [...] he may have sufficient trouble understanding it'.[47] As he boards the mothership as the credits roll and the music swells, Spielberg's identification is with his protagonist, and the viewer is similarly directed.

Star Wars and *Close Encounters* were perhaps the first 'kidult'-inflected mainstream products of the 'New Hollywood'. Critic Robin Wood has called such films 'regressive', identifying what he regards as

> the curious and disturbing phenomenon of children's films conceived and marketed largely for adults – films that construct the adult spectator as a child, or, more precisely, as a childish adult, an adult who would like to be a child.[48]

Roy is such an individual. His evident lack of empathy with his wife and son suggest an individual ill at ease with the complexities of adult life. An early scene shows his unsuccessful attempts to help his son with homework, with an awkwardness totally absent in his later, intuitive responses to the alien arrival. Shortly before his wife leaves, Roy is chastised by his son who calls him a 'cry baby' because of his emotional immaturity. In fact, it is only when he is freed from the distractions of family life that he is able to deduce the location of the alien landing. In the final analysis, it is not only Roy's ordinariness but his childlike view of the world that makes him the perfect candidate for 'abduction'. Both of these qualities mark him out as the representative of the mass audience: those emotionally regressed to childhood, and those still inhabiting it. Roy's departure with the aliens is certainly figured as the narratively 'correct' option. His guilt-free expression of childlike wonder as he enters the mothership confirms that he has found his true calling. His uncomprehending family have been narratively effaced – a positive thing, as it is presented, for they represented the chains of adult culture preventing his complete regression to symbolic childhood. Roy's ultimate trajectory confirms his everyman status, textually and contextually – childhood, of course, is a universal human experience.

'Kidult'-inflected franchises such as *Star Wars* (1977–2005), *Superman* (1978–87) and *Indiana Jones* (1981–2008) represented a new paradigm in Hollywood family entertainment. Possessing genuine cross-cultural, cross-demographic mass appeal, this new paradigm was founded upon largely-undifferentiated audience address, and by the early 1980s had almost totally subsumed the traditional, outmoded dual-addressed family movie. Yet none of these franchises were marketed as 'family' entertainment upon release. The 'family' brand was considered a liability, implying as it did a type of entertainment (and even a social structure) from which young audiences were trying to escape. The notion of film as family viewing appeared increasingly ridiculous, given that most young people attended movies independently, and tended to select entertainment that provided thrills and spectacle rather than a wholesome moral lesson. Even *Boxoffice* retired its long-running Blue Ribbon award for the best family film of the month in 1979. By this point, leading industry figures were abandoning the old, tired rhetoric of Hollywood cinema as a purveyor of entertainment for families. In late 1978, Marvin Goldman, president of the National Association of Theater Owners (NATO) and one of the industry's most outspoken advocates of family entertainment, was replaced by the more progressive Alan Friedberg. Goldman had believed that:

> Our industry has chased [audiences] away by gratuitous sex, profanity and violence. People want entertainment, fun, fantasies, escapism – not spilling intestinal organs on a giant screen, nor language a self-respecting sailor would not use, nor illustrated sex manuals.[49]

Friedberg, by contrast, insisted that the leading advocates for family films rarely attended theatres; that audiences were now dominated by the 16–24 demographic; and that 'contemporary youth today is not the kind of audience turned on by family films'.[50]

Critics coined terms like 'bubblegum blockbusters' to describe 'kidult'-inflected entertainments, but Peter Kramer has more accurately dubbed them 'family adventure movies'.[51] In their infancy, they were a specialised type of family film, that easily transcended the run-of-the-mill product, but they have since broadened-out considerably to a position of box office dominance. Despite this, Hollywood continues to differentiate its family product between high-end blockbusters and lower-budget offerings, catering for differences in age, culture and taste within family film audiences. Subsequent examples of the family-adventure movie include *Ghost Busters* (Ivan Reitman, 1984), *Back to the Future* (Robert Zemeckis, 1985), *Batman* (Tim Burton, 1989), *Jurassic Park* (Steven Spielberg, 1993), *Men in Black* (Barry Sonnenfeld, 1997), and, latterly, the *Harry Potter* (2001–11), *Lord of the Rings* (2001–3) and *Chronicles of Narnia* (2005–) franchises. Such films will usually produce at least one sequel, with the probability of a multimedia franchise if the initial film is sufficiently successful. By the late 1980s, the expectation for hit movies to spawn hit sequels had escalated to the point where *Ghost Busters II* (Ivan Reitman, 1989) – which grossed over $100 million at the box office – was considered commercially disappointing.[52] One of the key executive decisions now made when planning major blockbusters is whether a movie has franchise potential.[53] The higher the budget, the greater the necessity to extend the lifespan of a given movie product. The increasing proliferation of movie franchises is often attributed to the perceived importance of 'synergy' (which refers to the cooperation between diversified sections of the same horizontally-integrated conglomerate in perpetuating a given product). Former Disney CEO Michael Eisner suggested that 'if you don't have synergy, you have nothing but new products [...] If you have synergy, it goes on and on'.[54]

Lucas and Spielberg successfully demonstrated how to produce wildly successful family films, but their methods were not immediately replicated. Disney's films, in particular, were still mired in excessive and anachronistic juvenility. Over the course of the decade, the legendary 'Nine Old Men' – the nucleus of animators who had formed the backbone of Disney's animation division since the release of *Snow White* – gradually retired and were replaced by a new generation of animators. However, neither *Robin Hood* (Wolfgang Reitherman, 1973) nor *The Rescuers* (Reitherman et al., 1977) were well received, and Disney released no further animated features until 1981. Instead, it concentrated on quirky live-action productions such as *Return from Witch Mountain* (John Hough,

1978) and *The Cat from Outer Space* (Norman Tokar, 1978). Conscious that the studio was losing credibility among young audiences, executives took a significant gamble with the 1979 production, *The Black Hole* (Gary Nelson). Conceptualised as a space-opera version of *20,000 Leagues under the Sea*, the film's gestation period was lengthy, having originally been announced in 1975.[55] In 1978, Walt Disney's son-in-law and former football pro Ron W. Miller succeeded Card Walker as studio president. For Miller, luring an older (i.e. teenage) audience back to Disney movies was high on the agenda, and he regarded *The Black Hole* as a film capable of re-engaging the mass audience:

> that slightly older crowd – the audience we used to have in the 1950s with films like *20,000 Leagues under the Sea* [...] Ideally, this is the film that will take Disney to the all-important 15-to-30 year old group. The people who have seen *Star Wars* or *Close Encounters* two or three times.[56]

Disney's public perception as a purveyor of juvenile entertainment was an acknowledged problem within the corporation. Audience testing had revealed that 'the Disney name was actually off-putting to young adults since they associated it with a world of childhood from which they were trying to graduate'.[57]

With this in mind, and considering that *Star Wars*, *Close Encounters* and *Superman* had succeeded by galvanising an older demographic, *The Black Hole* was released under a PG rating – a notable watermark in the studio's production history. In the event, it was not a commercial success. While Disney's problematic brand identity surely impacted on attendances, it was also an artistic failure, paling in comparison with the two films it attempts to emulate – *20,000 Leagues under the Sea* and *Star Wars*. Although the visual effects are at least as impressive as those in *Star Wars*, the attempt to replicate that film's mass appeal fails because of a talky, prosaic script and lack of humour or identification figures. Although Disney assembled a strong cast of character actors (Robert Forster, Anthony Perkins, Roddy McDowell), they are forced to play vapid archetypes (the solid, taciturn hero who is less sympathetic than the antagonist; the idealistic scientist; the precocious robot). *The Black Hole* does not possess the 'kidult' elements required for mass-audience appeal. The ending – which reveals the titular black hole to be some kind of portal to hell – attempts grandiosity but is merely confusingly portentous. John Barry's music is perhaps the bleakest score ever to accompany a family film, and the especially doom-laden overture sets the tone for a strikingly unemotional production. Hindered by poor reviews, it ensured that Disney failed – as Peter Kramer puts it – 'to break out of the children's ghetto'.[58] Fortunately, motion pictures were no longer Disney's main source of revenue, constituting less than 10 per cent of the operating income of $200 million in 1982.[59] By 1984, Walt Disney World was reportedly the world's most popular tourist attraction, even if three-quarters of Disneyland's patrons were adults.[60] Miller was heavily criticised for losing touch with the company's core consumer base and was eventually ousted in late 1984 by a corporate team headed by Michael Eisner, former President of Paramount Pictures, and backed by Walt's nephew, Roy E. Disney. Only after Eisner and new president Frank Wells assumed office did Disney's fortunes begin to improve.

Adapting to the shifting demands of mainstream audiences was a problem faced by all the major studios. December 1980 – one month after the 1970s auteur movement took its last gasp with the spectacular failure of Michael Cimino's *Heaven's Gate* – saw the release of *Flash Gordon*, one of the most significant flops of the period. Its failure underlines the growing importance of style and tone over generic orientation. Had it been produced by George Lucas with the same spirit he imbued *Star Wars*, this 1950s comic-book adaptation might well have been enormously successful. As it was, no doubt mindful that a serious adaptation may have jarred with the comic aspects of the story, the filmmakers adopted a tone of high camp, all but guaranteeing its failure in a mainstream market grown accustomed to starry-eyed earnestness. The ironic mood was reinforced by deliberately eccentric casting: former football professional and Playgirl centrefold Sam J. Jones as Flash – with all his dialogue dubbed by an uncredited voice artist; Max von Sydow as dastardly intergalactic villain Ming the Merciless; veteran British film actor Peter Wyngarde, unrecognisable as Ming's right-hand man, Klytus; Israeli actor Topol as a mad scientist intent on saving the world; and Brian Blessed as a belligerent, bird-like prince.

Flash Gordon makes no attempt to replicate the polish of *Star Wars* and *Close Encounters*. The wide-eyed wonder of Spielberg's and Lucas's films mirrored the tone of national optimism surrounding the possibilities of space travel, but *Flash Gordon* trades on their inherent pomposity by offering faux-glitzy, cheap-looking sets belying its large budget, underscored by the campy soundtrack by rock band Queen. By imbuing the film with a mood of arch irony, its creators invite a sophisticated viewer response, but the fantasy narrative and vibrancy suggest a largely-incompatible juvenile audience. If there is a conclusion to be reached regarding post-*Star Wars* genre movies, it is that audiences will accept almost any generic form if the subject is attractively packaged: science fiction (*Star Wars*; *Close Encounters*; *Back to the Future*); fantasy (*Honey, I Shrunk the Kids*, Joe Johnston, 1989); pulp action-adventure (*Indiana Jones*); horror (*Arachnophobia*, Frank Marshall, 1990); domestic comedies (*Home Alone*, Chris Columbus, 1990); and even westerns (*Back to the Future III*, Robert Zemeckis, 1990). It is the means of communication, and not the generic orientation, that tends to determine audience response.

By the early 1980s, the family-adventure movie was well established. Lucas's and Spielberg's unique position in the industry was cemented by the box office success of their franchise collaboration, *Raiders of the Lost Ark* (1981). Their lucrative rapport with mass audiences afforded them considerable power. Having decided that they wanted to retain financial and artistic control of the franchise, they brokered an unprecedented deal with Paramount, in which the studio operated solely as a distributor.[61] Paramount's concern that it might not receive much in return for its distribution services proved unfounded. Like *Star Wars*, *Raiders of the Lost Ark* consciously evokes early twentieth-century pulp fiction, specifically the age of the comic strips and cheap movie serials of the 1930s. Perhaps to an even greater extent than the filmmakers' earlier projects, its hero, Indiana Jones (Harrison Ford), is an explicitly North American fantasy. Mild-mannered university archaeology professor by day and gung-ho adventurer by night, Indiana is far from infallible. It is part of the film's self-conscious approach that his occasional clumsiness belies his image of phallic omnipotence. Indeed, there is deliberate irony in the exaggerated double life he leads; the duality consciously evokes such all-American heroes as Superman and Batman. Perhaps the homage is too blatantly an exercise in technique; box office aside, *Raiders of the Lost Ark* was not received with quite the same chorus of critical approval as Spielberg's earlier works. As Morris notes: 'shot quickly and under Lucas's supervision and with Lucas retaining final cut, it was [...] Spielberg's least personal effort'.[62] Other critics regarded it as playing to the lowest common denominator. The film's four Oscars seem to validate this perspective: each emphasises its visual and aesthetic qualities, recognising its technical supremacy but relative lack of gravitas.

Nonetheless, the aura surrounding Lucas and Spielberg intensified as the decade progressed. As the family film reasserted its box office credentials, the filmmakers extended their influence to near-hegemonic proportions. Spielberg's production credits during the decade included the following movies tailored towards the family audience: *Poltergeist* (Tobe Hooper, 1982), *Gremlins* (Joe Dante, 1984), *The Goonies* (Richard Donner, 1985), *Back to the Future, An American Tail* (Don Bluth, 1986), *Harry and the Hendersons* (John Dear, 1987), **batteries not included* (Matthew Robbins, 1987) and *Who Framed Roger Rabbit* (Robert Zemeckis, 1988). Aside from his own *Star Wars* and *Indiana Jones* franchises, Lucas oversaw the production of *Labyrinth* (Jim Henson, 1986), *Howard the Duck* (William Huyck, 1986) and *Willow* (Ron Howard, 1988). The notion of two men dominating the family market – and thus capable of exerting a sizable influence upon children's culture as well as popular tastes – would doubtlessly elicit distaste in some quarters. However, as Stephen Prince notes, both men have also exercised their influence to bring the sometimes-unorthodox work of less established filmmakers to fruition.[63] Lucas's work during the 1980s included:

> Co-produc[ing] Akira Kurosawa's samurai epic, *Kagemusha* (1980), Francis Ford Coppola's period film *Tucker: The Man and His Dream* (1988), Lawrence Kasdan's *film noir* update *Body Heat* [1981], and, most remarkably, Haskell Wexler's *Latino* (1985), a pro-Sandinista film that was one of the few pictures in the period to explicitly criticise US support for the contra rebels fighting the Nicaraguan government.[64]

By the end of the decade, Spielberg himself was sick of making family films:

> Hitting 40, I really had to come to terms with what I've been tenaciously clinging to, which was a celebration of a kind of naivety that has been reconfirmed countless times in the amount of people who have gone to see *E.T., Back to the Future* and *Goonies* [...] I just reached a saturation point.[65]

Spielberg conceded: 'I have been in the candy factory for the last three years as a producer making sugar substitutes, and I've gagged on it myself.'[66] Reflexively, he attempted a more adult film with *Empire of the Sun* (1987) and even stated his intention to abandon his well-known desire of mounting a lavish adaptation of *Peter Pan*.

These family films, though, were the perfect fuel for the multiplexes. Multiplex theatres – small, featureless and architecturally uniform – compel audience attention towards the screen. Previously, conditions of exhibition had been pivotal to the movie experience. The 'picture palaces' of the classical era were identifiably middlebrow, designed to make the film-going experience as comfortable and prestigious as possible. Their architectural splendour, great size and facilities overtly positioned audiences as privileged observers, secure in the comfort of their well-furnished seats, rather than active participants in the action. In the multiplex, audiences are encouraged to *forget* their surroundings and position themselves *within* the film. Clearly, this immersive potential only works if there is congruity between the mode of spectatorship and the film being exhibited. However, the fact that the majority of contemporary Hollywood family films privilege sensorial appeal means that they are best suited to exploit this shift in the modes of spectatorship. I will discuss the intricacies of immersion in more depth in the final chapter.

The Hollywood Family Film in the 1980s: Proliferation and Generic Diversity

The development of ancillary markets in the early to mid 1980s was one of the major factors stimulating immense growth in the 'family' sector of the entertainment industry. With family-adventure movies illustrating the possibilities for massive profits in family-orientated programming, ancillary market potential – notably cable TV, merchandising and especially home video – took this trend to a new level. In the 1980s, the family film became the most lucrative production type in Hollywood cinema. Although the potential audience had been there since the 1970s, the technologies had not. As Balio notes:

> Home video and pay television [...] extended both the market and the revenue stream for filmed programming. It all started with the

launching of geosynchronous satellites in the mid-seventies. As Michelle Hilmes states [...] 'Satellite transmission capability finally began to transform television into a true "broadcast" medium, loosening its dependence on the nineteenth-century technology of wired transmission and giving it the ability to offer an almost limitless variety of channels and services'.[67]

The VCR became commercially available in the 1970s, but remained highly expensive, and did not achieve widespread market saturation. Both the hardware and software became more affordable in the 1980s. In 1984, VCRs were installed in 15 per cent of homes in the United States; this figure rose to 50 per cent in 1986.[68] To put the impact of these new technologies in perspective:

With the explosion of ancillary markets in the eighties [...] box office returns accounted for just 28 percent of total income – down from 54 percent in 1978 – with another 12 percent from pay cable and 40 percent from home video, which had contributed only a combined 4 percent in 1978.[69]

Paramount was the first studio to risk lowering prices for videotapes to stimulate demand, retailing *Airplane!* at $29.95 – much lower than the average price of around $70.[70] This strategy triggered a general price-drop and inaugurated the consumer practice of buying, rather than renting, videotapes. This had the biggest significance in the family market; as Thompson observes, 'kids could watch [family films] time after time on the electronic babysitter'.[71] The dominance of the family market in the home video sector prompted a broader industry embrace of family film production.

Considering the incubation period for a large-scale Hollywood film is typically at least two years, the beginning of the industry-wide family film craze can be traced to 1982 – a key year for several reasons. Special effects and computer animation were continuing to develop rapidly. *Star Trek II: The Wrath of Khan* (Nicholas Meyer), which was released in early June 1982, featured 60 seconds of computer graphics.[72] More significantly, the following month saw the release of *Tron* (Steven Lisberger) – Disney's attempt to re-establish itself at the forefront of industry innovation – which contained 40 minutes of computer graphics.[73] These films illustrated the continued technical strides the industry was taking in the creation of imagery that would have been thought impossible only a decade before. By far the most significant catalyst, however, was the release of Spielberg's *E.T.* Although Spielberg claims that *E.T.* was a 'personal film' and expressed surprise at its box office success, it was perfectly timed, and apparently calculated for mass-audience appeal.[74] With its considerable marketing potential, tie-in merchandise alone apparently grossed $1 billion.[75]

The increasing proliferation of family films brought with it a wide diversification of generic forms. Before *Star Wars*, family films were marked by relative product standardisation, but since the early 1980s they have been characterised by stylistic and generic differentiation. Loose generic patterns operating under the family film umbrella during the 1980s and 1990s included:

1. The family-adventure movie, as noted above.
2. The fantasy film – e.g. *Time Bandits* (Terry Gilliam, 1981), *E.T.*, *The Dark Crystal* (Jim Henson, 1982), *The NeverEnding Story* (Wolfgang Petersen, 1984), *Flight of the Navigator* (Randall Kleiser, 1986), *Labyrinth*.
3. The science movie – e.g. *WarGames* (John Badham, 1983), *Short Circuit* (John Badham, 1986).
4. The family-horror movie – e.g. *The Watcher in the Woods* (John Hough, 1980), *Something Wicked this Way Comes* (Jack Clayton, 1983), *Arachnophobia*.
5. The family-friendly teen pic – e.g. *Gremlins*, *The Last Starfighter* (Nick Castle, 1984), *Back to the Future* and its sequels, *Beetlejuice* (Tim Burton, 1988), *Bill and Ted's Excellent Adventure* (Stephen Herek, 1989).
6. Sword-and-sorcery films, e.g. *Conan the Barbarian* (John Milius, 1982), *Ladyhawke* (Richard Donner, 1985), *Legend* (Ridley Scott, 1985), *The Black Cauldron* (Ted Berman and Richard Rich, 1985), *The Princess Bride* (Rob Reiner, 1987), *Willow*.
7. The body-swap film – e.g. *Like Father Like Son* (Rod Daniel, 1987), *Vice-Versa* (Brian Gilbert, 1988), *Big* (Penny Marshall, 1988), *18 Again!* (Paul Flaherty, 1988).
8. The adult-driven domestic family film – e.g. *Uncle Buck* (John Hughes, 1989), *National Lampoon's Christmas Vacation* (Jeremiah

Chechik, 1989), *Home Alone*, *Hook* (Steven Spielberg, 1991), *Father of the Bride* (Charles Shyer, 1991), *Mrs. Doubtfire* (Chris Columbus, 1993), *Stepmom* (Chris Columbus, 1998).

9. The slapstick domestic comedy – e.g. *Kindergarten Cop* (Ivan Reitman, 1990), *Ghost Dad* (Sidney Poitier, 1990), *Beethoven* (Barry Levant, 1992), *Getting Even With Dad* (Howard Deutch, 1994).

10. The literary classic adaptation – e.g. *The Secret Garden* (Agnieszka Holland, 1993), *Little Women* (Gillian Armstrong, 1994), *A Little Princess* (Alfonso Cuarón, 1995).

11. The Christmas family movie – e.g. *National Lampoon's Christmas Vacation*, *Home Alone*, *The Muppet Christmas Carol* (Brian Henson, 1992).

12. The animated feature – e.g. *The Little Mermaid* (Ron Clements and John Musker, 1989), *Aladdin* (Ron Clements and John Musker, 1992), *Toy Story* (John Lasseter, 1995), *Antz* (Eric Darnell and Tim Johnson, 1998).

As will be seen, there is some overlap, and this list is intended to be indicative, rather than exhaustive. Nonetheless, it illustrates not only the degree of stylistic variation within contemporary family entertainment, but also its culturally-determined intermittency. The concept of commercially- and culturally-driven development seems particularly valuable. From the early to mid 1980s, family entertainment was dominated by family-adventure movies and fantasy films. Although 'real-world' concerns (such as divorce, and the threat of outside forces infiltrating family harmony) play a part in such fantasy films as *E.T.* and *Flight of the Navigator*, their narratives are still largely driven by the experiences of child protagonists. In the mid to late 1980s, this began to change. Narratives became driven by the experiences and anxieties of adults, most particularly middle-aged men. The seeds were sown by the body-swap cycle of films in 1987 and 1988. By the following year, even renowned teen film director John Hughes had moved into adult-driven family films with the release of *Uncle Buck*, and a spate of similar movies followed over the next few years. This shift from child- to adult-centric narratives was one of the defining features of late 1980s and early 1990s Hollywood family entertainment.

The reasons behind this preoccupation with adult concerns are numerous. A dominant factor was the size, power and influence of the baby boom generation, and its relationship with mass audiences. The cultural power of the baby boom generation has been best explored by Landon Y. Jones, who explains:

> For two centuries the birthrate in the United States and the world has steadily declined. It is still declining. There is only one exception: the single, unprecedented aberration we call the postwar baby boom. It was not, as is often thought, a short rise in the birthrate caused by returning GIs making up for lost time. It began that way in 1946, but instead of stopping in the 1950s (as in Europe), the tidal wave of births continued, affecting all races and classes with astonishing uniformity. This national euphoria – what I shall call the 'procreation ethic' – peaked in 1957, when more than 4.3 million babies were born. At least 4 million babies were born in each of the bumper-crop years from 1954 through 1964, the last real year of the baby binge. All totalled, 76,441,000 babies – one third of our present population – arrived in the 19 years from 1946 through 1964.[76]

Through sheer force of numbers, Jones argues, the baby boom drove the explosive emergence of the teenage market in the 1950s. In the 1960s, 'teenagers accounted for 55 percent of all soft drink sales, 53 percent of all movie tickets, and 43 percent of all records sold'.[77] The power of the baby boom generation was threefold: in addition to its demographic size, it was also the richest and best educated in US history.[78]

As the older sections of the baby boom generation matured to child-rearing age, it continued as the dominant voice in US culture:

> In the 1980s, the boom children are continuing their imperious ways. They are turning a youth-centred society into an adult-centred one as they make their particular concerns, whether housing prices or tax reform, into national obsessions. They are a generational tyranny.[79]

By the 1970s, the birth rate was in sharp decline. This 'baby bust' coincided with a period in US history where long-established norms of social behaviour appeared either outmoded, or in terminal decline. The institution of the family was at the forefront of this development. Most notably, divorce rates increased dramatically. Reynolds Farley suggests that North Americans in the 1970s 'adopted new views about personal fulfilment and about whether unhappily married couples should stay together'.[80] Baby boomers were getting married and having children later than previous generations, partially a corollary of gender-role reassignment since the counter-cultural movement of the 1960s.[81] Although sociologists such as Theodore Caplow and Stephanie Coontz have argued that actual changes in social and familial structures were less significant than is commonly thought, psychologically the baby boomers entered the 1980s, as Jones argues, as 'a generation of uncertainty, unsure about their role in society, unsure about marriage and family, unsure even about reproducing themselves'.[82] Priorities regarding the relationship between self and family significantly changed:

> The Good Times Generation never doubted its priorities: first family, then marriage, and finally self. But the baby boomers turned it upside down: their first priority was the self. Then came marriage, if it worked. And finally family, if that worked, too.[83]

In the 1970s and 1980s, 'the cult of the child [became] the cult of the adult'.[84]

There were significant socio-political factors behind this widespread retreat into domestic self-interest. The failure of the Vietnam War, and the subsequent resignation of President Nixon in 1974 following the Watergate conspiracy, sapped US confidence in its own supremacy.[85] In July 1979, President Carter broadcast his now-infamous 'crisis of confidence' speech to the nation.[86] Carter's identification of 'the loss of unity of purpose for our nation' was, in retrospect, a political error that contributed to his defeat to Ronald Reagan in the Presidential elections of the following year. Reagan 'turned this crisis of confidence into a successful presidential campaign', and came into office promising to 'cut income taxes, boost military spending, and make Americans "feel good"'.[87] The worst economic recession since the 1930s hit the USA in 1981, and lasted almost two years, yet the Reagan years were marked by an ever-widening gap between rich and poor.[88] Although Reagan professed to believe that 'America's true greatness lay less in material riches than in its values that gave pre-eminence to individual freedom', monetary income became the accepted measure of one's value to society.[89] The so-called 'cult of conspicuous consumption' is perhaps best exemplified by the yuppie class – a relatively young, upwardly-mobile executive class that prized money and status above all else.[90] By 1988, 'yuppie' had become a slur; *Newsweek* announced that the group were 'in disgrace' and even suggested that 'the 1980s were over, two years early'.[91] In spite of the public shame of the Iran-Contra affair – which implicated Reagan in the secret selling of arms to Iran to fund right-wing Sandinista rebels in overthrowing the democratically-elected communist government of Nicaragua – he remained overwhelmingly popular.[92]

It has become *de rigueur* in film criticism to invoke 'Reaganism' as the key to unlocking a deeper understanding of 1980s Hollywood films. Many critics have noted that the socially-critical auteur movement, which had flourished in the 1970s, withered and died during the Reagan era. Robin Wood contends that Spielberg's and Lucas's family-adventure movies typify 'Reaganite entertainment' in their defiantly optimistic veneer, which disguises an ideologically-conservative agenda.[93] Reagan became, as Cook argues, 'the perfect simulacrum of blockbuster heroes like Luke Skywalker and Indiana Jones'.[94] Although the analogy errs towards the teleological, popular culture and popular politics certainly fulfilled a cultural need, playing the emotions rather than challenging the intellect of the US public.

Hollywood films continued to reveal North American cultural anxieties, but the ideologies of unease were far more displaced. By 1980, as Edward Reiss explains:

> 'Middle America' was concerned about relative U.S. economic decline; loss of U.S. strategic superiority; the failure of détente, and perceived vacillation among NATO allies. Events in Iran, Afghanistan, and Nicaragua coincided with a wave of militarist revanchism in the USA and the resurgence of a 'New Right' which sought a technical or military solution, unilaterally enforceable by the U.S., to the problem of super-power relations [...] Presenting itself as the party of prudence, the Republican platform of 1980 called for a massive military build-up, 'more modern' ABM technologies and 'overall military and technological superiority over the Soviet Union'.[95]

Culture and politics became powerfully intertwined. The most significant expression of this symbiosis was Reagan's conception of the Strategic Defence Initiative (SDI), nicknamed 'Star Wars'. The SDI began life as a US military initiative designed to combat the threat of ballistic missiles. Under Reagan's regime, its scope was widened considerably. Dubbing the programme 'Star Wars', no doubt as a public-relations exercise, the President announced the SDI to the nation on 23 March 1983.[96] Reagan outlined a vision of using advanced technology to make nuclear weapons 'impotent and obsolete', promising to change 'the course of human history' with the programme's supposed ability to maintain an impervious 'shield' against nuclear missiles.[97]

The proposal was founded upon the idea of using orbiting satellites to shoot down enemy nuclear missiles upon launch, but Reagan's rhetoric greatly exceeded the abilities of the technology. On the day of the speech announcing it to the world, the head of directed energy weapons development informed a senate sub-committee that the SDI did not merit extra investment; such was its disappointing performance.[98] The whole concept of 'Star Wars' rested, as Reiss observes, on 'a strange mingling of science and culture, expertise and populism'.[99] Despite the paradox of the ultimate super-weapon being presented as 'inherently defensive', Reagan's offer of a water-tight defensive shield offered rhetorical appeal to a nation in search of comfort and security.[100] Furthermore, the promise of 'Star Wars' tapped into deeply-held mythologies surrounding US cultural history, such as intellectual, racial and technological supremacy, and the desire to expand the frontier (in this case deep space, rather than wagons west). The 'Star Wars' initiative also played on the nation's perceived vulnerability, appearing – falsely – to offer a scientific solution to a scientific problem. Although the scientific community widely discredited Reagan's public conceptualisation of the SDI, recognition of its failure was more of a slow realisation for the US public. From the start, 'Star Wars' was a rhetorical fabrication; an attempt to gain political capital from two dominant cultural themes of the period: unease surrounding the condition of US society, and the escapist promise of a better future as embodied in the fantasies of Lucas and Spielberg.

In this context, it is unsurprising that family films of the early 1980s reflected unease in Middle America regarding state-regulated scientific advance, intensified in its relationship with the domestic sphere. Mick Broderick and Tim Shary have both observed the abundance of early 1980s Hollywood films concerned either with the uses of nuclear power or the relationship between science and the wider social arena. Shary considers the 'science film' one of the five key genres in contemporary teen films, typified by such productions as *Weird Science* (Martha Coolidge, 1985) and *Real Genius* (John Hughes, 1985).[101] Whilst Broderick concedes that 'most nuclear movies eschew direct action by children in challenging the military-industrial complex', he argues that a selection of 1980s films reverse this trend.[102] Citing *WarGames*, *The Manhattan Project* (Marshall Brickman, 1986), *Project X* (Jonathan Kaplan, 1987) and *Terminator 2: Judgment Day* (James Cameron, 1991) as key examples, Broderick suggests that

> a repeated fear in such movies is the removal of human choice from the nuclear decision-making 'loop'. This becomes a narrative trope that the 'wisdom' of children and adolescents narratively seeks to redress.[103]

Noteworthy family films from this period that are similarly preoccupied with the use of scientific technology include *E.T.*, *Back to the Future*, *Flight of the Navigator* and *Short Circuit*. This variety of unease might be regarded as 'public-world' anxiety, as opposed to the more emphatically 'private-world' anxiety of the later adult-driven family films.

  E.T. combines elements of both. Perhaps the archetypal family film of the 'New Hollywood', it purports to cross demographic boundaries not

E.T. (1982)

by addressing children and adults as separate entities, but by tapping an appeal of the senses, consciously drawing upon 'awe' and 'wonder', offering sweeping orchestral music, cutting-edge visuals, and a self-conscious naivety in sentiment. Even a critic as hardened as Robin Wood is forced to admit that he 'enjoys being reconstructed as a child' in such a way.[104] I would, however, tend to agree with Kramer's assessment that the pleasures of 'regressive' texts are far from 'mindless' in nature.[105] On the contrary, a strong desire on the part of an emotionally-mature adult to watch a 'regressive' family film is likely to be emphatically self-conscious. Furthermore, the adult appeal in films like *E.T.* emanates partially from the textual dialectic between aspects of so-called 'pure fantasy' and the occasional infiltration of real-world, adult anxiety. All of Spielberg's family narratives maintain this dialectic between the fantastic and the mundane, persistently alluding to such emphatically adult concerns as divorce, family breakdown and outside intrusion, before drawing back and allowing the fantastic, the magical, to triumph.

These agendas ultimately serve to deepen the pleasurable association, particularly amongst adult audiences, as they concede the existence of an unpalatable alternative to utopian fantasy that is ultimately vanquished. It is ironic, given that Columbia's market researchers allegedly found that the film would interest no-one over the age of four, and advised scrapping the production, that adults, rather than children, were its core consumers.[106] Morris has argued that *E.T.*'s success stemmed partly from its appeal to a *specific* section of the adult audience, namely 'heterosexual childless couples in their late 20s and 30s'.[107] The story begins when a suburban schoolboy called Elliott (Henry Thomas) discovers a small alien in his backyard. Accidentally stranded on Earth by his mother-ship, the alien – E.T. – is adopted by Elliott and his family. Before long, the government becomes aware of the creature's presence and takes both Elliott and E.T. – whose relationship has somehow become symbiotic – for experimentation. Ultimately, Elliott, with the assistance of a gang of friends, manages to take the alien back to the forest in which he landed, and the alien ship promptly returns to collect him. In an ending closely mirroring the final sequence of *Close Encounters*, the mother-ship departs in a blaze of special effects as the humans look on in amazement. There is, however, a key difference between the films. The aliens in *Close Encounters*, however benevolent their intentions, are explicitly 'other', whereas E.T.'s 'alienness' is more cosmetic.

Symbolically, E.T. is a child, moving between the contrary poles of innocence and experience as the narrative structures of the film demands. His occasionally-glowing red heart is highly suggestive. But even where the film's regressive trajectory appears most strongly defined – in the simpatico relationship between E.T. and Elliott – the conflict between the public and private spheres powerfully emerges. It is soon established that this domestic environment is far from healthy. Elliott's unseen father has recently set up home with another woman in Mexico, leaving his emotionally-fragile mother, Mary (Dee Wallace), struggling to cope in his absence. Her refusal to believe that Elliott has met an alien prompts the sullen response, 'dad would believe me', a piece of dialogue doubtlessly reflecting adult remorse over the culpability of family breakdown. As Mary walks out, tearfully, Elliott's older brother, Mike (Robert MacNaughton), strikes back: 'why don't you grow up and think about how other people feel for a change?'

One of the most significant scenes in the movie – darkly incongruous in tone, if not in underlying message – occurs later in the film, when Mike and Elliott are seen sifting regretfully through artefacts of their young childhood, at a time when their father was still present:

> **Elliott:** Remember the time when he used to take us out to the ball games, and take us to the movies, and we had popcorn fights?
> **Mike:** [reassuringly] We'll do that again, Elliott.
> **Elliott:** [disbelievingly] Sure.

Unbeknownst to the boys, their conversation is being monitored. Although the precise identity of the intruders is not revealed, and we do not see their faces, we are left to assume that they are government spies, investigating E.T.'s arrival. As signalled by the unusually-ominous music, this is one of the few moments of genuine unease in the film. The fact that this intrusion is shown to take place at the moment of greatest family intimacy underlines the theme of power abuse, which is later reinforced when Elliott and E.T. are taken for experimentation, and hordes of scientists – rendered anonymous by their full-body protective suits – invade the house. Only one scientist, Keys (Peter Coyote), identifies with the family and eventually helps E.T.'s escape. Although the alien's departure signifies the ultimate triumph of fantasy over paranoia, these anxieties are not entirely effaced. *E.T.* – like most 1980s family films – is situated not in a Tolkienian world of imagination, but in a 'real', adult world, with its attendant threats, concerns and complexities.

WarGames and *Short Circuit* confront state power abuse even more explicitly. *WarGames* centres on school-age computer hacker David (Matthew Broderick). Accustomed to breaking into the school computer records to improve his substandard grades, he chances on a system called 'Global Thermo-Nuclear War', which he misinterprets as an innocent computer game. In reality, he has hacked into an automated government computer system regulating nuclear weapons. After his seemingly inno-cent gaming has succeeded in sparking a military panic, David is taken into custody, and the situation escalates to the brink of nuclear war before the boy uses his computing faculties to shut down the system. Although *WarGames* is positioned more towards the teenage than 'all-age' market, Badham's later film, *Short Circuit*, explores similar territory with a heavier 'family' emphasis. As with *WarGames*, it centres on a highly-advanced government-affiliated scientific endeavour that spirals out of control through irresponsibility and incompetence. In this film, it is a private corporation, Nova Laboratories, which is developing military hardware for the US military. Nova has constructed a specialised type of heavily-armed robot for use on the battlefield. As in *WarGames*, the technology is explic-itly offensive, with a potential for destruction on a massive scale.

The filmmakers obviously mistrust the government's motives and competency to handle dangerous technology. An early exchange sees the unscrupulous head of the facility, Howard Marner (Austin Pendleton) – significantly, a former scientist who has renounced his principles and now describes himself as 'a businessman' – attempting to secure support for the project in the Senate. The military's plan to use the robots as weapons is ineffectually but bitingly reproved by the robots' creator, Newton Crosby (Steve Guttenberg):

> **Military official:** It is the ultimate soldier. Obeys orders, never asks questions.
> **Crosby:** Originally, I had non-military purposes in mind. I designed it as a marital aid.
> **Marner:** [laughing nervously] Very funny. No, I think we'll all agree that Dr. Crosby has designed a weapon that will keep our world safe for all time.
> **Crosby:** Howard, what's safe about blowing people up?

This exchange evokes Reagan's rhetoric surrounding the supposedly-defensive function of the 'Star Wars' programme. The mood changes shortly afterwards, as a laboratory accident accidentally makes one of the robots – Number 5 (voiced by Tim Blaney) – sentient. Escaping from the lab, Number 5 encounters the dizzy Stephanie (Ally Sheedy), who mistakes him for an alien. Their early scenes together, in which Ally attempts to educate him in the ways of contemporary North American life, amiably recall *E.T.* Much of the film centres upon the pursuit of Number 5 by Nova's military arm, which believes the robot has gone rogue and represents a threat to the public. As with the pursuit of David in *WarGames*, the military has mistaken an innocent party for a dangerous foe, implying not only a hazardous lack of perception, but that *it* represents as much of a threat as the supposed enemies it zealously pursues. The film fuses socially-relevant themes such as the use of technology in a responsible way; domestic and worldwide military armament; adult relationships and budding romance – with a rather juvenile treatment in the scenes featuring Number 5, a creation clearly designed to thrill and amuse young children. Leaving aside the comic interaction between the robot and his human friends, the cultural frames of reference are strikingly grown-up.

Back to the Future – one of the highest-grossing movies of the decade – can be seen as an intermediate step between the childlike fantasy of *E.T.* and the adult-driven domestic narratives of the late 1980s. The film centres on down-to-earth teenager Marty McFly (Michael J. Fox). Although his school career and family life are floundering, Marty has a stable relationship with his long-term girlfriend and a close friendship with eccentric local inventor Doc Brown (Christopher Lloyd). After years of botched attempts and sourcing of materials, the Doc has finally succeeded in piecing-together a fully-functioning time machine, retrofitted to the chassis of a DeLorean sports car. Through a complex series of events, Marty accidentally transports himself 30 years back in time, to his own neighbourhood, circa 1955. There he meets his own mother and father, and discovers the reasons behind their failing relationship in the present: his mother, Lorraine (Lea Thompson), behind her demure exterior, is actually a devil-may-care rebel, whilst his father, George (Crispin Glover), is comically gauche, passive and inept. Marty realises that his own future – and that of his entire family unit – depends on him reshaping the present by forging a more successful relationship between the pair.

Back to the Future (1985)

In the process, he must encourage his father to become a more assertive, responsible figure, more attractive to Lorraine and a better father to himself, whilst conceiving a way of transporting himself back to 1985.

Like the adult-driven, small-town family dramas of the 1940s, *Back to the Future* uses nostalgia for a bygone age as a form of social commentary on the inadequacies of the present. As Coontz has observed, fascination and nostalgia for the 1950s was strongly marked in 1980s and 1990s US culture and society.[108] It was a period of relative social and ideological stability, before the counter-cultural movement of the 1960s, and polls have also shown that this period has been regarded as 'the best time for children to grow up'.[109] The 1950s embody more masculine than feminine fantasies of ideal domesticity, which is unsurprising, given that career opportunities for women were fewer, and that studies have suggested that the nuclear family structure was good for men's physical and emotional health.[110] Such nostalgia is here evident in its most superficial form as a repetitive, blatant identification with 1950s iconography. Marty possesses an affinity with James Dean denim jackets and rock 'n' roll, and a disregard for overbearing authority. At the same time, his apparent proclivity towards rebellion is deeply-rooted in conformity.

His relationship with his girlfriend is stable and loving (according to the Doc, freshly returned from a trip to the future at the end of the film, the relationship will eventually result in marriage). He also has a steady job, drives a car and still attends school. A more clean-cut rebel can scarcely be imagined. Although he is bafflingly regarded as a semi-delinquent by the authoritarian school principal, his actions and dialogue tend to mark him out as adult masquerading as child.

As if to disavow suggestions of an ideological agenda ill-befitting its self-appointed status as popcorn entertainment, the film features a number of satirical references to contemporary politics. The 1950s variant of the Doc, disbelieving Marty's contention that he has travelled back through time, asks the name of the President in 1985. Upon hearing the response, he exclaims, 'Ronald Reagan? The actor? Then who's vice-president? Jerry Lewis?' Later, the Doc remarks: 'no wonder your president has to be an actor. He has to look good on television'. Such comments may have chimed with viewers cognisant of Reagan's admission that his job reminded him of his acting days, in that it was 'something like shoot-ing a script'.[111] Moreover, these humorous allusions to political currents serve to divert attention from any actual agenda the film may be seen to promote, creating the illusion that it is both apolitical and open regarding its political affiliation (i.e. it does not have one). This theme is reinforced by a subplot concerning the electoral campaigns of two mayoral candidates, one from the 'present' and the other from 1955. Both promise 'progress', the 1950s candidate offering 'more jobs, better education, bigger civic improvements and lower taxes'. In all cases, however, these political allu-sions take place in the background, and the film is careful to show Marty's disconnection and apparent lack of interest in this dull and corrupt arena. Instead, Marty is closely affiliated with the Doc, whose homespun and benign eccentricity delineates him as the 'acceptable' face of scientific innovation and technical advance. The Doc stands in sharp contrast to the shady and morally-dubious state-regulated activities depicted in *WarGames* and *Short Circuit*.

Back to the Future's family drama unfolds against a striking backdrop of fantasy and expensive-looking special effects. This aesthetic innova-tion, however, ultimately serves to obfuscate the conventionality and ideological conservatism of the narrative. This is not really a fantasy movie; the impressively-realised time-travelling car is little more than a framing device which allows the filmmakers to delineate the disparate ideologies of past and present. The dissatisfaction at the heart of Marty's 1980s family is quickly established. The 24-year-old Lea Thompson's make-up depicts Lorraine as tired and downtrodden, and her emotional need for love and attention is obviously left unfulfilled by the pathetically ineffectual George, whose boorish appreciation of inane television is seen to drown-out the plaintive sentiments of his wife. Nothing short of a reversal of established history, as it is configured through Marty's brittle 1980s family unit, is satisfactory to the creative team behind the movie. The success of Marty's mission is signalled by the ending, which depicts a happy, functional family unit, underpinned by George's transformation into a confident, assertive patriarch. The purportedly feel-good emphasis of the movie is actually little more than a veneer, masking the unsubtle remodelling of the family unit to a state of ideological acceptability. With this in mind, the apparent guilelessness of the protagonist usefully diverts audience attention from these agendas. The conventionalism of its narrative, if recognised, is more likely to be seen as another pleasing evocation of its nostalgic qualities, rather than as a form of social commentary.

This shift towards the domestic arena was confirmed by the body-swap cycle, which responded to two major social concerns. The first was the visible emergence of the yuppie class, and the question of how this group of career-minded individuals would interact with the broader social sphere. The obvious distaste provoked by the yuppie archetype was counterpointed by the size and economic influence of this social group, which ensured its ongoing visibility. The second major concern, heavily related to the first, was the social and political obsession with childhood and parenthood. These issues moved to the forefront of US political campaigning, as the debate surrounding contemporary conditions of childhood and parenthood was deliberately intensified for electoral purposes. By 1994, according to the *Los Angeles Times*, 'candidates of both parties were "lining up" to join the family values bandwagon', while in 1996, politician Dan Quayle reported that 'America has truly reached a new consensus' to 'support the unified model of father, mother, and child'.[112] In the late 1980s, much of this attention surrounded the contemporary role of the father. In 1988, sociologist Frank F. Furstenberg proclaimed that 'fatherhood is in vogue'.[113] He argued that late 1980s fathers were subject to a labelling process dividing them between 'good dads' and 'bad dads'. The phenomenon emerged because 'the good provider role is on its way out [...] but its legitimate successor has not yet appeared on the scene'.[114] The realisation that more than half of all children in the United States would spend at least part of their childhood being brought up by a single parent provoked considerable unease.[115]

Although a number of body-swap titles emerged between 1987 and 1988, the film that made the biggest impact – and made the most money – was *Big*. Like *Back to the Future*, it utilises a pseudo-fantasy framework as a device with which to manoeuvre its characters into impossible situations. The story centres on 13-year-old Josh Baskin (David Moscow). Denied many of the pleasures of adulthood, and lacking the courage to speak to older girls, Josh fantasises about being an adult. Encountering a mysterious contraption at the local fairground which promises to grant wishes, he asks to be a grown-up. He is informed that his wish has been granted, but nothing appears to happen, so he returns home. The next morning, he awakens to find himself in the body of a 30-year-old man (Tom Hanks). Terrified, he turns to his mother for reassurance, but she runs him out of the house, believing him to be a burglar. Fortunately, Josh is spotted by successful toy manufacturer MacMillan (Robert Loggia). Impressed by his spirit, charm and vitality, MacMillan immediately offers him an executive position evaluating new toy lines. Also impressed by the

Big (1988)

freshness of the newcomer, fellow executive Susan (Elizabeth Perkins) quickly falls in love with Josh and they begin a relationship. Although initially successful, the relationship gradually falls apart, due to a combination of Susan's insecurities and Josh's emotional immaturity. He finally tells Susan the truth about his true nature. They part company, and Josh – suddenly and inexplicably a child again – returns home to his family.

As may be gauged from this synopsis, *Big* is highly convoluted. Concerned with exploring the relationship between childhood and adulthood in the contemporary world, it certainly struck a chord with audiences and the Academy (who nominated the film for Best Screenplay) alike. The blurb on the back cover of the home video release – 'You'll never forget Tom Hanks in "Big" – a special comedy that'll make you feel years younger' – heavily implies a largely adult target audience. This is consistent with the fact that Josh does not really represent childhood, but rather an adult's conception of childhood, characterised by frozen smiles and clumsy gestures, sexual innocence and general naivety regarding adult relationships, and an obsession with mindless play to an extent bordering on caricature (especially for a 13-year-old). Josh is the polar opposite of such cocksure, wised-up and cynical teen film protagonists as Ferris Bueller and Jeff Spicoli, characters not much older than Josh, but clearly concocted for very different audiences. Even child protagonists such as Elliott in *E.T.* or David (Joey Cramer) in *Flight of the Navigator* are not shown to be as – for want of a better term – 'childish' as Josh Baskin.

The movie's agendas become apparent soon after Josh assumes his position on MacMillan's executive board. His success in the corporation, it is implied, stems from the fact that he alone retains the innocence embodied by the 'essential' child. He can still have fun, and is generous and loving. Initially, Susan is only slightly more sympathetic than her joyless, soulless colleagues. We learn that she has had several unfulfilling affairs with office co-workers, and presents herself as bored with the lifestyle and looking for something deeper. Misconstruing her interest as purely platonic, he innocently invites Susan to spend the night at his flat. When they arrive at the apartment, which is littered with childish toys, Susan is introduced to his bunk-bed and allocated the bottom bunk. Josh wishes her goodnight, without as much as a kiss on the cheek; Susan misunderstands his incomprehension for respect and restraint, and her fascination with him deepens further. As the narrative unfolds, however, Josh begins to lose his childish innocence as he becomes more deeply enmeshed within the back-stabbing corporate structure inhabited by the high executive. The implication is clear – the yuppie lifestyle is inherently harmful on two levels: upon the individual, and upon society. At the same time, the qualities Josh embodies are themselves equated with 'ideal' adulthood. When Josh's rival Paul (John Heard) asks Susan 'what is so special about Baskin?', Susan can only respond: 'he's a grown-up'. Later, as the cracks in Josh's and Susan's relationship begin to widen and he decides to reveal that he is only a child, Susan again misunderstands, replying: 'Oh, and who isn't? You think that there isn't a frightened kid inside of me, too?' By implication, then, the self-aggrandisement and excessive professional ambition constitutive of the yuppie are not only corrupt, but inherently immature. It takes the artless, unaffected 'wisdom' of childhood to bring that fact into focus. In the midst of such observations – which purportedly offer a therapeutic function for adult audiences, but which were surely lost on many juvenile viewers – the realities of childhood become obscured to the point of invisibility.

Consolidation vs. Innovation: The Family Film in the 1990s

Throughout the 1980s, Hollywood studios had avoided publicising their 'all-age' productions as 'family' entertainment. This aversion to the 'family' label had abated by the early 1990s, partly in response to the increasing socio-political capital surrounding the concept of the family in North America at the time. Although the previous decade-and-a-half produced some immensely profitable family entertainment franchises, the actual volume of family films as a percentage of total studio output had remained comparatively low. To put it another way, although a *material* template for the diversified 'family' franchise had been established, and the seeds of its future industrial dominance were sown, the *structural* centrality of family entertainment was largely a product of early 1990s behind-the-scenes deal-making and industrial realignment. Between the mid-1980s and mid-1990s, all of the major Hollywood studios except Disney were either acquired by larger multinational corporations or merged with other media companies to create the diversified, international media conglomerates that exist today. It was this wave of conglomeration, and the desire to exploit the template established by Fox's *Star Wars* and Warner Bros.'

Superman franchises – and not, as Janet Wasko, and others, have argued, a result of rival studios' attempts to 'emulate the Disney model' – that led to the development of films and franchises that could be realised across multiple media platforms, targeting an increasingly-accessible world market.[116]

In 1991, it was announced that Time Warner was planning to create a 'Family Film' division. It was a development of the utmost significance – especially with hindsight – yet aroused very little surprise in the industry or the trade press. *Variety* observed that it reflected 'industry-wide aware-ness that survival in the 1990s may be a matter of creating wholesome, family-oriented entertainment', and that similar discussions regarding 'increasing production of family films, if not creating family film divisions' were ongoing at Universal, Paramount, TriStar and Columbia.[117] The same article noted that Peter Guber, then head of production at Sony, was 'seriously interested in pursuing programming that has strong family appeal', partly because of the growing value of so-called 'aftermarket business' such as home video.[118] By this point, the development of 'Family Film' divisions evidently was considered logical, if not inevitable, given the increasing proliferation and box office value of family entertainment, coupled with the global outlook of the media conglomerates.

By 1993, Warner Bros. and Twentieth Century Fox all had 'Family Film' divisions in operation.[119] As Warner's executive Rob Friedman explained: 'the industry has identified a growing family audience [...] the baby boomers are now parents, and the family orientation is growing as a busi-ness'.[120] Disney's Tom Deegan responded: 'the family market has always been there, but Hollywood has just chosen to ignore it in the past'.[121] Some 'baby boomer' executives even went so far as to identify a moral compunction to produce wholesome entertainment for families in an age of violence and uncertainty, and were doubtless encouraged by the 'family values' policies promulgated by leading US politicians.[122] A more tangi-ble motivation was an influential report advocating greater production of family entertainment from research company Paul Kagan Associates. It pointed out that half of the films to gross $100 million at the box office were PG-rated, and argued that 'there is an underexploited segment that could be costing the studios millions of dollars: family comedies and dramas that are rated PG'.[123] 'The resurgence of family pictures is no coin-cidence', admitted Warner Bros. executive Bruce Berman, in March 1993:

We've begun to realise there's a big audience out there. Kiddie films are no longer seen as movies that adults have to deal with for 75 or 80 minutes. Quality films reaching parents and kids is the primary target.[124]

MGM marketing executive Bob Dingilian pointed to the greater commercial lifespan of such films when compared with more adult categories, arguing that their 'visual' quality contributed to overseas popularity.[125] Nevertheless, there was still some scepticism towards the format. Director Ron Shelton bemoaned Hollywood's embrace of 'the lowest common denominator', while fellow filmmaker Paul Mazursky did not believe the 'cycle' would continue for more than a couple of years.[126] Nonetheless, by 1994, even such unlikely figures as Chuck Norris and Roger Corman were trying to establish a foothold in the family market, utilising the potentialities of direct-to-video production.[127]

In spite of these revolutionary behind-the-scenes developments, in front of the camera, Hollywood largely continued its production strategies from the late 1980s. The initial fruits of the studios' new 'Family Film' divisions were mostly mid-budget literary classic adaptations, including *The Secret Garden*, *Lassie* (Daniel Petrie, 1994) and *Black Beauty* (Caroline Thompson, 1994). Otherwise, the early 1990s were dominated by adult-driven domestic comedies, most notably *Home Alone*, *Hook* and *Mrs. Doubtfire*; knockabout family comedies such as *Kindergarten Cop*, *Ghost Dad* and *Beethoven*; Disney animated features, notably *Beauty and the Beast* (Gary Trousdale and Kirk Wise, 1991), *Aladdin* and *The Lion King* (Roger Allers and Rob Minkoff, 1994); and family-adventure blockbusters, such as *The Addams Family* (Barry Sonnenfeld, 1991), *Batman Returns* (Tim Burton, 1992) and *Jurassic Park* (Steven Spielberg, 1993). There is little more to be said of the family-adventure movie, which progressed along similar lines to its late 1970s and 1980s predecessors. However, the continuing re-emergence of the animated feature requires further discussion.

After a prolonged slump in the 1970s and 1980s, Disney was brought decisively back into the Hollywood mainstream by a fresh and commercially-astute new creative team during the mid-to-late 1980s. This resurgence was kick-started by the Disney/Warner Bros. collaboration *Who Framed Roger Rabbit*, which fused animation and live action to high acclaim, and subsequently *The Little Mermaid*, which was, as Tino Balio notes, 'Disney's first open attempt to court baby boomers and their children'.[128] *Beauty and the Beast* – one of Disney's most confident and assured feature films – was even more profitable, as was *Aladdin*. As with family-adventure movies, animated features have the ability to mobilise mass audiences by transcending normative demographic boundaries. Furthermore, the format is flexible enough to adapt to the mores of the cultural context, while rising above, to a certain degree, the apparently taste-specific restrictions imposed by genre. By mid-decade, Disney had a major competitor in the animation field in DreamWorks SKG, co-founded by Steven Spielberg, producer Jeffrey Katzenberg and music mogul David Geffen. Other forms of animation were emerging: stop-motion, Claymation and (with the release in 1995 of Pixar's *Toy Story*) computer-generated. By this point, the adult-driven domestic comedy was in decline, and animated features began to fill the vacuum. Disney, DreamWorks and Pixar (which distributed via Disney) were all producing a wide roster of critically- and commercially-successful animations, including *A Bug's Life* (John Lasseter, 1998), *The Prince of Egypt* (Brenda Chapman and Steve Hickner, 1998) and *Toy Story 2* (John Lasseter, 1999). Disney also managed to reassert its place in the mainstream live-action family market, remaking many of its 1960s films, such as *The Nutty Professor* (Tom Shadyac, 1996), *Flubber* (Les Mayfield, 1997), *Doctor Doolittle* (Betty Thomas, 1998) and *The Parent Trap* (Nancy Meyers, 1998).

The leading family genre during the first half of the decade, however, was the adult-driven family comedy. After the massive success of *Home Alone* in 1990, the genre reached its apotheosis with Spielberg's *Hook* and Chris Columbus's *Mrs. Doubtfire*. The release of *Hook*, in December 1991, saw Spielberg finally bring his vision of *Peter Pan* to the screen. Watching the film with the benefit of historical perspective, it seems clear that he intended it as a grand modern parable about the condition of the contemporary North American family. At the time, *Hook* was said to be the second most expensive production ever (after *Terminator 2: Judgment Day*) with a $79 million production budget.[129] Perhaps Spielberg felt that the prestige treatment, all-star cast and even the long gestation period were necessary to convey the gravitas demanded by the strength of sentiment. Spielberg intended to film the story as early as 1985, but lost enthusiasm for the project after the birth of his son: 'suddenly I couldn't be Peter Pan any more. I had to be his father'.[130] As with *Big* – another movie sacrificing clarity of story in order to give full rein to its socio-political agendas – the plot is markedly convoluted. *Hook* centres on Peter Banning (Robin

Williams), a beleaguered yuppie who devotes so much of his time to his stressful job that he barely sees his family, and often misses significant moments in the life of his children. As the narrative unfolds, it emerges that Peter Banning was once Peter Pan. Many years earlier, in one of his occasional visits to the 'real' world, he met Moira (Caroline Goodall), and, falling instantly in love, renounced Neverland, started a family and gradually lost his memory of his magical past. Peter is forced to return to Neverland when his old nemesis, Captain Hook (Dustin Hoffman), kidnaps his children, Jack (Charlie Korsmo) and Maggie (Amber Scott). This forces him to relinquish his uptight-executive identity and re-engage with his inner child and the identity he has renounced.

Peter Banning ultimately succeeds in working through his problems. He uses his visit to Neverland as a catharsis; a timely reminder that his essential child – the values of play and fun represented by Pan – has been lost, but can be re-discovered. Perhaps more significantly, in terms of the film's blatant address to the adult sections of the audience, Peter's childlike qualities are ultimately able to co-exist with his adult skills. One of the most therapeutic scenes is Peter's war of words with his successor as head of the Lost Boys, Rufio (Dante Basco). It is his 'adult' skills with wordplay, using his expertise as a lawyer, which allow him to defeat Rufio and re-emerge, victorious, as Peter Pan. Spielberg has admitted to personally identifying with the figure of the modern father who is too busy with his career to give the required attention to his children, and to feeling 'guilty and wanting to do something about it'; *Hook* serves as his platform.[131] In this light, *Hook* becomes, at least conceptually, a release valve for the anxieties of a generation; the fears and failures that had bedevilled the baby boomers for over a decade. The film also attempts to resolve these anxieties, for whilst Banning may have temporarily lost touch with his inner self, he has also gained skills as an adult to compensate for that loss. The ideal state, the film self-servingly implies, is a composite between the wonder and imagination of childhood, and the responsibilities and skills of an adult man.

Hook had a mixed reception upon release. It was, as Morris observes, 'severely panned by critics for excessive blockbuster values' and 'became synonymous with Hollywood's shortcomings'.[132] On the other hand, after a sluggish start, it made strong profits and obviously struck a chord with audiences.[133] Presumably, it was a similar audience base that made *Mrs. Doubtfire* – again starring Robin Williams as a patriarch desperately trying to make good on his family obligations – a massive hit. Although devoted to their three children, Daniel (Williams) and his wife, Miranda (Sally Field), have fallen out of love. Out-of-work actor Daniel is perennially childish and irresponsible in his demeanour, whilst Miranda is stolidly earnest. After a hostile divorce played out in the courts, Miranda is given sole custody of the children, a ruling which devastates Daniel. Ever the performer, though, and not to be outdone, he learns that Miranda is seeking a nanny to look after the children after school, and sees his opportunity. With the help of his brother – a prosthetics expert, who makes him a rubber mask and full-body suit – Daniel invents a character called Mrs. Doubtfire, a firm but kindly elderly Scottish widow, and concocts the perfect nanny. Before long, the whole family has embraced Daniel's creation.

As with *Uncle Buck*, *National Lampoon's Christmas Vacation* and *Hook*, *Mrs. Doubtfire* expends far more time developing convincing characterisations for its adult protagonists than for its children. Earlier films in the cycle privileged adult agendas with a self-preoccupation bordering on the obsessive. *Mrs. Doubtfire*, whilst retaining themes of divorce and

Mrs. Doubtfire (1993)

social breakdown, fuses these preoccupations with a recurrent strain of grotesque humour, emphasising sight gags and slapstick; the kinds of visual comedy widely assumed to appeal specifically to children. There are a number of sequences showing Daniel's body suit in jeopardy, including a comic sequence where he sets fire to one of his rubber breasts whilst cooking. In another scene, Daniel accidentally knocks his mask out of a window on to the road below, and looks on in horror as it is flattened by a passing truck. Immediately thereafter, to maintain his masquerade for the benefit of a visiting court liaison officer, he sticks his face into a cream pie to obscure his true physiognomy. In short, Daniel is constructed as a figure of fun, and it is surely significant that he is, by trade, a children's entertainer. Although his irresponsible character traits are clearly defined, it is equally established that he is a morally good man who never transgresses the projected frontier between childishness as foolish bravado and childishness as familial disregard. In fact, Daniel emerges in a better light than Miranda, whose po-faced rejection of childish play threatens not only Daniel's sense of fun, but also that of the audience. Miranda exemplifies the patronising, misogynistic belief, identified by Susan Faludi, that 'women are unhappy precisely because they are free'; that 'women are enslaved by their own liberation'.[134] Increased freedom to embark upon a successful career seems to have done little for Miranda but make her as tense and guilt-ridden as her male yuppie counterparts. As parents, Daniel and Miranda resemble the opposing, unreconstructed facets of Peter Banning's persona in *Hook*; one is happy and fun but lacking in responsibility; the other is miserably aware of the impossibility of reconciling professional and domestic duty.

Despite its massive success, a number of elements in *Mrs. Doubtfire* suggest the impending end of the adult-driven domestic family comedy. Firstly, the grotesquery implicit in the character of Mrs. Doubtfire carries the film away from the self-absorption of earlier films in the genre. Secondly, the film evidences a greater sense of acceptance regarding new social structures. *Big* and *Hook* implied a need to regress to the symbolic properties of childhood as a means of coping with modern life. In *Mrs. Doubtfire*, a film more grounded within realistic pragmatism, the difficulties posed by family breakdown and status anxiety are facts of life which must be accepted. There is a sense that the social issues and concerns triggering the emergence of this cycle of films had either dissipated or changed their form; the political battle for equality between men and women, for instance, has not so much been won or lost, as obscured. Moreover, attitudes towards divorce and family structures were changing: *Mrs. Doubtfire* is the first mainstream family movie willing to concede the potential *benefits* a divorce might bring to the long-term welfare of a family. The film does not end with Daniel and Miranda reconciling – for a film that places such value upon the truth of its social representations, this would place too great a strain on credulity. Yet they do arrive at an understanding, based upon their shared love for their children. Although Daniel's/Mrs. Doubtfire's direct-to-camera address at the end of the movie – in which, via his new television show, he gently explains that divorce (and, by implication, the emergence of alternative family structures) need not spell the end of 'family' – is ostensibly directed to his own children watching at home, it also appears designed to impress the message upon children watching in theatres around the world.

The natural end of the adult-driven domestic comedy again demonstrates that production patterns are determined not solely by box office, but also by the cultural and political concerns of the social context. The genre's absence from production schedules after the early 1990s left something of a gap within the family film market, which was ultimately filled by the upsurge in production of 'kidult'-orientated family-adventure movies. The crucial lesson learned by the majors during this period was that cutting-back on mid-level productions and re-orientating towards a smaller volume of 'family'-suitable 'event' films was the required strategy. This was a major turning point. Since 1995, as Richard Maltby has observed, Hollywood's output has fallen almost exclusively into two categories: 'big-budget international movies and smaller-budget movies with less dependence on the international market'.[135] The fact that profitable overseas markets – such as post-Soviet Russia and Latin America – were opening up was an added incentive: why would studios confine themselves to the North American market when a huge global audience was waiting to be addressed?

Hollywood executives began abandoning child-orientated family films in favour of action-adventure fare that could be pitched universally. A high-level Sony executive announced, portentously: 'the death of the family movie – that is the footnote for summer 1996'; Twentieth Century Fox executive Bill Mechanic explained:

> We made a strategic move to get out of the kid business, as we've
> known it, a year ago. Kid-oriented movies have been in trouble. [*The*]
> *Nutty Professor* [1996] and *Independence Day* [1996] have become the
> kid movies, the new family films.[136]

Disney's Joe Roth traced the beginnings of this shift to *Raiders of the
Lost Ark*, which was, he argued, 'the beginning and the end of family
films in America'.[137] This astute remark encapsulates the new reality of
'family' entertainment: the highly culturally-specific 'dual' appeal that
characterised 'family' films until the 1970s has been supplanted by a
more escapist, 'undifferentiated' mode of audience address. Buffy Shutt,
president of marketing for Universal, argued that the tonal shift in family
movies paralleled a wider cultural embrace of 'youth culture' across
demographics:

> We grew up in a youth culture: we're youth oriented and we still think
> we're hip and young [...] Parents and kids now dress similarly, listen
> to the same music [and] have the same pop culture meeting grounds.
> My parents wouldn't think of watching Elvis or the Grateful Dead with
> me. That wouldn't happen now.[138]

Producer Brian Henson spoke for the majority when he argued, simply:
'there's really no such thing as a children's movie'.[139] At the start of the
decade, the majors typically released about 30 films a year, but only
around half that number by the end.[140] As Balio suggests, 'the goal of
every studio was to gross $1 billion worldwide each year', with block-
busters providing much of this income.[141] As the following chapter will
show, it is with such 'kidult'-orientated blockbusters that Hollywood has
strengthened its grip on the global film market.

7

THE FAMILY AUDIENCE AND THE GLOBAL MEDIA ENVIRONMENT

In the first decade of the twenty-first century, the true importance of 'family' media to Hollywood's industrial, cultural and commercial identities became fully apparent. Family entertainment has come to define mainstream Hollywood cinema. Its prominence is part of a broad, complex socio-cultural embrace of the 'kidult' – particularly in Western countries – also visible in other (co-dependent) media, such as television, popular fiction, comics, video games, toys and many other forms of merchandise. However, nowhere is the influence of 'kidult' culture more marked than in Hollywood cinema, where extensive corporate and artistic reorganisations have taken place as a direct result. Although there is no doubt that 'families' are still important consumers, if we regard Hollywood family entertainment primarily as internationally-distributed mass media – rather than trivial amusements for parents and their children – we are closer to the reality. Significantly, in many non-English-speaking markets, the 'family film' label is not used, even in translation. Instead, such terms as 'children's film', 'action film' or, most strikingly, 'American film' are employed, in recognition of the fact that such generalised mass entertainment has become virtually synonymous – beyond Western markets, at least – with Hollywood itself.

As Paul Grainge observes, Hollywood 'has been seen as an exemplary model of capitalist restructuring in its move from a studio system to a flexibly specialised part of a global image business'.[1] The point is, of course, that the increasing globalisation of the major studios' industrial

191

organisation and the increasing globalisation of their filmic products are far from separate phenomena. The most cursory glance at box office statistics confirms that, without exception, the most successful entertainment franchises of recent years have been pitched at international 'family audiences'. They include the live-action fantasy franchises *Harry Potter* (2001–11), *The Lord of the Rings* (2001–3) and *The Chronicles of Narnia* (2005–); the computer-generated animated franchises *Toy Story* (1995–), *Shrek* (2001–10) and *Ice Age* (2002–); and the action-heavy, family-suitable blockbuster franchises *Pirates of the Caribbean* (2003–) and *Avatar* (2009–). Yet their formidable combined box office performance only tells half the story. Whilst the family movie remains at the heart of most contemporary entertainment franchises, it is never an end in itself.

Most major family films either generate multimedia franchises or are based on existing properties. Narratively speaking, Warner Bros.' *Harry Potter* and *Lord of the Rings* franchises are comparatively traditional adaptations of pre-existing literary material, whereas Disney's *Pirates of the Caribbean* and DreamWorks' *Transformers* (2007–) are 'adapted' from nothing more substantive than a theme park ride and successful toy line, respectively. They have been developed as multimedia franchises because their core brand images are widely accessible, possess an existing consumer base, and lend themselves easily to cross-media exploitation. There is already a great deal of academic literature on the anatomy of contemporary multimedia franchises, and clearly, family entertainment can no longer be understood solely in terms of a single, generative filmic text. Kramer has observed that 'most of Hollywood's superhits since 1977' are 'children's films for the whole family and for teenagers, too'.[2] While this is perfectly true, Hollywood's exploitation of its family entertainment has developed to the point that it transcends cinematic typology. More aptly – if less conveniently, for critical analysis – it can be regarded as a spectrum of widely-intelligible, interrelated products based around core brand images. Robert C. Allen correctly anticipated its increasing centrality when in 1999 he identified the 'family film' as the 'earliest and clearest expression' of 'the rise of post-Hollywood cinema'.[3]

Perhaps the most visible and striking statistic is that as many as 27 out of 30 – or 90 per cent – of the top-grossing films of all time globally (unadjusted for inflation) are family films.[4] Equally significantly, all were produced and/or distributed by the 'big six' major Hollywood studios (i.e. Walt Disney Studios, Warner Bros., Paramount, Twentieth Century Fox, Sony and Universal), which together comprise the MPAA. These companies account for the vast majority of international box office hits and major cinematic franchises, despite typically producing less than 30 per cent of all films distributed annually in the United States.[5] Each studio endeavours to craft a handful of high-concept blockbuster family films annually which can be exploited synergistically and thus develop into major franchises. Furthermore, the respective blockbuster releases of the major studios – with very few exceptions – are indistinguishable from one another. These companies exert a near-hegemonic control over global film distribution, which, when combined with some highly protectionist policies, have ensured that rivals – both domestic and international – are effectively closed out of the world market.

Since the turn of the century, the major Hollywood studios have been pursuing policies of increasing product standardisation. A growing proportion of mainstream films are rated PG or PG-13 by the MPAA for the US market, evidencing a continued shift towards the middle ground. A 2004 Harvard School of Public Health study argued that 'a movie rated PG or PG-13 today has more sexual or violent content than a similarly rated movie in the past', and accused the MPAA of tolerating more extreme content in family-friendly ratings.[6] The following year, *Variety* reported that R-rated films, 'once the studios' mainstay, are on the decline, both in numbers and in lure'.[7] In 2004, PG-rated films outperformed R-rated films for the first time since 1984.[8] However, a closer examination reveals that the overall proportion of films rated R – which prevents children under the age of 17 attending without adult supervision – has remained relatively stable at just under 60 per cent; the difference is that far fewer *blockbusters* are now released with an R rating.[9] In 1980, 55 per cent of the top 20 films of the year were R-rated; by 1995, this figure had fallen to 30 per cent and by 2009, 10 per cent.[10] This trend contrasts dramatically with industry practice between the late-1960s and the early 1980s, when the R rating was widely perceived as a badge of honour, and a 'family' rating constituted a virtual guarantee of commercial oblivion. Indeed, for the US release of *Chariots of Fire* (Hugh Hudson, 1981), the distributors allegedly inserted profanity in one scene, in order to avoid an unwanted G rating. Today, as Jennifer Geer has observed, marketers are eager to represent their products as 'family' entertainment because the associations have become so positive.[11] While the R rating retains some of its connotations with independent-minded artistry, the days when a 'family'-friendly rating was considered inimical to commercial success are long past. One Hollywood marketing executive wryly observed: 'you're leaving tens of millions of dollars on the table with an R rating. Why? For artistic integrity? Get real'.[12]

The media industry has consciously attempted to broaden public perceptions of family entertainment. One of the ways in which this has been achieved is by implementing the PG-13 rating. The MPAA introduced the PG-13 category following protests in the USA that *Indiana Jones and the Temple of Doom* (Steven Spielberg, 1984) was too violent for PG. It was felt that cultural standards of acceptability had broadened since the introduction of the rating system in 1968 to such an extent that a new category was needed. Consequently, the PG-13 rating was created as a buffer between PG and R, ostensibly allowing entry for children under the age of 13 only if accompanied by an adult. A PG or PG-13 rating has become almost a prerequisite for live-action blockbuster success. Fully 60 per cent of the top 30 films of all-time now fall into the PG-13 category, including such unambiguously family-orientated films as *The Simpsons Movie* (David Silverman, 2007), *The Golden Compass* (Chris Weitz, 2007) and *Harry Potter and the Deathly Hallows Part 2* (David Yates, 2011).[13]

Increasingly, industrial and synergistic considerations directly determine film form. Nowhere is this more apparent than in mainstream Hollywood's wholesale embrace of fantasy subjects since the turn of the millennium. There are three primary reasons why fantasies are attractive subjects. Firstly, it is a highly visual form that presents an ideal pretext for the kinds of visual-orientated appeal demanded by international consumers. Such films arouse sensual as well as intellectual responses; as cognitive theorist Torben Grodal observes: 'when we watch a film, our heart rhythms change, we sweat, and our muscles alternately tense and relax throughout'.[14] The heightened importance of spectacle and visual appeal can be seen in the extraordinary success of James Cameron's 3D blockbuster *Avatar*, which was released in 2009 and, at the time of writing, is the highest-grossing film ever. It received rave reviews, despite critical consensus that the plot, dialogue, characterisation and performances were clichéd at best, and at worst downright banal. Geoff King has argued that the ever-increasing reliance on spectacle has not – as is often assumed – destroyed classical narrative conventions, but immersive, regressive blockbusters can certainly make narrative *appear* irrelevant.[15] Viewers marvelling at technical virtuosity are, presumably, less likely to be concerned with narratives that are too childish, derivative or pedestrian.

Secondly, because its horizons are generally non-terrestrial, fantasy lacks the socio-cultural specificity that executives fear will alienate non-Western audiences. The *Lord of the Rings* and *Harry Potter* franchises, although inevitably retaining Western emphases, are not as clearly 'American' in origin as, say, *Star Wars* or *Indiana Jones*. Disney executive Mark Zoradi argues that 'the fantasy genre travels exceptionally well, partly because there's nothing that makes it geographically unique [...] and its themes are pretty universal – good vs. evil, loyalty, the family sticking together'.[16] Thirdly, a richly-detailed fictional world affords almost limitless opportunities for merchandise and other ancillary revenues. What David Bordwell has termed 'world-building' is central to Hollywood's treatment of fantasy. 'World-building' describes the intricate construction of a fictional universe, intended to imbue fantasy narratives with as much depth and identification as possible, and although it can be traced as far back as *2001: A Space Odyssey* (Stanley Kubrick, 1968), it has reached its apotheosis in more recent fantasy franchises.[17] The success of *Harry Potter* and *The Lord of the Rings* rests partially on the complexity and believability of the fictional worlds they inhabit. Although retaining their powerful visual appeal, the *Harry Potter* films occupied a progressively complex, ambiguous fictional landscape, reflecting simultaneously the demands of the narrative, the physical and emotional growth of the protagonists and the parallel 'growing up' – the desire for deeper forms of identification and of structural and emotional fulfilment – among its consumers. World-building implicates the active viewer in manufacturing a fully-realised fictional meta-universe, which is then recapitulated not only in spin-off media but also via word-of-mouth, conventions and fan fiction. Presumably, these richly-detailed fictional worlds offer credible alternatives to a real world often lacking in structure, coherence and purpose. An extended fictional universe not only deepens the multivalent experiences of the movie, but, moreover, creates almost endless merchandise opportunities. As Grainge has observed, Warner Bros., with its stake in the *Harry Potter* and *Lord of the Rings* franchises, led the way in world-building at the turn of the millennium 'with serials, spin-offs and genres that were based quite specifically on the filmic realisation of a pre-sold, inveterately marketable, narrative universe'.[18]

Hollywood's family entertainment strategies over the last decade have been markedly influenced by three enduring, broad-appeal franchises that first hit cinemas in 2001. *Harry Potter and the Sorcerer's Stone* (Chris Columbus), *The Lord of the Rings: The Fellowship of the Ring* (Peter Jackson) and *Shrek* (Andrew Adamson, Vicky Jenson) collectively generated almost 10 per cent of the $8 billion worldwide gross for the year.[19] Their extraordinary popularity, coupled with recognition of the fact that they are 'the perfect fuel for the synergy machine', stimulated the development of other lavish family entertainment franchises possessing similar qualities.[20] Whilst all three franchises evidence the now-standard Hollywood hybridisation of classical 'family' and 'kidult' entertainment characteristics, each attempts to mobilise a slightly different audience base. *Harry Potter* is the archetypal 'crossover' entertainment (i.e. it appeals equally to adults and children). The franchise was already well-established by the time Warner Bros.' adaptation reached the screen, with J. K. Rowling's book series (1997–2007) having already attained 'cultural phenomenon' status. Therefore, the film series trades considerably on the existing popularity of the broader multimedia franchise, as well as appealing more generally to fans of fantasy and blockbusters.

Harry Potter and the Sorcerer's Stone (2001)

In contrast, much of the discourse surrounding *The Lord of the Rings* centred upon its status as a 'cult franchise', as an ambitious series of adaptations of J. R. R. Tolkien's 1950s fantasy novels. Directed by New Zealander auteur Peter Jackson, financed by 'independent' studio New Line (actually owned by Time Warner) and filmed by a Wellington-based production crew, the franchise was marketed partially as an antidote to *Harry Potter* (which was released only one month earlier). Perhaps of greater interest to mass audiences (beyond its cult appeal) are the films' qualities as action-adventure entertainment. On the contrary, like most Hollywood animated features, *Shrek*'s modes of audience address are comparatively differentiated. Whilst the humour is broad, it clearly attempts to appeal independently to adult and juvenile audiences. Drawing on fairy-tale convention for comedic, 'postmodern' effect, it was recognised upon release as a landmark in computer animation and was awarded the inaugural Academy Award for Best Animated Feature in 2002, a measure of the growing significance of feature animation within contemporary Hollywood.[21]

The 'Kidult'-Orientated Hollywood Blockbuster

Hollywood cinema, as Richard Maltby has often observed, deals in 'economies of pleasure'. Yes, it is a cultural institution, but it is primarily concerned with making money by offering the highest concentration of potential consumers a unique, pleasurable experience. As Carl Plantinga observes:

> Movie viewing is first and foremost a pleasurable experience, suffused with affect. Audiences are willing to pay for this experience with money, time, and effort, and in exchange they expect to be fascinated, shocked, titillated, made suspenseful and curious, invited to laugh and cry, and in the end, given pleasure.[22]

As we have seen, the Hollywood family movie – which offers all of the above with the additional promise of basic comfort and reassurance – has been one of the primary instruments in this endeavour. Yet its modes of audience appeal have necessarily changed in accordance with shifting socio-cultural values. Western societies are now dominated by a youth-orientated (or, perhaps more aptly, a 'kidult'-orientated) cultural aesthetic, of which the 'juvenilisation' of Hollywood cinema is merely a part. It is the ubiquity of this cultural paradigm that allows mature, intelligent adults who attend supposed 'children's films' to be deemed behaviourally normative. In order to attract audiences from a broad range of cultural, racial, geographic and demographic backgrounds, Hollywood films must transcend such socially-constructed barriers by appealing to universal human drives and requirements. This is primarily achieved by evoking basic affective responses (to stimuli), and by arousing more cognitively-determined emotional responses.

Pre-cognitive affects are primarily sensual in nature, and include largely unconscious feelings of tension, shock, revulsion and visceral excitement. Emotional responses – such as fear, pity and happiness – are more complex, in that they involve a higher degree of cognitive processing. This is to understand emotions in the psychological sense, as 'transient disturbances, initiated by the subject's construal or appraisal of a disruptive situation that relates to the subject's concerns', rather than as static or permanent states.[23] As Plantinga observes, the responses films attempt to elicit vary considerably depending on genre and target audience. He postulates that 'while mystery emphasises cognitive play and fantasies of intellectual mastery, the action/adventure genre appeals to visceral excitement and physical mastery, the melodrama genre to sympathy, and parody and irony to reflexive pleasures'.[24] Yet he also stresses that 'no genre emphasises one pleasure wholly at the expense of the others', as commercial cinema must usually offer pluralistic audiences multiple avenues of access.[25] Most family films are specifically designed to evoke both sensual and emotional responses. Producers of blockbuster films often compare their products with 'rollercoaster rides', which implies a desire to evoke a satisfyingly diverse combination of cognitive and pre-cognitive responses. While all films appeal to the sensory and emotional faculties in some sense, mainstream Hollywood family entertainment presents a very calculated and blatant fusion of uplifting emotional stimulation and stirring sensorial appeal. The power of these sensory and emotional cues is obvious. Whilst we must not overlook the fact that Hollywood's international dominance stems partially from its so-called 'competitive advantages' on the world stage, nor can we ignore the undoubted global appeal of the entertainment values it packages and exports.

Global audiences have continued to increase in importance since the turn of the century.[26] In 2008, *The Golden Compass* made the headlines because of the enormous superiority of its international box office performance over that of the US domestic market.[27] It was the first film to gross $300 million in foreign revenue without hitting $100 in North America.[28] *Variety* suggested that overseas distributors marketed it more effectively as a family movie than did domestic marketers.[29] The Italian distributors claimed that they targeted the 8–13 demographic, whilst in the USA, 'the pic's biggest demographic was young adult males, who came looking for the next "Lord of the Rings", left disappointed and told their friends not to bother'.[30] On a purely practical level, overseas audiences are especially attuned to family blockbuster titles because, on average, they attend fewer movies than their US counterparts. International audiences therefore tend to privilege 'event' movies with family (i.e. mass) suitability.[31] Additionally, numerous foreign markets enforce strict codes of censorship, so the least offensive Hollywood films stand a better chance of avoiding censure.

Many live-action Hollywood blockbusters attempt to 'immerse' audiences as fully as possible within the cinematic experience. This desire has always been present; big screens, low lighting and loudness – ever-present conditions of movie exhibition since the early twentieth century – are all designed to hold audience attention. The more involved audiences are, the deeper the experience, and the more likely they will part with their money in return for something they cannot find anywhere else. Contemporary Hollywood family blockbusters advance this policy in two distinct ways: firstly, by offering ever-increasingly impressive forms of spectacle; and secondly, with the calculated removal of socio-cultural allusions which might detract from their purportedly universal reach. Where changes are most noticeable on a concrete level are the reduction of local humour, and parochial allusions to internal politics and culture. References to international political currents – such as the climate change allegory in *Avatar* – remain acceptable, as they trade on global (rather than simply domestic) matters of importance. This agenda does not extend to populist and cosmetic brand-based aspects of national identity – the comic-book Americana of *Indiana Jones* and *Star Wars*, or the genteel 'Englishness' of *Harry Potter* – examples of exoticism which might be profitably exported internationally.

DreamWorks' *Transformers* series (2007–) is perhaps the most brazenly 'kidult'-orientated franchise in the history of popular cinema. It started life as a successful toy range produced by Hasbro, which licensed the property to a Japanese animation company and was adapted into a successful, syndicated television show. Hasbro then struck a distribution deal with DreamWorks for a motion picture based on the toy line. Steven Spielberg served as co-executive producer with Hasbro CEO Brian Goldner, ensuring a high-profile incubation period, and blockbuster specialist Michael Bay was signed to direct. The film was finally released in 2007 to box office success and predictably mixed critical reaction, and Goldner, evidently satisfied, congratulated Bay for making an 'extremely toyetic picture'.[32] The original film has since been followed by the sequels *Transformers: Revenge of the Fallen* (2009) and *Transformers: Dark Side of the Moon* (2011). Both attracted scathing reviews but extremely strong box office returns, with the latter grossing well over $1 billion internationally. The particular curiosity of these films is that they stake no claim to social and cultural use value. Even 'family'/'kidult' hybrids such as the *Harry Potter* and *Chronicles of Narnia* franchises implicitly assert their importance as arbiters of morality and social stability. In *Transformers*, characters and situations exist only as pretexts for unrelenting, inarticulate spectacle. Such an approach is eminently characteristic of Bay, who has described his directorial style as 'fucking the frame'. Yet what is more significant is that the franchise can achieve success on such a grand scale solely on this level of audience address. Responses to such films are likely to be heavily

Transformers (2007)

predicated on pre-cognitive effect; what I call an appeal of the senses, and sometimes referred to as 'the low road'. Undoubtedly, the appeal of this franchise depends heavily on its novelty value. Most theatre audiences will be aware that they are paying for unremitting spectacle and very little else, with few of the non-aesthetic traditional modes of appeal (e.g. cognitive play; emotional stimulation) in evidence. The success of the films, therefore, depends heavily on their ability to fulfil that unwritten contract and perform the audacious feat of satisfying the senses for the duration of the movie. Clearly, the profitability of the *Transformers* franchise, and others that will follow in a similar vein, rests on the capacity to provide a packaged experience that transcends those offered by alternative media platforms (such as video games). The need to remain at the forefront of technological development, therefore, is palpable.

Whilst *Transformers* may be the ultimate 'kidult' entertainment – with all the positive and negative connotations that follow – it is also something of an easy target. Whilst few Hollywood action-adventure franchises present their wares in quite the same unashamed style, a 'kidult'-orientated aesthetic – even when presented alongside such typical family entertainment characteristics as moral didacticism and overt sentiment – has become necessary in order to secure the widest spectrum of global audiences. One pertinent example of an avowed 'family' franchise that actually possesses a 'kidult' aesthetic is Walden Media's *Chronicles of Narnia* series. Its evident religiosity (Walden Media is owned by evangelical billionaire Philip Anschutz, and the franchise was apparently regarded by the Christian establishment as a potential 'discipleship tool') undeniably deviates from the more typical, implicitly secular, approach exemplified by *Harry Potter*.[33] Nevertheless, it would be a mistake to assume that it constitutes a return to a traditional conception of family entertainment as a straightforward vehicle for educative and ideological content. Like their literary sources, these films contain many thinly-veiled affirmations of the moral and philosophical superiority of faith and spiritual belief over hollow pragmatism. However, their 'kidult' elements are rarely obscured. All of the films in the series to date have added entirely new subplots to the original narratives in order to provide a stronger action-adventure aesthetic. They have also made liberal use of computer-generated animation, particularly in the form of *Lord of the Rings*-style CGI battles. *The Voyage of the Dawn Treader* (Michael Apted, 2011) – like most current Hollywood blockbusters – was adapted into 3D. The Christian allusions may, indeed, constitute an attempt to recruit a new generation of believers, but the filmmakers are not so naive as to believe that such a policy has any hope of success without sweetening the pill.

A similar duality of purpose can be seen in *Avatar*, although the moral and didactic elements of this film are almost always subsumed by the potency of its aesthetic appeal. Its convoluted narrative concerns humanity's attempts to plunder mineral wealth from a fertile alien planet after exhausting its own resources. The plot is scarcely worth detailing; many critics viewed it as a crude allegory of the United States' exploitation of less powerful nations possessing precious natural resources, while others identified criticism of neo-conservatism.[34] Even in cases such as this, where they betray their cultural and political origins, family blockbusters may yet emerge unscathed because of their powerful, primary function as 'total entertainment'.[35] Although 3D is far from a new innovation, CGI has considerably deepened its potential. As Kenneth Turan of the *Los Angeles Times* enthused:

> In Cameron's hands, 3D is not the forced gimmick it's often been, but a way to create an alternate reality and insert us so completely and seamlessly into it that we feel like we've actually been there.[36]

The success of the CGI and 3D can be seen in Turan's assessment of the film as 'a total immersion experience'.[37] Other critics have drawn even more grandiose conclusions from the success of the phenomenon. Scott Foundas saw the movie as a 'rebirth' in context of the supposed 'death of cinema', while Shawn Levy declared, portentously: 'starting today you live in a post-"Avatar" movie world'.[38] Only with greater historical perspective will we be able to assess the long-term impact of these technologically-driven, family-suitable 'experiential' films. At the time of writing, the jury is still out concerning 3D. Despite the big hits, several high-profile 3D films have flopped, and the notorious 3D-induced headache remains an obstacle to universal acceptance. Yet it is also clear that such innovations are temporal technologies, forming only part of a broader, ongoing agenda. The industrial need to develop new technologies (allowing new modes of exhibition) in the quest to sufficiently differentiate cinema from other media will continue.

Thus far, this chapter has mainly been concerned with changes in Hollywood's family blockbusters and how they have impacted upon the theatrical experience. Yet contemporary family entertainment franchises are defined equally by so-called 'ancillary' consumer products, and broader processes of cultural reception. Hollywood studios have recently targeted two areas for cross-media tie-ins in the family entertainment business: comic books and toys. The comic book adaptation has been one of the most profitable genres of recent years, emerging as a sub-genre of the wider Superhero movie boom which began with *X-Men* (Bryan Singer, 2000), and continued with the *Spider-Man* (2002–) and *Batman* (2005–) franchises, *Hulk* (Ang Lee, 2003), *Fantastic Four* (Tim Story, 2005) and *Superman Returns* (Bryan Singer, 2006). Although some Superhero movies are original properties, most have derived from Marvel's and DC Comics' archives. Because of the large, hitherto-unexploited range of licensable characters they own, unsurprisingly these companies became desirable targets for acquisition. Disney's announcement in August 2009 that it had bought Marvel for $4 billion created a considerable furore in the media and among the general public (although Marvel's closest competitor, DC Comics, has been a subsidiary of Warner Communications since the early 1970s).[39] Paramount, Sony and Fox already have long-term distribution deals based on Superhero characters, with Sony holding the rights to *Spider-Man* and Fox to *X-Men* and *Fantastic Four*. Irrespective of the longevity of the superhero cycle, the durability of these properties across different media – books, comics, action figures, computer games, theme park rides – makes them reliable and enduring sources of capital. Instant box office success is scarcely the sole motivation for these acquisitions.

The second major trend in cross-media tie-ins has been toys. The biggest US toy companies, Hasbro and Mattel, have developed filmic adaptations of some of their biggest toy properties. For many years, toy manufacturers have held a tight grip on children's television. Early children's television shows of the 1950s and 1960s exploited the lack of regulation by blatantly advertising commercial products within the fabric of the shows. In 1969, the Federal Communications Commission (FCC) increased regulation in US children's television after finding that ABC's *Hot Wheels* was nothing more than a 'program length commercial'.[40] Under Reagan's administration in the 1980s, though, the FCC deregulated children's television, and toy-driven shows like *He-Man and the Masters of the Universe* flourished. Marketing consultant Gary Pope argues that modern children's television shows 'are just giant toy ads'.[41] Nevertheless, early attempts by toy and game manufacturers to exploit motion pictures such as *Clue* (Jonathan Lynn, 1985) and *Masters of the Universe* (Gary Goddard, 1987) proved unsuccessful, and the toy and film-making industries have not collaborated successfully on a broad scale until recently. The most famous and successful 'toyetic' franchise to date, of course, is *Transformers*.

Tie-in merchandise is carefully designed to cut across demographics, exploiting not only nostalgia for the original toy lines and television shows but also the large number of adults who still buy toys themselves. Many consumers of the *Transformers* films, and no doubt of the forthcoming *He-Man* adaptation, were raised on these products, and as *Variety* observes: 'adult toybuyers don't just drive toy sales, they drive enthusiasm that can be turned into films'.[42] There was an 8 per cent increase in action figure revenue in 2008 from the previous year, which was attributed partly to

> toy manufacturers and their showbiz partners [...] rolling out toys for people who, one might gently suggest, are too old for toys. Some of the product is breathtakingly expensive, or based on R-rated movies or painfully obscure characters – and they're selling bigtime.[43]

Likewise, video games – also long considered a primarily juvenile amusement – increasingly target adult gamers.[44] Recent statistics show that 72 per cent of North American households play computer and video games.[45] Additionally, 82 per cent of video gamers are over 18 years old (with an average age of 37), and as high a proportion as 42 per cent of all gamers are women.[46] These figures are not wholly surprising, given the ongoing convergence between movies, television, video games, toys and other forms of 'kidult'-orientated media, which, in spite of stereotyping, apparently appeal almost as much to adult females as to male adolescents. Modern synergistic expansion is based on the philosophy that very few demographics are a closed market for any given product.

The Contemporary Animated Feature

Until the mid-1990s, animated features remained – in spite of their box office potential – anomalies in mainstream Hollywood. The production process was difficult, time-consuming and labour-intensive, and the pejorative associations with 'children's entertainment' were seemingly immutable. In fact, of the major Hollywood studios, only Disney showed any prevailing interest (and had any sustained success) in the medium. This has changed entirely with the industry-wide adoption of CGI, which has almost invalidated the traditional, firmly-drawn distinctions between live-action and animated filmmaking. Several major studios have developed their own animation divisions, thereby opening up the market. Chris Meledandri was a key figure in Fox's successful incorporation of animation in the early part of the decade, and his production company, Illumination, allowed co-owner Universal rapid entry into the market. Again, advances in technology have made the format an attractive investment. CGI animations are easier to adapt for digital 3D projection than live-action films; in 2008, DreamWorks announced that all its future productions would be released in 3D.[47] As *Variety* suggests, computer-generated animations are currently the industry's most reliable genre, despite such box office failures as DreamWorks' *Flushed Away* (David Bowers and Sam Fell, 2006) and Disney's *Meet the Robinsons* (Stephen J. Anderson, 2007) and *Mars Needs Moms* (Simon Wells, 2011).[48] It should be noted, however, that the power of the Disney brand is still a significant competitive advantage globally, in spite of the convergence in major studio output since the early 1990s. A recent survey of global responses to the Disney brand found that consumption of its products is almost universal,

Toy Story (1995)

with a general consensus among respondents worldwide that the corporation promotes values of 'fun and fantasy'; 'happiness', 'magic' and 'good over evil'.[49] Furthermore, criticism of the firm is strongly opposed, especially in the United States and Japan.[50] The other major studios do not yet possess this degree of brand loyalty, although it is possible that this may eventually change. Computer-generated animation is far more a level playing field than hand-drawn animation, and is less associated with a specific house style.

Several of the points made earlier concerning the sensorial appeal of live-action Hollywood family blockbusters also apply to computer-generated animations. As CGI technology has improved, the visual contrast between live action and animation has diminished accordingly, and many such films are similarly calculated to evoke thrills and exhilaration. Indeed, such entirely computer-generated blockbusters as *The Polar Express* (Robert Zemeckis, 2004), *A Christmas Carol* (Zemeckis, 2009) and *The Adventures of Tintin* (Steven Spielberg, 2011) are basically action-adventure films which utilise the potentialities of CGI for aesthetic and economic purposes. As the technologies involved in the manufacturing process (such as performance capture) have advanced, the films in question have become less identifiably 'cartoonish' and therefore less apt to be defined automatically as juvenile entertainment. Nonetheless, this undoubted trend towards a more 'kidult'-orientated visual appeal in Hollywood feature animations is only partial. Most such films attempt an updated version of the traditional 'dual-address', in which adults and children are addressed separately, rather than the 'undifferentiated address' now prevalent in live-action blockbusters. The *Shrek* and *Toy Story* films, for instance, are playful and cleverly-written, possessing broad but lively humour, and an abundance of cultural and meta-textual references to amuse grown-ups, as well as some prominent voice actors. Furthermore, they possess didactic elements reminiscent of classical-era Hollywood family entertainment. The *Toy Story* films reaffirm the values of friendship and family, whilst the *Shrek* films remind viewers of the importance of not judging others by their appearance. Of course, such didacticism offers parents the gratification of seeing the kinds of moral lessons they may attempt to impart to their children practically and attractively reinforced on the screen. Yet – for all the prevailing conservatism of the Hollywood feature animation – such left-field animations as *Corpse Bride* (Tim Burton, 2005), *Coraline* (Henry Selick, 2009), *The Fantastic Mr. Fox*

(Wes Anderson, 2009), *Cloudy with a Chance of Meatballs* (Phil Lord, 2009) and *Rango* (Gore Verbinski, 2011) display intelligence and imagination in abundance. It is ironic that such qualities continue to flourish in a supposedly child-orientated format, whilst being conspicuously lacking in many live-action blockbuster productions allegedly more attuned to 'adult' sensibilities. Indeed, the fact that the 'family' market exerts such attraction to well-respected 'auteur' filmmakers such as Martin Scorsese, Tim Burton and Wes Anderson perhaps reflects the parallel decline of mature, adult-orientated filmmaking in mainstream Hollywood.

One of the main reasons why feature animation is such an attractive commercial proposition is the home video market, which has always relied disproportionately on family entertainment. After initial resistance, Disney embraced the strategy of 'sell-through' – pricing the video cheaply in order to sell the maximum number of copies – starting with *Pinocchio* in 1985.[51] The entire run of 300,000 copies sold out, earning the company $8 million.[52] However, it was not until the early 1990s that studios began manufacturing what became known as 'kidvids'. In 1994, Disney released *The Return of Jafar* (Tad Stones), a direct-to-video sequel to its 1992 theatrical hit *Aladdin*. The venture was highly successful, selling over 7 million copies, placing it within the top-ten all-time best-selling videos.[53] Direct-to-video animations can be made relatively cheaply. The budget of *The Return of Jafar* was estimated at $6 million. Producer-director Tad Stones admitted that 'we didn't have Disney's best animators working on *Jafar*', but pointed out that 'you don't compare a TV movie-of-the-week to *Schindler's List*'.[54] Direct-to-video has since become common industry practice. In 2000, *Variety* noted that 'even a modest-selling video premiere can generate $25 million–$50 million in revenue for a studio'.[55] This dominance actually accelerated as DVD replaced VHS as the leading home video technology. By 2004, the annual revenue from 'kidvids' had increased to $3 billion.[56] One of their major strengths is relative immunity to theatrical market forces, such as the industry recession of 2008/09. Marc Rashba, Vice President of marketing for Sony Home Entertainment, suggests that 'family audiences, even in this sort of down market [...] continue to support family titles overall on DVD'.[57]

Hitherto, 'kidvids' have been largely a North American phenomenon, but international producers have also attempted to exploit the format. In October 2003, the British Broadcasting Corporation (BBC), the UK Film Council and the Children's Film and Television Foundation (CFTF) announced a cooperative initiative to produce a series of British family films, promising £900,000 over a three-year period to develop both live-action and animated productions.[58] Jenny Borgars, head of the Film Council development fund, explained: 'big-budget successes such as "Chicken Run" and "Harry Potter" have shown that there is an audience for distinctively British family-friendly films'.[59] The fund is now closed, although the CFTF website reports that five projects are in development as of early 2012.[60] In 2006, the Australian government-funded Film Finance Corporation (FFC) announced its intention to develop more home-grown 'broad-appeal movies and children's pics'.[61] Effectively a public body because of its state sponsorship, Chief Executive Brian Rosen told *Variety* that the FFC was responding to a public call for greater family films.[62] Such films are also being strongly encouraged in Scandinavian countries, some of which offer state subsidies for home-grown productions. Denmark produced nine such movies in 2006. Charlotte Giese, head of the Danish Film Institute's Children and Youth department, admitted that 'it means a lot to us that Danish children are watching Danish films'.[63] Certainly, a backlash over the near-hegemony of Hollywood productions in the global arena is almost inevitable. As Hollywood blockbusters have re-orientated to international tastes, a growing number of smaller industries internationally have chosen to target family audiences on the local level, eschewing the displaced, generic culture of global mass entertainment.

Cultural Tradition and Globalised Family Entertainment

Ironically, one of the few domestic markets capable of significant profitability is North America. Arguably the most interesting – though by no means the most lucrative – family film cycle of the previous decade was the rejuvenated slapstick domestic comedy. Twentieth Century Fox's remake of *Cheaper by the Dozen* (Shawn Levy, 2003) was a surprise success, and re-launched the genre, which – in its most recent incarnation – comprised such films as *Daddy Day Care* (Steve Carr, 2003), *Johnson Family Vacation* (Christopher Erskin, 2004), *Cheaper by the Dozen 2* (Adam Shankman, 2005), *Yours, Mine and Ours* (Raja Gosnell, 2005), *Are We There Yet?* (Brian Levant, 2005), *RV: Runaway Vacation* (Barry Sonnenfeld,

2006), *Are We Done Yet?* (Steve Carr, 2007) and *Daddy Day Camp* (Fred Savage, 2007). These films, unsurprisingly, achieve the majority of their success in the US market, where even the domestic critical consensus has been explicitly hostile. Like previous Hollywood family comedies, such films are admittedly didactic, but the recurrence of this didacticism pertains less to an inherited motif than the films' defiant insistence upon promoting conservative, avowedly 'American' values and traditions as a counterpoint to the international inflection of the most profitable Hollywood family entertainment.

Correspondingly, each of these films presents a quintessentially 'American' protagonist, generally male, and often the head of a large family. *Cheaper by the Dozen*, *Daddy Day Care* and *RV* star Steve Martin, Eddie Murphy and Robin Williams, respectively – three of the biggest Hollywood stars of the 1980s and 1990s, each now entering late middle-age and settling into less anarchic, more paternalistic personae. Steve Martin, particularly, has repeatedly returned to the same archetype, having largely divorced himself from the subversive stand-up which launched his career. Having been hand-picked to play the family patriarch and college baseball coach in *Parenthood* (Ron Howard, 1989) because of his 'everyman' qualities, and having starred in Charles Shyer's 1991 remake of Minnelli's 1950 production, *Father of the Bride*, Martin's role in *Cheaper by the Dozen* as a family patriarch and college football coach appears calculated. Robin Williams's return to family entertainment in *RV* is similarly noteworthy. Unlike Martin's role in *Cheaper by the Dozen*, *RV* offers Williams the opportunity to play against expectation, before finally reaffirming ideological and formal conventionality.

The opening sequence of *RV* sees Williams playing to type. We see a young girl, Cassie (Erika-Shaye Gair), sitting on her bed laughing and enjoying a puppet show performed by a familiar voice, just out of sight of the camera. The performer, of course, turns out to be Williams – or rather his character, Bob Munroe – ever the doting, seemingly asexual patriarch, comfortingly familiar to viewers because of his famous performances in family films over the years. After Bob's wife, Jamie (Cheryl Hines), comes in to complain about him keeping Cassie awake, an exchange ensues:

> **Cassie:** I'm never gonna get married.
> **Bob:** Why not?
> **Cassie:** Cause I always wanna stay with you.

Bob: Well, you know, one day you're gonna grow up, meet a wonderful guy and you're gonna get married. But you and I will always be best friends.

Immediately thereafter, the narrative jumps a decade into the future. We see Bob, driving his now-dysfunctional, argumentative family around town. Cassie has become a rebellious teenager (as played by JoJo Levesque) and Bob and Jamie now also have a teenage son, Carl (Josh Hutcherson). Bob and Cassie are no longer 'best friends'; far from it. The opening scene's image of domestic harmony is ironically situated, seemingly designed to lull the audience into the mistaken belief that proceedings will be as warmly comforting and sentimental as Williams's 1990s family movies.

RV positions itself as revealing what happens *after* the 'happy ever after', with experience replacing innocence and domestic sentiment giving way to contemporary realism. This is not to say that sentimentality does not reassert its dominance as the narrative unfolds, and like *Cheaper by the Dozen* and *Are We There Yet?*, the film offers a jarring juxtaposition of sentiment and gross-out humour. One sequence loaded with symbolism sees the hapless Bob/Williams sprayed with raw sewage as he tries to drain a septic tank, as the cosy idealism of the 1990s family comedies gets assaulted with a hefty dose of unpleasant reality. And yet, the film ultimately presents an ending as saccharine as any presented in Williams's earlier films. Would it be overly cynical to suggest that the filmmakers posit an illusion of down-and-dirty realism to deflect attention from the ideological conventionality? Consider the plot. Bob's job as a soda company executive is under threat from a younger, hungrier employee backed by his odious boss. Bob decides that he will be on hand for an all-or-nothing business meeting out in the sticks to convince a small, independent soda company to merge with his larger organisation, where he will face-off against his professional rival in a battle for his boss's affections. Bob, under pressure to reunite his increasingly-estranged family, decides that he will bring them along under the pretext of a road-trip holiday, keeping them in the dark about the nearby business meeting, intending to keep the two worlds separate. Ultimately, after a series of slapstick set pieces, the family manages to reconnect. Bob's conscience finally gets the better of him and he quits the environmentally-questionable soda company. Serendipitously, he is offered an executive position in the more environmentally-friendly firm, which is persuaded to remain independent – an obvious symbol of the widening dichotomy between domestic- and international-flavoured family entertainment.

The Hollywood slapstick family comedy often pointedly rejects international media culture, invoking local and domestic cultural mores as a bulwark against encroaching globalisation. This calculated parochialism manifests itself in a neatly symbolic scene in *Are We There Yet?* Protagonist Nick Persons (Ice Cube) runs a sports memorabilia store, immaculate and full of classic collectables from the sports of baseball, basketball and American football. His shop is a virtual tribute to twentieth-century US recreational history. As if to deliberately disrupt Nick's reveries, a couple of kids walk in asking for Yu-Gi-Oh! (Japanese manga). Nick furiously retorts:

> Look, you come in here every day asking the same questions. We ain't got no Pokémon, no Digimon, no Buffy, no SpongeBob, no Beanie Babies.

When Nick angrily chases the children from his shop, his co-worker, Marty (Jay Mohr), sarcastically notes: 'you know, you really got a way with kids'. He makes a good point. Nick's disdain for contemporary children's media culture reflects that of the filmmakers, who have crafted an old-fashioned family movie driven by adult protagonists, sentimentality, a romantic subplot and slapstick comedy to keep the children entertained. There are two points to be made regarding this genre. The first is that family movies have moved on since the early 1990s success of *Home Alone* and *Mrs. Doubtfire*: international audiences accustomed to fantasies and blockbuster spectacles no longer appear satisfied with comedic representations of North American family life. Some such films are so flag-waving in their US cultural inflection that they automatically discount a sizable international audience. The second point is that the genre is actively *intended* for the domestic market, and can still yield a significant profit if outlay is kept to a minimum. Such material has traditionally found a popular niche in the south, and in more rural areas where conservative politics exercise a firmer grasp. US fundamentalist religious organisations, such as Ted Behr's Christian Film and Television Commission and *Movieguide*, also strongly petition for 'wholesome' and 'traditional' family fare. The problem faced by producers is largely hostile critical feedback, which in turn elicits negative word-of-mouth. The box office failures of

Are We Done Yet? and *RV* triggered the end of this particular cycle, but the rhetorical attraction of its core values will endure.

Such socio-culturally-specific entertainment is becoming increasingly isolated in a media marketplace where family entertainment takes many different forms. The diversity of product attests to the strength and depth of the market, but also the range of platforms now available. The explosion in children's television is a significant factor. Nickelodeon, a 24-hour channel showing parent-approved programming, completely changed the children's media landscape. In 1996, it ranked number one in the US daytime ratings for the first time. In recent years, Disney has emerged as a serious competitor. The Disney Channel was launched in 1997, and in 1998, Showtime and HBO's Family Channel announced greater investment in original programming.[64] By the turn of the decade, Disney was operating four platforms, each aimed at a different niche, allowing the company to reach 'every conceivable demo': ABC Family (est. 2001), the Disney Channel (est. 1997), Toon Disney (est. 1998; now Disney XD) and ABC Kids (est. 1997).[65] This increasing competition has led to greater product diversity but also intensified the need for precision in demographic targeting. Television networks have begun to focus more aggressively upon younger demographics, which led to the increasing prominence of the pre-school and 'tween' audiences from early-to-mid-decade. As Dade Hayes points out:

> In the kids-and-family racket, business has boomed of late, and yet the old label 'fun for the whole family' is about as relevant as a G rating. Nielsen's long-established, overlapping age ranges – 2 to 11 years old, 6 to 11 and 9 to 14 grow more archaic by the hour.[66]

Sales in pre-school entertainment have surged in recent years. By 2007, one in three DVDs sold in the USA – or 51 million – was intended for the pre-school market.[67] The emergence of the 'tween' is almost as striking. Although definitions of the 'tween' demographic vary, it is usually regarded as the audience 'in-between' childhood and adolescence. Nickelodeon executive Cyma Zarghami said in 2002: 'I feel like this demo has been around for a long time, but attention on it hasn't been as focused as it is now.'[68] Although the 'tween' demographic arose from network and cable television, it has emerged as a viable theatrical audience section with *Hairspray* (Adam Shankman, 2007), *Hannah Montana: the Movie* (Peter Chelsom, 2009) and the *High School Musical* (2006–8) series.

Where the influence of children's television has been apparent is in the greater stylistic range evident in contemporary family films. Several stylistically-unconventional children's TV shows have been adapted into feature films, such as *The Rugrats Movie* (Igor Kovalyov and Norton Virgien, 1998), *The Wild Thornberrys Movie* (Cathy Maskasian and Jeff McGrath, 2002), *The SpongeBob SquarePants Movie* (Stephen Hillenberg, 2004), *Alvin and the Chipmunks* (Tim Hill, 2007) and *The Smurfs* (Raja Gosnell, 2011). Producers now realise that family entertainment need not be uniform and formally conventional to achieve big success, as Burton's adaptation of *Charlie and the Chocolate Factory* (2005) proves. Bearing interesting comparison with the 1971 original, *Willy Wonka & the Chocolate Factory* (Mel Stuart), Burton's adaptation adds several new plot elements, as well as reconfiguring the central figure of Wonka (here played by Johnny Depp). Although Gene Wilder's portrayal in Stuart's film is certainly eccentric, Depp's character is uncomfortably, almost distastefully weird. Made-up to look like Michael Jackson, he makes the character of Wonka camp and almost sinisterly childlike. *Charlie and the Chocolate Factory* embodies a palpable sense of ironic detachment and invites the viewer to take a step backwards, exercise their analytical skills and look beyond the surface gloss, just as the visitors to the chocolate factory are forced to interrogate the authenticity of the sights with which they are presented.

These days, of course, consumers are assuredly media-savvy, and the fact that the visitors feel compelled to air their cynicism regarding the seemingly-magical surroundings of the factory reflects common awareness of the technological possibilities of, say, computer graphics, to create such fantastic environments. In a later scene, viewers are shown a flashback of Wonka's unhappy childhood, in which he was prevented by his authoritarian father (Christopher Lee) from eating sweets. Afterwards, the camera cuts to Wonka's distracted face, whereupon he explains, 'I'm sorry, I was having a flashback', a tongue-in-cheek reference to the clichéd Hollywood 'flashback scene'. In the book, Wonka is a ruthless moraliser, who for all his bizarre eccentricity is clearly a grown-up figure of authority. As played by Depp, Wonka is more of a child than Charlie (Freddie Highmore). He is impulsive and amoral; perhaps even dangerous. One of the most influential auteurs currently working in Hollywood, Burton can rarely allow the

Charlie and the Chocolate Factory (2005)

sweeter, more narratively-conventional moments to pass without ambiguity, even at the film's conclusion, where Wonka is 'adopted' by the Bucket
family. In this way, the film plays simultaneously to mass audiences and to
fans of fantasy and genre filmmaking, as well as those who regard Johnny
Depp and Tim Burton as cult heroes of left-field Hollywood.

Indeed, the success of *Charlie and the Chocolate Factory*, and Burton's/
Disney's *Alice in Wonderland* (2010), indicate that there is substantial
mileage in mainstream family entertainment which appears to eschew
the obviousness and vulgarity of the lowest common denominator. Such
films present pleasing spectacle and an emotional hit, while purportedly
providing for more sophisticated, cine/media-literate audiences raised
on a more varied entertainment diet than previous generations. While
Burton's films have always walked the line between artistic innovation and populism, and his more recent, family-orientated films reveal
an apparent preoccupation with mainstream blockbuster success, the
attraction of stylistic and thematic oddness is surely not confined to the
intelligentsia or the artistically aware, but is likely to appeal to anyone
who does not like to think of themselves as an unsophisticated consumer
of lowest common denominator entertainment. Nevertheless, the relative

214

commercial obscurity of the comparatively cerebral productions *Coraline* and *The Fantastic Mr. Fox* illustrates that eccentricity is only really a marketable commodity when it is little more than a veneer, in films which remain ideologically and emotively conventional.

For the Hollywood studios, the huge global success enjoyed by its contemporary blockbuster franchises represents the culmination of a strategy that began in the early 1930s. The family film was conceived as part of a demagogic campaign to establish Hollywood's credentials as a producer of high-class entertainment for everyone. Its function has always been twofold: to attract the broadest spectrum of audiences while protecting the industry from external threats (such as censorship legislation). This duality of purpose is still clearly in evidence in contemporary family entertainment, although undeniably the tension between these two basic functions has increased in recent years. It is likely that the future will see a continuation and perhaps deepening of the present dichotomy between the big international blockbusters – of which family films constitute a large proportion – and smaller-scale films more affiliated with local and national cultural traditions, eschewing the universalised tone of the internationally-pitched productions. Such small-scale operations cannot, at present, realistically compete with the resources of Hollywood, and will succeed only by differentiating their product to appeal to smaller niches within the 'family' market – as successfully accomplished by the pan-European *Asterix and Obelix* (1999–) franchise, which has proven highly popular in Western Europe. The alternative is funding and/or distribution from Hollywood. The Australian family production, *Babe* (Chris Noonan, 1995), and the Japanese feature animation, *Spirited Away* (Hayao Miyazaki, 2001), belong to a very select list of international films that attracted significant major studio distribution, and thereby achieved significant global box office success.

Some audience sections, of course, remain immune to the perceived pleasures of globalised family entertainment. Others continue simultaneously to enjoy entertainment forms such as the noir, the art house, the erotic, the perverse: genres and styles existing outside of this most mainstream facet of media culture. Moreover, the nature of family entertainment and the styles utilised in its construction are subject to flux, as cultural mores and technological advances impose their own changes. Throughout these changes, however, the basic commercial philosophy of family entertainment remains constant.

CONCLUSION

In Hollywood cinema, styles are constantly changing, but the mission – selling entertainment to the masses – remains the same. Considering Hollywood's ongoing pursuit of entertainment capable of engaging universally (within the obvious practical constraints of that word), it is unsurprising that the family film – which seeks to appeal equally to all consumer groups – has emerged as its quintessential mode of production. Furthermore, only by examining its entire history is it possible to recognise the overall patterns in the Hollywood family film, both in terms of strategy and production methods. As such, it is important to evaluate the relationship between change and continuity, and examine how this dialectic functions in contemporary Hollywood family films, looking towards a future in which their dominance is likely to further extend.

Unquestionably, the most important historical variable has been the shift from a chiefly adult-orientated to a chiefly youth-orientated cultural model. Family films from the 1930s to the 1960s were made for a predominantly adult-centred, North American middlebrow public. Since the late 1970s, family films – and US popular culture in general – have been made to satisfy a youth- or 'kidult'-orientated international market. This shift underscores the importance of the socio-cultural environment in shaping film content. Family films in the modern style would not have been possible during the studio era, partly because of technological limitations, but largely due to the absence of a cultural consensus in the way 'kidult' entertainment now dominates the Western

217

media landscape. Crossover hits, such as *Snow White and the Seven Dwarfs*, were very much exceptions to the rule. In general, metropolitan, small-town, middle-class and working-class audiences all possessed their own, divergent, requirements. The 'family audience' in its broader extension remained inaccessible until North America embraced a less stratified taste consensus. The emergence of the teenager as a powerful consumer group is certainly pivotal in this regard, although the suburbanisation of the United States (which brought greater uniformity in lifestyle) and the popularisation of television (a more democratic format which enabled greater cultural interaction) were similarly important. The universality of television prepared US audiences for the undifferentiated address of post-1970s family films in a way that would not earlier have been possible.

The most significant changes that have elevated family films above other entertainment formats have been social and industrial, rather than textual. Changes in lifestyle, particularly in the USA, have led to greater conformity in cultural taste, as have developments in mass communication. As a result, although cultural diversity remains on many levels, globally-active mass audiences, motivated by increasingly uniform entertainment impulses, have become attainable. Bypassing more sophisticated thought processes, contemporary family films are capable of temporarily suspending many – although not all – of the differences in age, race, religion, culture and class separating potential consumers across the world. Family blockbusters are tailor-made for this role. Although movies have always provided some quantity of 'immersion', modern family blockbusters actively bombard the senses with CGI special effects, even projecting outwards into the theatre via 3D. Some CGI-heavy fantasies, in fact, delight in the spectacle of huge, fearsome monsters leaping towards the camera, mouth open, as if to consume the screen, and in so doing eradicate this physical barrier between film and audience.

It is well to keep in mind that spectacle has always been important in family movies dating back to the feature animations and fantasies of the 1930s (the tornado that swept up Dorothy Gale's house in *The Wizard of Oz* was remarkably sophisticated in its day). In doing so, we can resist the temptation to regard the spectacular aspects of contemporary family movies as epochal, and instead view them as logical technological and aesthetic progression, in which techniques allowing deeper forms of audience immersion have grown progressively more sophisticated. However, the increasing prominence of spectacle certainly does not *efface* narrative, nor the expectation for good stories well told, well paced and excitingly plotted. Geoff King is correct when he argues that we must resist a superficial analysis stating that 'narrative is in some way absent or displaced by spectacle' – this is a common critical confusion which, when interrogated, has little basis in reality.[1] In fact, technological sophistication notwithstanding, there is an enduring desire for an engaging story, and this is one of the most important continuities not only between films past and present, but the broader cultural histories of literature and narrative.

Instead of concentrating solely on content, it is useful to comment on the continued importance of family films to Hollywood and to Western culture. Almost from its very beginnings, Hollywood's size and resources, and the extent of its international distribution networks, suggested its ability to harness the potential of cinema as a mass medium capable of uniting audiences from all walks of life through a form of appeal that – unlike other dominant arts, such as literature and the theatre – was truly universal in scope. Hollywood's agenda of mass audiences united by mass-appeal movies has rarely been fully appreciated in academia, partly because, until the 1970s, it often remained invisible. Critics have instead lauded classical-era Hollywood genres such as film noir and screwball comedies for their creative diversity, lamenting the absence of such sophisticated maturity in the 'New Hollywood'. In doing so, they fail to appreciate sufficiently the commercial side of Hollywood's operations. To survive and prosper, studios need to address as large an audience as possible; the main reason left-field or niche movies are distributed by the global media conglomerates is because no film is capable of appealing to everyone, and there will always be a limited demand for the unusual and the sophisticated. To suggest otherwise risks misconceiving the film and media industries' true agendas. The prospect of family films ultimately eradicating minority-appeal films is remote, but this has not prevented them from banishing 'niche' filmmaking to the periphery of mainstream consumption. With the emergence of the 'global village' and a tangible taste consensus, the market for such products has declined commensurately.

However, family films are equally defined by the socio-cultural values they represent. These ideologies are both a considerable asset and an insurmountable obstacle in terms of attracting global audiences. For much of their history, their potency and appeal were at the very heart of Hollywood family films. Since the shift towards globally-orientated modes of appeal, these values – many of them explicitly deriving from the US national consciousness – have proven to be awkwardly incongruous with the supposed universality of the format. Family films have always tried to give mainstream audiences what they want and expect. Their conservatism tends to reflect an ideological populism which adheres to the most important tenets of the United States' national identity – freedom, individualism, political and racial superiority, the importance of family and community, and the 'American Dream' of meritocratic self-advancement. Family films reflect the perceived requirements of their dominant consumers: social and economic recovery during the 1930s Depression; the nostalgic 'return to the soil' throughout the 1930s and 1940s; the rejection of youth culture during the 1960s, implicit in the renewed interest in 'traditional' entertainment; the surge in escapist fantasy in the late 1970s period of national malaise; the preoccupation with baby boomer anxieties in the late 1980s and early 1990s; the conservative rejection of globalised popular culture in 2000s domestic comedies; and immersion in contemporary entertainment franchises. For most of their history, family films have been made largely for a North American audience, and only relatively recently have their modes of appeal been reconfigured to accommodate international audiences. Although it is true that many foreign audiences willingly buy-in to a branded representation of 'America' when they consume Hollywood movies, and producers want to preserve this aggressively confident self-image, equally they wish to avoid both the mundane qualities of day-to-day life, and elements of the national character that may detract from the propaganda of 'pure entertainment'. There has also been a clear trend towards a more liberal inclusivity, although much progress has still to be made in this area, given the legitimate accusations of misogyny, racism and homophobia that have long been levelled at the format.

Much of this book has addressed family films in terms of the consensus they seem to represent, and their ability to reflect majority tastes and values. Increasingly, though, as Hollywood reconfigures its family-orientated products for global tastes, there are points of opposition. Firstly, we must consider the North American marketplace. In Chapter 7, I talked at length about certain recent Hollywood family films that reject fantasy and universality in favour of traditional studies of US domestic life, such as *Are We There Yet?* and *RV.* These narratives are almost *anti*-blockbuster in spirit, both in terms of filmmaking style and the cultural values they articulate. Whereas family blockbusters disavow associations of strong, flag-waving Americanism, these domestic comedies reaffirm 'traditional' US ideologies concerning the strong, structurally-isolated nuclear family. Many low-budget, low-key independent productions are similarly defined by their opposition to blockbuster production values and mainstream tastes. For reasons of artistry as well as commerce, such films are rarely family orientated, but seek to mobilise audiences whose interests lie outside mainstream action or adventure material. Although contempo-rary domestic-orientated family comedies usually embody conservative political ideals, whereas independent films often tend towards more liberal ideologies, these politically-opposed factions are – to some extent – unified by their disdain for the family blockbuster. It is no coincidence that indie films exploded on to the market at almost precisely the same time as the major Hollywood studios embraced media conglomeration and family entertainment as in-built principles.

However, cultural resistance to family entertainment is most strongly marked in overseas territories. Western Europe is Hollywood's most lucrative foreign theatrical market, and has, in general, assisted in its dominance by actively encouraging Hollywood co-productions and distri-bution deals. However, a big-budget, pan-European family-orientated venture – *Asterix and Obelix vs. Caesar* (Claude Zidi, 1999) – curbed the trend by achieving substantial box office success without US funding or distribution, or, indeed, a wide release in US theatres. A French, German and Italian co-production based on the long-running French comic strip, the film returned over $100 million, less than $1 million of which stemmed from US theatres.[2] It has since spawned a successful movie franchise, but it is very much the exception to the rule, both in terms of its extraordinary success and its populist approach (which appropriates, rather than counterpoints, the style of Hollywood family movies).

Far more important to Hollywood's future in the global arena are China and India. Both are enormous markets which, despite repeated over-tures, have proven frustratingly difficult to crack. US commentators have been anticipating China's imminent arrival as a massive foreign market for years.[3] It was felt that the internet would force China's development towards democracy, which would, in turn, lead to a loosening of existing

221

trade restrictions, but this has not yet materialised (partly because of the local dominance of the state-operated Internet search engine, which censors a great deal of politically- and culturally-sensitive content). Furthermore, the Chinese state currently only allows domestic distribution of 20 foreign films per year, and piracy is rife.[4] Although *Avatar* broke the all-time Chinese box office record in early 2010 with grosses of approximately $70 million, this only equated to around half its UK theatrical grosses, which, in turn, amounted to a fraction of its US box office performance.[5] Since its programmes of economic 'liberalisation' in the early 1990s, India has appeared more politically and commercially open, yet imported films have struggled to overcome the domestic hegemony of locally-made productions. In response, Hollywood has resorted to manufacturing Bollywood-style films for the Indian market, but thus far, this initiative has achieved only limited success.[6] Ironically, the real challenge Hollywood studios now face in extending their global market share is producing films capable of local – rather than global – appeal. Hollywood family films are doing their job very well; they are dominating global box office charts and keeping the US film industry firmly on top (with a greater than 60 per cent stake in the global box office).[7] What globalised family films *cannot* accomplish is serving minority needs for localised, culturally-specific entertainment, and in this area Hollywood has proven less than successful. In India, for example – a territory dominated by domestic productions – Hollywood's market share in 2006 was a mere 5 per cent.[8]

To a large extent, successful foreign distribution of Hollywood movies depends on politics and ideology at the local level. Hitherto, family films have been too capitalistically 'American' to fully succeed in China, for reasons of state ideology, and in India, for reasons of national culture. Many other international territories are economically underdeveloped and therefore negligible markets.[9] Historically, as poorer countries have expanded their economies within capitalist frameworks and foreign trading has increased, Hollywood has simply assumed control of the market. Advanced global capitalism – no respecter of cultural democracy and diversity – generally allows the largest and most powerful corporations to expand their reach, either through absorption or eradication of competitors. This is precisely what occurred in post-communist Russia. After the fall of the Soviet Union, long-standing restrictions on Hollywood films were dropped, and the studios rapidly overcame local competition:

by 2003, Hollywood's market share in Russia had reached 75 per cent (compared with 82 per cent in Britain, 70 per cent in Spain, 65 per cent in Italy and 52 per cent in France), and by 2006 the country was, according to *Variety*, 'the hottest theatrical [film] market in Europe'.[10] For the same reasons, Western capitalist enterprise is eagerly awaiting the end of communist China, not for ideological reasons, but because a democratic government could conceivably pave the way for unlimited commercial access to the world's most populous nation. Of course, it is probable (as Michael Curtin argues) that such emerging economies as China and India will eventually be able to seriously challenge Hollywood's dominance.[11] Currently, it seems that any substantive challenge is still distant, contingent as it is on overcoming considerable competitive advantages, such as the availability of technical and creative resources, the Hollywood studios' well-protected global distribution networks, and the brand value of Hollywood entertainment itself. Between 1990 and 2005, Hollywood's proportion of the world market doubled.[12] This is unsurprising, given that the USA possesses what has been called 'the most protectionist culture in world history'.[13]

The fact that China and India – the two most populous countries in the world – continue to resist Hollywood entertainment is telling. It underlines an irresolvable paradox, namely that no matter how internationally-flavoured Hollywood family films become, they will always respond to US values, customs and tastes. The media conglomerates clearly do not believe, as do economists Jonathan Knee, Bruce Greenwald and Ada Seave, that 'all profitable media is local', but it is well to remember that around 35 per cent of the global box office still derives from the US domestic market.[14] This necessitates a certain pandering to local cultural tradition in order to satisfy the desires of an enormously powerful domestic audience which overwhelmingly rejects imported entertainment (foreign movies now constitute less than 1 per cent of the North American box office, down from a high of around 10 per cent in the 1960s).[15] When asked for his predictions regarding the future trajectory of family films, Disney executive Andy Bird replied:

> 'Family films'/entertainment/brands are going to become even more important/relevant in the future. As the world becomes more fragmented, 'family time' will become more precious. In my house, some nights all four members of the family (I have two boys aged 12 and

14) are on their individual computers. We've instilled family time to watch films together or play 'Scrabble'...It's the only time we get together and I think this will become even more of a premium going forward.[16]

His response tells us two things. Even now, it seems, Hollywood executives perceive traditionally-flavoured family entertainment as a palliative for economically-developed, Western societies in which social fragmentation and family togetherness is a concern. Equally significant, Bird's description strongly evokes traditional, conservative family fare (e.g. Disney animation, North American domestic comedies) rather than family-branded 'total entertainment', with its undifferentiated address, acceptance of moderate violence and swearing, and PG-13 ratings.

The divergence between these two manifestations reveals an internal conflict regarding the uses of the family brand. The growth of 'total entertainment' may ultimately become problematic for its survival; already there are intimations that the industry is having difficulty reconciling the brand's easy familiarity with the blatant corporatism of the product. Former Disney head of production Oren Aviv, speaking of the most recent instalment in the *Pirates of the Caribbean* series prior to release, spoke of the need to 'get the story right', because

you can't get bigger [...] The movies got bigger and bigger and very complicated [...] I want to kinda reboot the whole thing and bring it down to its core and to its essence which is the characters.[17]

Aviv's response indicates that Hollywood is concerned about brands becoming *solely* defined by spectacle, recognising the harm such perceptions might entail. There is a desire to preserve the 'integrity' of such multimedia franchises by establishing an opposition between family films still supposedly governed by principles of co-viewing ('for all the family') and social usefulness, against those which are lamentably brand-based, purely escapist and socially worthless ('for everyone'). Given that all the major studios continue to release both family-adventure movies and more child-orientated, wholesome fare under the 'family' banner, the dichotomy is entirely artificial, but the distinction surely appeals to the many fans and critics who still believe – as did the moral and educational reformers of the 1920s and 1930s – that popular culture ought to project authenticity, solidarity and demonstrate social conscience. Such is the current value of the 'family' brand that – in contrast to its contaminating associations before its rejuvenation in the 1980s – marketers are eager to apply it to their products as often as possible, sometimes inappropriately. As Jennifer Geer notes, the North American DVD release of the adult-orientated period melodrama *Finding Neverland* (Marc Forster, 2004) overtly positions it as a family film.[18] This practice is now commonplace and is perturbing for consumers, who may be misled by such cynical marketing strategies, but also potentially for the Hollywood studios, which must ensure that the brand is not misused, and retains its credibility and potency.

Ultimately, these questions boil down to a battle for brand ownership. The brands and intellectual properties are owned by producers, but as artefacts of North American popular culture and reflectors of social mores since the 1930s, family films also belong to their consumers. Because awareness of these movies is almost universal in the Western world, ownership is extremely valuable. Political, religious and civic bodies have always regarded the Hollywood family movie as a cultural rather than commercial format, largely because of the association with the concept of the 'family', which has enduring political appeal. The Christian right, for instance, historically has supported the 'traditional' family film because it represents society freed from perceived threats, such as divorce and family breakdown, career-minded women, gays, racial and ethnic minorities, and foreigners. Certainly, it is hard to imagine a form of popular culture more attractive to such bodies than the family film, so explicitly 'American', pro-'family', pro-tradition, hostile to change and, through conspicuous absence, implicitly hostile to outsiders – all filtered through the facade of amiability. As family films have become less *identifiably* driven by political agenda, organisations such as Walden Media have stepped in to plug the gap. The battle for ownership of the family brand, the desire to exploit its potential for ideological uses, and the ongoing need to extend the scope of its signification, may be defining characteristics in the years to come.

We may also ponder as to where the corporate strategies of global expansionism and universalism outlined in the latter part of this book will ultimately lead. While there can be no serious argument that family entertainment franchises are inherently unprofitable, considerable risks are attached. Moreover, Hollywood's determination to *exploit* its 'family' brands has led to an over-reliance on synergy and expansionism in the pursuit of universalism. Some of the most notable media acquisitions of the last few years – Disney's acquisition of Pixar Animation Studios for $7.4 billion in 2006 and Marvel for $4 billion in 2009 – were clearly motivated by the need for additional licensable properties and synergistic outlets in the pursuit of the global 'family' market. Although costly in the extreme, the executives who orchestrated these acquisitions clearly believed them to be sound investments. In the aftermath of the Pixar deal, Disney executive Dick Cook enthused: 'you can't come close to calculating what [this acquisition] means in the long term for the company in terms of new characters, stories, and lands for films and parks and publishing and more'.[19] However, Wall Street analysts thought that Disney overpaid, while Knee, Greenwald and Seave cite a number of prominent media mergers and acquisitions that failed to yield any perceptible synergistic benefits. Furthermore, corporate overspending is so prevalent that the potential benefits of synergies are sometimes outweighed or invalidated by the costs of acquisition. It would not be unreasonable to suggest, then, that the enormous profitability of several prominent Hollywood family franchises represents a glamorous – and slightly misleading – upside to a broader agenda of global media expansionism that is frequently marked by underperformance. Disney – so often represented as the very model of the diversified, synergistically-active, family-orientated international media conglomerate – actually provides one of the most salient examples of the potential risks associated with such strategies of vertical and horizontal integration.

Disney's resurgence during the late 1980s and early 1990s has often been attributed to CEO Michael Eisner's forward-thinking embrace of synergy. However, a closer examination reveals that it had more to do with conservative cost-cutting and price-rising strategies, and Disney's subsequent difficulties from the mid-1990s onwards coincided with Eisner's attempts to (over)extend the media conglomerate.[20] In 1995, he oversaw Disney's most radical corporate realignment in decades: the acquisition of US television network ABC for an estimated $19 billion. It should have been the apotheosis of Eisner's tenure, enabling a whole array of reciprocally beneficial synergies and tie-ins. However, Disney significantly overpaid and subsequently entered a long period of underperformance as a result. Knee, Greenwald and Seave identify such expansionist and universalistic strategies as primary markers of 'bad mogul' behaviour.[21]

That is a matter for debate. However, Hollywood family entertainment has undoubtedly become the material manifestation of a broader universalistic agenda, of which conglomeration, expansionism and synergy are the corporate equivalents. They are two sides of the same coin.

For popular and academic criticism, now is the ideal time to take notice of family films, not only because of their enormous historical significance – which is more than reason enough – but their increasingly important role in popular entertainment. A very pertinent question is which critical and theoretical frameworks are best suited to such investigation. Genre criticism has shown little or no interest, and excessively formalist interpretations of its scope serve to impede the study of such a pluralistic format. In contrast, socio-cultural approaches seem fertile, as does cognitive neuroscience, which helps us to understand why contemporary, 'kidult'-infected family films possess such an appeal to audiences of all ages and backgrounds. If, as I would suggest, the appeal of family films derives from an exploitation of innate needs coupled with a reflection of pertinent socio-political currents, an approach that fuses elements of culturalism and cognitivism would best suit future academic study into internationally-orientated family films.

Leaving aside the current and probable future dominance of the Hollywood family film, its position in US culture and film history since the 1930s has been enormous. Commercial cinema has always been one of the most important cultural formats for children, and certainly unrivalled as the dominant medium for a dual audience of adults and children. Furthermore, family films have always been far more than simply escapist, and have functioned on many levels: pedagogical, escapist, reflective, regressive, demagogic, conservative and utopian. This does not mean we should lose sight of their basic function. Family movies exist to make money; cultural significance is a fortunate by-product which keeps the bandwagon rolling, and their appeal to children should not risk obfuscating this fact. However, their continued success, across many incarnations, points to a cultural need for basically affirmative, happy stories which evoke pleasure in many forms, emotional and aesthetic. While Hollywood family movies remain artefacts of North American culture and society, they respond to basic, innate human needs, which is why they exert such a powerful attraction to audiences globally.

NOTES

Introduction

1   Of the top ten highest-grossing films of all time worldwide as of Autumn 2011 (unadjusted for inflation), only *Titanic* (#2) and *The Dark Knight* (#10) are not family films. All of the remainder (#1 *Avatar*, #3 *Harry Potter and the Deathly Hallows Part 2*, #4 *The Lord of the Rings: The Return of the King*, #5 *Transformers: Dark Side of the Moon*, #6 *Pirates of the Caribbean: Dead Man's Chest*, #7 *Toy Story 3*, #8 *Pirates of the Caribbean: On Stranger Tides* and #9 *Alice in Wonderland*) are designed for 'all-age' appeal. See *Box Office Mojo*, 'All Time Worldwide Box Office Grosses': <http://boxofficemojo.com/alltime/world/> [accessed 12 September 2011].

2   Personal correspondence between the author and Andy Bird, 26 March 2009.

3   Ruth Vasey, *The World According to Hollywood, 1918–1939* (Madison, Wisconsin: The University of Wisconsin Press, 1997), p. 4.

4   Kristin Thompson, *Exporting Entertainment: America in the World Film Market, 1907–1934* (London: British Film Institute, 1985), pp. 61–63.

5   Theatre and television have long been widely marketed and received as such, but for an interesting examination of the modern theme park as an example of 'family entertainment', see 'Theme Parks: The American Dream and the Great Escape', *The Economist*, Saturday 11 January 1986, pp. 83–84.

6   Peter J. Dekom, 'The Global Market', in Jason E. Squire (ed.), *The Movie Business Book* (New York: Fireside, 1992), pp. 418–430.

7   Questions of film suitability often centre on children, which are seen as the most vulnerable audience. However, mainstream family films must avoid

offending *any* audience group, whether on ideological, racial or religious grounds.

8   See Cary Bazalgette and Terry Staples, 'Unshrinking the Kids: Children's Cinema and the Family Film', in Cary Bazalgette and David Buckingham (eds), *In Front of the Children* (London: British Film Institute, 1995), pp. 92–108; Robert C. Allen, 'Home Alone Together: Hollywood and the "Family" Film', in Melvyn Stokes and Richard Maltby (eds), *Identifying Hollywood's Audiences: Cultural Identity and the Movies* (London: British Film Institute, 1999), pp. 109–134; also four essays written by Peter Kramer: 'Would You Take Your Child to See This Film?: The Cultural and Social Work of the Family Adventure Movie', in Steve Neale and Murray Smith (eds), *Contemporary Hollywood Cinema* (London: Routledge, 1998), pp. 294–311; '"The Best Disney Film Never Made": Children's Films and The Family Audience in American Cinema since the 1960s', in Steve Neale (ed.), *Genre And Contemporary Hollywood* (London: British Film Institute, 2002), pp. 185–200; 'It's Aimed at Kids – the Kid in Everybody: George Lucas, Star Wars and Children's Entertainment', in Yvonne Tasker (ed.), *Action and Adventure Cinema* (London: Routledge, 2004), pp. 358–370; 'Disney and Family Entertainment', in Linda Ruth Williams and Michael Hammond (eds), *Contemporary American Cinema* (Maidenhead: Open University Press, 2006), pp. 265–271.

9   Kramer, '"The Best Disney Film Never Made": Children's Films and the Family Audience in American Cinema since the 1960s', p. 186.

10 Richard Maltby, *Hollywood Cinema* (London: Blackwell, 2003), p. 89.

11 Lincoln Geraghty and Mark Jancovich (eds), *The Shifting Definitions of Genre: Essays on Labelling Films, Television Shows and Media* (London: McFarland, 2008).

12 Allen, 'Home Alone Together: Hollywood and the "Family" Film', p. 113.

13 See, for example, Kathy Merlock Jackson's *Images of Children in American Film: A Sociocultural Analysis* (London: Scarecrow Press, 1986); Neil Sinyard's *Children in the Movies* (London: Batsford, 1990); and Karen Lury's *The Child in Film: Tears, Fears and Fairy Tales* (London: I.B.Tauris, 2010).

14 See, for example, Ian Wojcik-Andrews, *Children's Films: History, Ideology, Pedagogy, Theory* (New York and London: Garland Publishing, 2000); Timothy Morris, *You're Only Young Twice: Children's Literature and Film* (Urbana: University of Illinois Press, 2000); and *Contemporary Children's Literature and Film: Engaging with Theory*, eds Kerry Mallan and Clare Bradford (Basingstoke: Palgrave Macmillan, 2011).

15 As a result, I have concerned myself more with live-action than animated productions. Animated features constitute a very small percentage of Hollywood family films across this historical period, and, as noted, have already received a great deal of scholarly attention.

Chapter 1: The Emergence of the Hollywood Family Feature, 1930–9

1   See Lee Grieveson, 'A Kind of Recreative School for the Whole Family: Making Cinema Respectable, 1907–09', *Screen* 42, no. 1 (2001), pp. 64–76, for a discussion of Hollywood producers' early interest in the 'family' audience.

2   Edgar Dale, *The Content of Motion Pictures* (New York: Macmillan, 1935), p. 17.

3   See Russell Merritt, 'The Nickelodeon Theatre, 1905–1914: Building an Audience for the Movies' in Ina Rae Hark (ed.), *Exhibition, The Film Reader*, (London and New York: Routledge, 2002), pp. 21–29.

4   'Children's Films for Children', *The New York Times*, 20 June 1915, p. x5.

5   Garth Jowett, *Film: The Democratic Art* (Boston, Toronto: Little, Brown and Company, 1976), p. 121.

6   Ibid, pp. 126–127.

7   Will H. Hays, *The Memoirs of Will H. Hays* (New York: Doubleday), p. 377.

8   'Results of National High School Students' Poll', quoted in Richard Koszarski, *An Evening's Entertainment: The Age of the Silent Feature Picture* (Berkeley, Los Angeles and London: University of California Press, 1990), p. 29; Alice Miller Mitchell, *Children and Movies* (Chicago, Illinois: University of Chicago Press, 1929), pp. 18, 42–45; Edgar Dale, *Children's Attendance at Motion Pictures* (New York: Macmillan, 1935), pp. 4, 26.

9   'Results of National High School Students' Poll', p. 29; Miller Mitchell, *Children and Movies*, pp. 98, 105.

10   Koszarski, *An Evening's Entertainment: The Age of the Silent Feature Picture*, pp. 290, 306.

11   Andre Sennwald, 'Children and the Cinema: A Brief Glance at the Nursery and its Perplexing Relation to the Screen', *The New York Times*, 23 December 1934, p. x5.

12   Raymond William Stedman, *The Serials: Suspense and Drama by Instalment* (Norman: University of Oklahoma Press, 1971), p. 51.

13   Miller Mitchell, *Children and Movies*, p. 5.

14   'Test Movies on Children', *The New York Times*, 19 March 1922, p. 14.

15   Quoted in Jowett, *Film: The Democratic Art*, p. 129.

16   'Films for Children', *The New York Times*, 1 February 1920, p. xxx3.

17   'Humanizing the Movies', *The New York Times*, 18 January 1922, p. 13; Larry May, *Screening out the Past: The Birth of Mass Culture and the Motion Picture Industry* (New York and Oxford: Oxford University Press, 1980), p. 205.

18   Vasey, *The World According to Hollywood, 1918–1939*, p. 64.

19   'Children's Films for Children'.

20   Jowett, *Film: The Democratic Art*, p. 148.

21   Ibid, p. 129.

22   Ibid.

23   Richard deCordova, 'Ethnography and Exhibition: The Child Audience, The Hays Code and Saturday Matinees', in Gregory A. Waller (ed.), *Moviegoing in America: A Sourcebook in the History of Film Exhibition* (Oxford: Blackwell Publishers, 2002), pp. 159–169.

24   Ibid.

25   Ibid.

26   Ibid.

27   Hays, *The Memoirs of Will H. Hays*, p. 389.

28   *The Neighborhood and its Motion Pictures: A Manual for the Community Worker Interested in the Best Motion Pictures for the Family* (New York: MPPDA, 1930), p. 3.

29   Ibid, pp. 30, 33.

30   Will H. Hays, *The President's Report to the Motion Picture Producers and Distributors of America, Inc.* (New York: MPPDA, 1932), p. 13.

31   P. S. Harrison, 'The Producers' New Code of Ethics', *Harrison's Reports*, 5 April 1930, vol. xii, no. 14.

32   P. S. Harrison, 'The Effects of the Code on the Minds of the American Public', *Harrison's Reports*, 12 April 1930, vol. xii, no. 15.

33   Ibid.

34   Donald Crafton, *The Talkies: American Cinema's Transition to Sound, 1926–1931* (New York: Scribners, 1997), p. 539.

35   Douglas Hodges, 'Remember Youth or Lose B.O. of Tomorrow, Declares Barker', *Exhibitors Herald-World*, 8 November 1930, p. 44.

36   Hays, *The Memoirs of Will H. Hays*, p. 443.

37   *Exhibitors' Herald-World*, 29 November 1930, p. 1.

38   *Exhibitors' Herald-World*, 6 December 1930, p. 62.

39   *Photoplay*, vol. XXXIX, no. 1, December 1930, p. 4.

40   'Excerpts from Reviews by N. Y. Dailies of New Pictures on B'way this Week', *Variety*, 20 December 1930, p. 2.

41   'The Shadow Stage', *Photoplay*, vol. XXXIX, no. 1, December 1930, pp. 52–53.

42   'Juvenile Appeal of New Pictures Proves Talking Films Will Stay: Darmour', *Exhibitors Herald-World*, 20 December 1930, p. 37.

43   'Loew's Play for Kids', *Variety*, 14 July 1931, p. 14.

44   'Serials Bring the Kids', *Motion Picture Herald*, 28 March 1931, p. 36.

45   Martin Quigley, 'For the Whole People', *Motion Picture Herald*, 4 April 1931, p. 7.

46   'Kid Pictures Are All Washed Up; Await "Sooky" As the Final Indicator', *Variety*, 15 December 1931, p. 7.

47   Ibid.

48 Will H. Hays, *The Motion Picture in a World at War: Twentieth Anniversary Report to the Motion Picture Producers and Distributors of America Inc.* (New York: MPPDA, 1942), p. 40.

49 Hays, *The Memoirs of Will H. Hays*, p. 445; Balio, *Grand Design: Hollywood as a Modern Business Enterprise*, pp. 13–16.

50 Vasey, *The World According to Hollywood, 1918–1939*, pp. 124–125.

51 Chapin Hall, 'Hope Placed in Cowboy Films to Attract Children to Theaters', *The New York Times*, 21 February 1932, p. X4; 'Mary Pickford Back From Europe; Proposes to Appear in "Alice in Wonderland", Animated by Walt Disney', *The New York Times*, 31 March 1933.

52 Ben Shylen, 'Announcing a Tried and Proven Plan for Rebuilding Family Patronage', *New England Film News*, 3 March 1932, pp. 3–4.

53 'Family Pix Only Name, Not Reality, Hays Aide Finds Hollywood', *Variety*, 16 May 1933, pp. 35, 87.

54 Vasey, *The World According to Hollywood, 1918–1939*, pp. 128–129.

55 Garth S. Jowett et al., *Children and the Movies: Media Influence and the Payne Fund Controversy* (Cambridge: Cambridge University Press, 1996), p. 7.

56 Gregory D. Black, 'Changing Perceptions of the Movies: American Catholics Debate Film Censorship', in Melvyn Stokes and Richard Maltby (eds), *Hollywood Spectatorship: Changing Perceptions of Cinema Audiences* (London: British Film Institute, 2001), pp. 79–90; Vasey, *The World According to Hollywood, 1918–1939*, p. 130.

57 Chapin Hall, 'Attack on Movies Stuns Hollywood', *The New York Times*, 8 July 1934, p. E1.

58 Churchill, 'Hollywood Heeds the Thunder', *The New York Times*, 22 July 1934, p. Sm1.

59 Jowett, *Film: The Democratic Art*, p. 254.

60 Richard Maltby, 'Sticks, Hicks and Flaps: Classical Hollywood's Generic Conception of its Audiences', in Melvyn Stokes and Richard Maltby (eds), *Identifying Hollywood's Audiences: Cultural Identity and the Movies* (London: British Film Institute, 1999), pp. 23–47.

61 Joan Shelley Rubin, *The Making of Middlebrow Culture* (Chapel Hill and London: The University of North Carolina Press), 1992, p. xi.

62 Susan Ohmer, 'The Science of Pleasure: George Gallup and Audience Research in Hollywood', in Richard Maltby and Melvyn Stokes (eds), *Identifying Hollywood's Audiences* (London: British Film Institute), 1999, pp. 61–80.

63 William Lewin, 'Higher Screen Standards for Youth: Filming of Classics Urged by English Teachers', *The New York Times*, 15 July 1934, p. xx4.

64 William Lewin, 'Movies Bow to Schools: The Film World Launches a New Cycle of Classics Long Favoured by Educators', *The New York Times*, 1 September 1935, p. xx7.

65 Ibid.; Anne Moray, *Hollywood Outsiders: The Adaptation of the Film Industry, 1913–1934* (Missouri: University of Minnesota Press, 2003), p. 159.

66 'Educating the Film Fan', *Variety*, 30 May 1933, p. 5; 'Body Drops Nine Other Aides', *Variety*, 14 November 1933, p. 4.

67 Melvyn Stokes, 'Female Audiences of the 1920s and early 1930s', in Melvyn Stokes and Richard Maltby (eds), *Hollywood Spectatorship: Changing Perceptions of Cinema Audiences* (London: British Film Institute, 1999), pp. 42–60.

68 Joel W. Finler, 'Box Office Hits 1914–2002', *The Hollywood Story* (London and New York: Wallflower Press, 2003), pp. 356–363. *Gone with the Wind* (1939), *Snow White and the Seven Dwarfs* (1937) and *San Francisco* (1936) were the top three films at the box office of the decade.

69 'Hays Sees an Era of Literary Films', *The New York Times*, 27 March 1934, p. 24.

70 Ibid.

71 Tino Balio, *Grand Design: Hollywood as a Modern Business Enterprise 1930–1939* (Berkeley, Los Angeles and London: University of California Press, 1993), pp. 179, 187.

72 Richard Maltby, 'The Production Code and the Hays Office', in *Grand Design: Hollywood as a Modern Business Enterprise 1930–1939*, pp. 37–72.

73 Margaret Farrand Thorp, *America at the Movies* (London: Faber and Faber, 1945 (1939)), p. 142.

74 Balio, *Grand Design: Hollywood as a Modern Business Enterprise 1930–1939*, p. 192.

75 Finler, 'Box Office Hits 1914–2002'.

76 Hays, *The President's Report to the Motion Picture Producers and Distributors of America, Inc.*, p. 8.

77 'Showmen's Reviews', *Motion Picture Herald*, 11 November 1933, pp. 27–30.

78 'Alice in Wonderland', *Variety*, 26 December 1933, p. 19.

79 P. S. Harrison, 'Little Big Shot', *Harrison's Reports*, 5 October 1935, vol. xvii, no. 40.

80 Nicholas Sammond, *Babes in Tomorrowland: Walt Disney and the Making of the American Child 1930–1960* (Durham and London: Duke University Press, 2005), pp. 112–113.

81 Steve J. Wurtzler, 'David Copperfield (1935) and the U.S. Curriculum', in John Glavin (ed.), *Dickens on Screen* (Cambridge: Cambridge University Press, 2003), pp. 155–170.

82 Richard Ford, *Children and the Cinema* (London: Allen and Unwin, 1939), pp. 211–212.

83 Wurtzler, 'David Copperfield (1935) and the U.S. Curriculum', pp. 155–156.

84 Ibid.

85 Hays, *The Memoirs of Will H. Hays*, p. 487.

86   Ford, *Children and the Cinema*, pp. 211–212.

87   Lewin, 'Higher Screen Standards for Youth: Filming of Classics Urged by English Teachers'.

88   Lewin, 'Movies Bow to Schools: The Film World Launches a New Cycle of Classics Long Favoured by Educators'.

89   Ibid.

90   'Producers Keeping Promises, Aver "Decency" Protagonists', *Boxoffice*, 5 October 1935, p. 4.

91   Ibid.

92   Hall, 'Attack on Movies Stuns Hollywood'; Douglas W. Churchill, 'Sweetness and Light: Hollywood Reverts to Elsie Books, to Pollyanna and to Kate Wiggin', *The New York Times*, 22 July 1934, p. sm1.

93   'The Public IS Pleased', *Boxoffice*, 6 April 1935, p. 4.

94   Andre Sennwald, 'Children and the Cinema: A Brief Glance at the Nursery and Its Perplexing Relation to the Screen', *The New York Times*, 23 December 1934, p. x5.

95   Andre Sennwald, 'Children and the Cinema: Containing the Heretical Suggestion That Children Know Their Own Minds', *The New York Times*, 9 June 1935, p. x3.

96   'Hays Finds Public Backs Clean Films', *The New York Times*, 11 October 1934, p. 29.

97   'What the Picture Did for Me', *Motion Picture Herald*, 16 November 1933, pp. 55–59.

98   'What the Picture Did for Me', *Motion Picture Herald*, 16 November 1935, pp. 68–70.

99   'Family Films Predominate First Nine Month Current Year, Checkup Shows', *Boxoffice*, 26 October 1935, p. 8; 'Family Films in Last 1936 Quarter Shatter Record', *Boxoffice*, 26 December 1936, p. 8; 'Producers Keep "F" Films in Fore During 1937', *Boxoffice*, 1 January 1938, p. 12. Of course, the attribution of a rating of suitability to any given film was essentially subjective and varied according to chosen criteria. For example, the *Christian Science Monitor* – a more conservative publication – placed the proportion of family films during 1936 at a relatively lowly 42 per cent. See 'Family Films Rise to 42 P.C. with Council's Five-Year Aid', *The Christian Science Monitor*, 28 April 1937, p. 15.

100 David Thomson, 'Shirley Temple', *A Biographical Dictionary of Film* (London: Andre Deutsch, 1994), pp. 743–744.

101 Bruce A. Austin, *Immediate Seating: A Look at Movie Audiences* (Belmont, CA: Wadsworth, 1989), p. 36.

102 See Dale, *Children's Attendance at Motion Pictures*, p. 73. Dale estimated that minors accounted for approximately one-third of all tickets bought during the early-1930s.

103 Graham Greene, 'Wee Willie Winkie; The Life of Emile Zola', originally published 28 October 1937 in *Night and Day*, and reprinted in David Parkinson (ed.), *The Graham Greene Film Reader: Mornings in the Dark* (Manchester: Carcanet, 1993), p. 234.

104 Norman J. Zierold, *The Child Stars* (New York: Coward-McCann, 1965), p. 61.

105 See particularly Theodore Caplow et al., *Middletown Families: Fifty Years of Change and Continuity* (Minneapolis: University of Minnesota Press, 1982), pp. 4–5, 18.

106 Anthony J. Badger, *The New Deal: The Depression Years, 1933–1940* (London: Macmillan, 1989), p. 247.

107 Lionel Robbins, *The Great Depression* (London: Macmillan, 1934), p. 16.

108 Mark Roth, 'Some Warners Musicals and the Spirit of the New Deal', *The Velvet Light Trap*, no. 17, winter 1977, pp. 1–7.

109 Badger, *The New Deal: The Depression Years, 1933–1940*, p. 8.

110 Charles Eckert, 'Shirley Temple and the House of Rockefeller', in Christine Gledhill (ed.), *Stardom: Industry of Desire* (London and New York: Routledge, 1991), pp. 60–73.

111 Frank S. Nugent, 'Little Miss Broadway', *The New York Times*, 23 July 1938, p. 10:4. Ironically, in Nugent's later career as a Hollywood screenwriter, he provided the script for one of Temple's few successful – albeit relatively minor – adult roles, in John Ford's *Fort Apache* (1949).

112 'What the Picture Did for Me', *Motion Picture Herald*, 26 August 1939, pp. 78–79.

113 Balio, *Grand Design: Hollywood as a Modern Business Enterprise 1930–1939*, p. 27.

114 Quoted in Maltby, 'Sticks, Hicks and Flaps: Classical Hollywood's Generic Conception of its Audiences', p. 27.

115 Ibid.

116 Thorp, *America at the Movies*, p. 19.

117 Churchill, 'Hollywood Heeds the Thunder'.

118 'What the Picture Did for Me', *Motion Picture Herald*, 23 February 1935, pp. 79–84.

119 'What the Picture Did for Me', *Motion Picture Herald*, 10 April 1937, pp. 85–87.

120 Thomson, 'Will Rogers', *A Biographical Dictionary of Film*, pp. 646–647.

121 '"U" Plans Series of "Family" Pix', *Variety*, 27 March 1939, pp. 1, 6; 'Negro Counterparts of "Hardy Family" Pix', *Variety*, 29 November 1939, p. 1.

122 David M. Considine, *The Cinema of Adolescence* (Jefferson and London: McFarland, 1985), p. 13.

123 Aljean Harmetz, *The Making of the Wizard of Oz* (New York: Alfred A. Knopf, 1977), p. 11.

124 Bosley Crowther, 'The Courtship of Andy Hardy', *The New York Times*, 10 April 1942, p. 21:2.

125 Bosley Crowther, 'Andy Hardy's Double Life', *The New York Times*, 12 January 1943, p. 23:3.

126 Frank S. Nugent, 'The Too Familiar Family', *The New York Times*, 19 February 1940, p. x5.

127 'Movies are Guilty of "Escapism", Can be Proud of It, Hays Finds', *The New York Times*, 29 March 1938, p. 23.

128 Andre Sennwald, 'Children and the Cinema: Containing the Heretical Suggestion that Youngsters Know Their Own Minds', *The New York Times*, 9 June 1935, p. x3.

129 *Variety*, 4 December 1947, p. 2,

130 Finler, 'Box Office Hits 1914–2002'.

131 'The New Pictures', *Time*, 30 April 1934.

132 The scene was cut after protests from the Legion of Decency, but the footage still exists, and occasionally features in modern showings and home video releases of the film.

133 Ford, *Children and the Cinema*, p. 129.

134 P. S. Harrison, 'Let's Go Collegiate', *Harrison's Reports*, 4 October 1941, vol. xxiii, no. 40.

135 Thorp, *America at the Movies*, p. 16.

136 Thorp, *America at the Movies*, p. 16.

137 Ibid.

138 James Shelley Hamilton, 'Modern Times', March 1936, reprinted in *From Quasimodo to Scarlett O'Hara: A National Board of Review Anthology*, pp. 217–220.

139 Thomson, 'Sir Charles Chaplin', p. 124.

140 Harmetz, *The Making of the Wizard of Oz*, pp. 3–4.

141 Ibid.

142 Ibid, p. 288.

143 Ibid, pp. 20–21.

144 Ibid.

145 Ibid, p. 22.

146 Ibid, p. 23.

Chapter 2: Walt Disney and the Beginnings of Feature Animation

1 Eric Smoodin, *Animating Culture: Hollywood Cartoons from the Sound Era* (New Brunswick, New Jersey: Rutgers University Press, 1993), p. 15.

2 Ibid, p. 12.

3   Paul Rotha and Richard Griffith, *The Film Till Now: A Survey of World Cinema* (Middlesex: Feltham, 1967), p. 517.

4   'Merchandising: The Mighty Mouse', *Time*, Monday 25 October 1948.

5   Ivan Spear, 'A Fairy Tale to Glowing Life upon the Screen', *Boxoffice*, 25 December 1937, p. 18.

6   Cited in Margaret Farrand Thorp, *America at the Movies* (London: Faber and Faber, 1945 (1939)), p. 16.

7   Timothy R. White, 'From Disney to Warner Bros.: The Critical Shift', in Kevin S. Sandler (ed.), *Reading the Rabbit: Explorations in Warner Bros. Animation* (New Brunswick, New Jersey and London: Rutgers University Press), 1998, pp. 38–48.

8   Fleischer Studios, which specialised in animated shorts, started life in 1921 as Inkwell Studios, formed by brothers Max and Dave Fleischer. Although the company never quite rivalled Disney and Warner Bros., their Betty Boop, Koko the Clown and Popeye series, as distributed by Paramount, were highly popular.

9   Michael Barrier notes that although *Gulliver's Travels* was 'modestly profitable', Paramount had to stop distributing *Mr. Bug Goes to Town* in 1946, having only recouped around one-third of the production costs. See *Hollywood Cartoons: American Animation in its Golden Age* (Oxford: Oxford University Press, 2003), pp. 296, 305.

10 Richard Schickel, *The Disney Version* (Chicago: Elephant Paperback, 1997), p. 298.

11 Barrier, *Hollywood Cartoons: American Animation in its Golden Age*, p. 302.

12 Schickel, *The Disney Version*, p. 29.

13 Smoodin, *Animating Culture: Hollywood Cartoons from the Sound Era*, p. 97.

14 James Shelley Hamilton, 'Pinocchio', March 1940, reprinted in *From Quasimodo to Scarlett O'Hara: A National Board of Review Anthology*, pp. 342–343.

15 'What the Picture Did for Me', *Motion Picture Herald*, 15 May 1943, pp. 50–54.

16 Steven Watts, *The Magic Kingdom: Walt Disney and the American Way of Life* (Boston and New York: Houghton Mifflin Company, 1997), pp. 448–449.

17 Schickel, *The Disney Version*, p. 38.

18 Ibid.

19 Ibid, p. 28.

20 Smoodin, *Animating Culture: Hollywood Cartoons from the Sound Era*, p. 101.

21 Ibid, pp. 101–102.

22 Ibid.

23 Ibid, pp. 203, 204.

24 Watts, *The Magic Kingdom: Walt Disney and the American Way of Life*, p. 264.

Chapter 3: The Middlebrow Family Film, 1940–53

1   Austin, *Immediate Seating: A Look at Movie Audiences*, p. 36.
2   Gilbert Seldes, 'Majority and Minority Audiences', February 1938, reproduced in *From Quasimodo to Scarlett O'Hara: A National Board of Review Anthology*, pp. 389–390.
3   'The Biscuit Eater', *Variety*, 6 April 1940, p. 3.
4   'Analysis of What Pix Scare Kids at Nat'l Board of Review Conclave', *Variety*, 11 December 1940, p. 11.
5   Ibid.
6   Ibid.
7   Ibid.
8   'Product Digest', *Motion Picture Herald*, 6 March 1943, p. 82.
9   'The Human Comedy', *Variety*, 3 March 1943, p. 14.
10 'The New Pictures', *Time*, 22 March 1943.
11 'Dog and Pony Pictures Click – Sequels Coming', *Variety*, 27 October 1943, p. 5.
12 'ANIMAL CRACKERS', *Variety*, 22 October 1943, p. 3.
13 '12 HORSE OPERAS AND ANIMAL PIX ON MAJOR SKEDS', *Variety*, 30 August 1944, p. 12.
14 Bruce Babington and Peter Evans, *Blue Skies and Silver Linings: Aspects of the Hollywood Musical* (Manchester: Manchester University Press, 1985), p. 144.
15 Ibid, p. 161.
16 'The New Pictures', *Time*, 25 August 1947.
17 Stephanie Coontz, *The Way We Never Were: American Families and The Nostalgia Trap* (New York: Basic Books, 1992), p. 99.
18 Ibid, pp. 97, 101.
19 Ibid, p. 109.
20 Thomas M. Pryor, 'Life with Father', *The New York Times*, 16 August 1947, p. 6:6. The predominantly middle-class readership of the *New York Times*, of course, is precisely reflected by the implied audience for films of this variety.
21 See Theodore Caplow et al., *Middletown Families: Fifty Years of Change and Continuity* (Minneapolis: University of Minnesota Press), pp. 225–229.
22 Martha Wolfenstein and Nathan Leites, *Movies: A Psychological Study* (New York: Atheneum, 1970 (1950)), p. 124.
23 'MPAA Children's Show Plan Provides for 28 Reissues', *Boxoffice*, 14 September 1946, p. 14.
24 Ibid.

25   'Children's Films Gain in Momentum', *The New York Times*, 19 September 1947, p. 26.

26   Ibid.

27   'Conflicting Report Cards', *Time*, 23 January 1950.

28   'Films for Children Urged on Hollywood', *The New York Times*, 23 April 1950, p. 64.

29   'How Not to Go Broke', *Time*, 25 June 1951.

30   Ibid.

31   Kenneth T. Jackson, *Crabgrass Frontier: The Suburbanisation of the United States* (New York and Oxford: Oxford University Press, 1985), p. 4.

32   Ibid, p. 280.

Chapter 4: The Traditional Family Film in Decline, 1953–68

1   Douglas Gomery, *Shared Pleasures: A History of Movie Presentation in the United States* (Madison: University of Wisconsin Press, 1992), pp. 85, 87.

2   Charles Champlin, *The Flicks: Or, Whatever Happened to Andy Hardy?* (Pasadena, California: Ward Ritchie Press, 1977), p. 28.

3   Austin, *Immediate Seating: A Look at Movie Audiences*, p. 38.

4   Gordon Gow, *Hollywood in the Fifties* (London: A. Zwemmer Ltd, 1971), p. 7.

5   David Bordwell, Janet Staiger and Kristin Thompson, *The Classical Hollywood Cinema: Film Style and Mode of Production to 1960* (London: Routledge, 1985), pp. 320–330.

6   Ibid.

7   Steve Neale, 'Hollywood Blockbusters: Historical Dimensions', in Julian Stringer (ed.), *Movie Blockbusters* (London: Routledge, 2003), pp. 47–60.

8   Finler, 'Box-Office Hits 1914–2002'.

9   Austin, *Immediate Seating: A Look at Movie Audiences*, p. 36.

10   Bruce Babington and Peter William Evans, *Biblical Epics: Sacred Narrative in the Hollywood Cinema* (Manchester: Manchester University Press, 1993), p. 5.

11   Thompson, *Exporting Entertainment: America in the World Film Market 1907–1934*, p. 1.

12   Thomas H. Guback, *The International Film Industry: Western Europe and America Since 1945* (Bloomington: Indiana University Press, 1969), p. 71.

13   Ibid, pp. 10–11.

14   Ibid.

15   Ibid.

16 'Disney's "Treasure Island" (RKO) Wins August Blue Ribbon Award', *Boxoffice*, 9 September 1950, p. 28.

17 'FAMILY PIX AS B. O. BACKBONE', *Variety*, 6 September 1950, pp. 1, 22.

18 'Mayer, Schary, Rodgers Star as MGM Winds Big Sales Meet', *Variety*, 11 February 1949, p. 3.

19 'MGM Wins Most Blue Ribbons in 20 Years of These Awards', *Boxoffice*, 10 January 1953, p. 11.

20 Schickel, *The Disney Version*, pp. 19, 316.

21 'Interview with Fletcher Markle', 25 September 1963, reproduced in Kathy Merlock Jackson (ed.), *Walt Disney: Conversations* (Jackson: University Press of Mississippi, 2006), pp. 89–103.

22 'Interview of Walt Disney by Cecil B. DeMille', 26 December 1938, reproduced in *Walt Disney: Conversations*, pp. 13–14.

23 Thomas Hine, *The Rise and Fall of the American Teenager* (New York: Avon Books, 1997), p. 8.

24 Ibid, p. 10.

25 Jon Lewis, 'Movies and Growing up...Absurd', in Murray Pomerance (ed.), *American Cinema of the 1950s: Themes and Variations* (New Jersey and London: Rutgers University Press, 2005), pp. 134–154.

26 See, for example, Fredric Wertham, *Seduction of the Innocent* (New York: Associated Faculty Press, 1972 (1954)).

27 Murray Pomerance, 'Movies and the 1950s', *American Cinema of the 1950s: Themes and Variations*, pp. 1–20.

28 Hine, *The Rise and Fall of the American Teenager*, p. 237.

29 Ibid, p. 238.

30 Thomas Doherty, *Teenagers and Teenpics: The Juvenilisation of American Movies in the 1950s* (Philadelphia: Temple University Press, 2002), p. 57.

31 Ibid, p. 56.

32 Ibid, pp. 90–158.

33 Ibid, pp. 17–18.

34 Ibid, p. 125.

35 Lynn Spigel, *Make Room for TV: Television and the Family Ideal in Postwar America* (Chicago and London: University of Chicago Press, 1992), p. 81.

36 Ibid.

37 Ibid.

38 Robert C. Allen, *Speaking of Soap Operas* (Chapel Hill and London: The University of North Carolina Press, 1985), pp. 10–11.

39 Spigel, *Make Room for TV: Television and the Family Ideal in Postwar America*, pp. 137, 141.

40 Ibid, pp. 154–155.

41 Ibid, p. 173.

42   Gerard Jones, *Honey, I'm Home! Sitcoms: Selling the American Dream* (New York: St. Martin's Press, 1992), p. 86.

43   Ibid, p. 93.

44   Ibid, p. 92.

45   Jonathan Munby, 'A Hollywood Carol's Wonderful Life', in Marl Connelly (ed.), *Christmas at the Movies* (London and New York: I.B.Tauris, 2000), pp. 39–57.

46   'Youthful Ideas For Filmization Imbue Vet Megger Taurog', *Variety*, 6 December 1954, p. 2.

47   Gregory D. Black, 'Changing Perceptions of the Movies: American Catholics Debate Film Censorship', in Melvyn Stokes and Richard Maltby (eds), *Hollywood Spectatorship: Changing Perceptions of Cinema Audiences* (London: British Film Institute, 2001), pp. 79–90.

48   Fred Hift, 'Prod'n Code Weighs Peace (And Its Price) With Legion of Decency', *Variety*, 18 May 1955, p. 3.

49   Thomas M. Pryor, 'Johnston Backs Production Code', *The New York Times*, 21 May 1955, p. 11; 'Production Code is Revised; Provisions More Flexible', *Boxoffice*, 15 December 1956, p. 8.

50   Stephen Farber, *The Movie Rating Game* (Washington, DC: Public Affairs Press, 1972), p. 12.

51   Thomas M. Pryor, 'Family Film Fare Urged by Rhoden: New National Theatres' Head Cites Need for Appealing to Children in Audiences', *The New York Times*, 8 November 1954, p. 25.

52   'LAUGHING IT UP FOR LADDIES: TV COMICS VEER TO MOPPET TIE', *Variety*, 24 November 1954, p. 23; 'SHOW BIZ NEGLECTING KIDS; TV MAKES EFFORT, PIX A WASHOUT', *Variety*, 13 November 1957, pp. 1, 79.

53   'Children's Film Library, Down to 0, Assured of New Supply of Prints', *Variety*, 29 February 1956, p. 24.

54   'Children's Film Library Will Be Revitalised', *Boxoffice*, 14 January 1956, p. 14.

55   'SECRET FEAR OF "FAMILY" FILMS', *Variety*, 24 February 1960, p. 3.

56   Ibid.

57   'DO ADULTS WANT "ADULT" FILMS?', *Variety*, 19 October 1960, p. 1.

58   'EXHIBS TRULY "FAMILY" MEN? TRADE SEES LOT OF LIP SERVICE', *Variety*, 2 November 1960, p. 5.

59   'COT LOTS OF HOT TOT PLOTS', *Variety*, 30 November 1960, p. 7.

60   'Kids & Family Get Lip Service', *Variety*, 25 January 1961, p. 3.

61   Ibid; 'Adult Cinematics: TV Problem', *Variety*, 5 June 1963, p. 27.

62   Doherty, *Teenagers and Teenpics: The Juvenilisation of American Movies in the 1950s*, p. 128.

63   Schickel, *The Disney Version*, p. 354.

64   Ibid, p. 345.

65 Ibid, p. 298.
66 Quoted in Watts, *The Magic Kingdom: Walt Disney and the American Way of Life*, p. 332.
67 JerryGriswold,'Pollyanna:Ex-Bubblehead',*TheNewYorkTimes*,25October1987: <http://www.nytimes.com/1987/10/25/books/pollyanna-ex-bubblehead .html?sec=&spon=> [accessed 31 March 2009].
68 Schickel, *The Disney Version*, p. 344.
69 'Around the World in 80 Days', *Variety*, 24 October 1956, p. 6.
70 Fredric Jameson, *Signatures of the Visible* (New York and London: Routledge, 1992), p. 13.
71 R. D. Laing and A. Esterson, *Sanity, Madness and the Family* (London: Penguin Books, 1964).
72 See Watts, *The Magic Kingdom: Walt Disney and the American Way of Life*, p. 452.
73 Bruce Babington, 'Song, Narrative and the Mother's Voice: A Deepish Reading of Julie Andrews', in Bruce Babington (ed.), *British Stars and Stardom: from Alma Taylor to Sean Connery* (Manchester: Manchester University Press, 2001), pp. 192–204.
74 Schickel, *The Disney Version*, pp. 362–363.
75 Finler, 'Box-Office Hits 1914–2002'.
76 Schickel, *The Disney Version*, p. 361.
77 Douglas Gomery, *The Hollywood Studio System: A History* (London: British Film Institute, 2005), p. 269.
78 Tino Balio, *United Artists: The Company That Changed the Film Industry* (Madison, Wisconsin: University of Wisconsin Press, 1987), p. 133.
79 Finler, 'Box-Office Hits 1914–2002'.
80 'Films Selected to the National Film Registry, Library of Congress 1989–2008', *National Film Preservation Board*: <http://www.loc.gov/film/nfrchron. html> [accessed 1 April 2009].
81 Maurice Isserman and Michael Kazin, *America Divided: The Civil War of the 1960s* (Oxford and New York: Oxford University Press, 2000), pp. 3–4.
82 'NO FAMILY BIZ FOR FAMILY FILMS', *Variety*, 21 October 1964, pp. 7, 30.
83 '"Nice, Unwashed, Pot-Smoking Kids' Will Go For Fantasia", Predicts NGT', *Variety*, 18 November 1970, p. 7.
84 Ibid.
85 Thomas Schatz, 'The New Hollywood', *Movie Blockbusters*, pp. 15–44.
86 Guback, *The International Film Industry: Western Europe and America Since 1945*, p. 12.
87 Schatz, 'The New Hollywood', pp. 16–17.
88 Geoff King, *Spectacular Narratives: Hollywood in the Age of the Blockbuster* (London: I.B.Taurus, 2000), p. 9.

Chapter 5: The Independents: Pal, Harryhausen and Radnitz

1 Thomson, 'Stanley Kramer', pp. 405–406.
2 Thomas Fernsch, *The Man Who Was Dr. Seuss* (New York: New Century Books, 2001), pp. 104–105.
3 Gail Morgan Hickman, *The Films of George Pal* (South Brunswick and New York: A. S. Barnes and Company, 1977), pp. 17–22.
4 Ibid, p. 30.
5 Ibid, p. 35.
6 'The New Pictures', *Time*, 5 January 1959.
7 Hickman, *The Films of George Pal*, p. 157.
8 Charles H. Schneer, interviewed for the independently-made documentary *The Harryhausen Chronicles*, 1998.
9 Ray Harryhausen and Tony Dalton, *An Animated Life* (London: Aurum, 2003), p. 103.
10 Ibid, p. 121.
11 The earliest usage of the term I have found is in the following article: 'LAUGHING IT UP FOR LADDIES: TV COMICS VEER TO MOPPET TIE', *Variety*, 24 November 1954, p. 23.
12 '2008 Entries to National Film Registry Announced', *Library of Congress*, 30 December 2008: <http://www.loc.gov/today/pr/2008/08-237.html> [accessed 17 December 2010].
13 'The 7th Voyage of Sinbad', *Variety*, 26 November 1958, p. 6; 'The 7th Voyage of Sinbad', *Film Daily*, 25 November 1958, p. 6.
14 'The 7th Voyage of Sinbad', *The Hollywood Reporter*, 25 November 1958, p. 3; Melvyn Maddocks, 'The 7th Voyage of Sinbad', *The Christian Science Monitor*, 18 December 1958, p. 7.
15 'Jason and the Argonauts', *Variety*, 5 June 1963, p. 6; Howard Thompson, 'Jason and the Argonauts Seek Golden Fleece at Loew's State', *The New York Times*, 8 August 1963, p. 19:1.
16 'A Dog of Flanders', *Variety*, 23 December 1959, pp. 3, 6.
17 'LIP SERVICE TO FAMILY FILMS', *Variety*, 1 April 1964, p. 7.
18 Ibid.
19 Ibid.
20 Richard Oulahan, 'News! A Film Fit for Kids!: Island of the Blue Dolphins', *Life*, 19 June 1964, pp. 14–17.
21 'Stern Touts, Radnitz Derides Code; Warn Show-A-Rama of Negatively Fixated Bias against "Family" Pix', *Variety*, 8 March 1972, p. 5.
22 'CLEAN-FUN-RADNITZ REGRETS MPAA RATINGS', *Variety*, 19 March 1969, p. 21.

23   'RADNITZ FAMILY PIC PAYOFF', *Variety*, 25 March 1970, p. 3.

24   Charles Champlin, 'Another Entry from Apostle of Family Films', *Los Angeles Times*, 25 May 1969, p. o1.

25   'OATS MAY BRING BACK FAMILY', *Variety*, 13 August 1969, p. 5.

26   Ibid.

27   Gary Arnold, 'Readers Digest to Co-Produce Family Films', *The Washington Post*, 28 June 1972, p. E6.

28   'Radnitz-Mattel Slate 8 Family Pix Over 3 Years', *Variety*, 14 July 1971, pp. 1, 12.

29   Charles Champlin, 'Top 10 Films – And Then Some – In An Actor's Year', *Los Angeles Times*, 31 December 1972, p. J1; 'Sounder', *Variety*, 16 August 1972, p. 16.

30   Carlton Jackson, *Picking up the Tab: the Life and Movies of Martin Ritt* (Bowling Green, Ohio: Bowling Green State University Popular Press, 1994), p. 122.

31   Ibid, p. 124.

32   'Hollywood Producer-Director Seeking Negro Stories', *Jet*, 16 June 1966, p. 58.

33   Correspondence between the author and Tony Dalton and Ray Harryhausen, 9 February 2011.

34   Harryhausen and Dalton, *An Animated Life*, p. 262.

35   'Clash of the Titans for the Young in Heart Only', *Variety*, 10 June 1981, p. 18.

36   Correspondence between the author and Tony Dalton and Ray Harryhausen, 9 February 2011.

37   'Joe Camp Thesis: Badly-Made Pics Give G Built-in Yawn', *Variety*, 12 February 1975, p. 34.

38   Ibid.

39   Mary Sue Best, 'New Era in Family Films? Canine Star Points the Way', *The Christian Science Monitor*, 2 April 1975, p. 25.

40   'Joe Camp's Idea: "Families" (Kids Separately Considered) Not Patronizing G-Rated Films', *Variety*, 30 November 1977, p. 5.

41   'Radnitz: MPAA "Hypocritical" And Old Family Films Extinct', *Variety*, 23 June 1976, p. 7.

Chapter 6: The Modern Family Film and the New Hollywood, 1977–95

1   David A. Cook, *Lost Illusions: American Cinema in the Shadow of Watergate and Vietnam, 1970–1979* (Berkeley, Los Angles and London: University of California Press, 2000), p. 9.

2   Tino Balio, *Hollywood in the Age of Television* (Boston: Unwin Hyman, 1990), p. 260.

3   Cook, *Lost Illusions: American Cinema in the Shadow of Watergate and Vietnam, 1970–1979*, p. 67.

4   Kramer, '"The Best Disney Film Never Made": Children's Films and The Family Audience in American Cinema since the 1960s', p. 191.

5   Ibid.

6   Farber, *The Movie Rating Game*, p. 39.

7   'Entertainment Industry Market Statistics', *Motion Picture Association of America*, 2007, p. 13.

8   Ryan Gilbey, *It Don't Worry Me: Nashville, Jaws, Star Wars and Beyond* (London: Faber and Faber, 2003), p. ix.

9   Balio, *Hollywood in the Age of Television*, p. 261.

10 'Valenti Hits Audience Hypocrisy', *The Los Angeles Times*, 28 April 1969, p. G17.

11 Farber, *The Movie Rating Game*, p. 24.

12 Norman Goldstein, '"Family" Tag Irks Director of "Colt"', *The Los Angeles Times*, 12 November 1968, p. C17.

13 Steve Toy, 'MAJOR FILMS FADING OUT NUDITY', *Variety*, 3 December 1971, pp. 1, 20.

14 Ibid.

15 Ibid.

16 Gregory Curtis, 'From Fellini to Deep Throat', *Texas Monthly*, January 1975, pp. 72–73.

17 Cited in Kramer, 'Disney and Family Entertainment', pp. 265–279.

18 Kramer, '"The Best Disney Film Never Made": Children's Films and The Family Audience in American Cinema since the 1960s', p. 188.

19 Farber, *The Movie Rating Game*, p. 3.

20 Kramer, 'Disney and Family Entertainment', pp. 269–270.

21 Cook, *Lost Illusions: American Cinema in the Shadow of Watergate and Vietnam, 1970–1979*, p. 15.

22 Ibid.

23 Gomery, *The Hollywood Studio System: A History*, p. 214.

24 Justin Wyatt, *High Concept: Movies and Marketing in Hollywood* (Austin: University of Texas Press, 1994), p. 7.

25 Ibid, p. 13.

26 Cook, *Lost Illusions: American Cinema in the Shadow of Watergate and Vietnam, 1970–1979*, p. 46.

27 Cited in Austin, *Immediate Seating: A Look at Movie Audiences*, p. 3.

28 Ibid, pp. 47–48.

29 Marcus Hearn, *The Cinema of George Lucas* (New York: Harry N. Abrams, Inc., 2005), p. 80.

30 Ibid.

31 Ibid, p. 81.
32 Ibid, p. 78.
33 Cited in Kramer, '"The Best Disney Film Never Made": Children's Films and The Family Audience in American Cinema since the 1960s', p. 190.
34 Hearn, *The Cinema of George Lucas*, p. 107.
35 'Star Wars: The Year's Best Movie', *Time*, 30 May 1977.
36 'Lucas' "Star Wars" (20th Fox) Chosen Blue Ribbon Award Winner for May', *Boxoffice*, 18 July 1977, p. 14.
37 'Movies around Town', *New York*, 28 August 1978, pp. 15–16.
38 Austin, *Immediate Seating: A Look at Movie Audiences*, p. 22.
39 Hearn, *The Cinema of George Lucas*, p. 89.
40 Cited in Gary R. Edgerton, *American Film Exhibition and an Analysis of the Motion Picture Industry's Market Structure 1963–1980* (New York and London: Garland Publishing, Inc., 1983), p. 175.
41 Cook, *Lost Illusions: American Cinema in the Shadow of Watergate and Vietnam, 1970–1979*, p. 23.
42 Hearn, *The Cinema of George Lucas*, p. 89.
43 Cook, *Lost Illusions: American Cinema in the Shadow of Watergate and Vietnam, 1970–1979*, p. 51.
44 Ibid, p. 46.
45 Susan Royle, 'Steven Spielberg in his Adventures on Earth', in Lester D. Friedman and Brent Notbohm (eds), *Steven Spielberg: Interviews* (Jackson: University of Mississippi Press, 2000), pp. 84–106.
46 Ibid, p. 97.
47 Murray Pomerance, 'The Man-Boys of Steven Spielberg', in Murray Pomerance and Frances Gateward (eds), *Where the Boys Are: Cinemas of Masculinities and Youth* (Detroit and Michigan: Wayne State University Press, 2005), pp. 133–154.
48 Robin Wood, *Hollywood from Vietnam to Reagan* (New York: Columbia University Press, 1986), p. 163.
49 'New NATO Prez: Wholesome Films Bore Mod Youth?', *Variety*, 6 December 1978, p. 5.
50 Ibid.
51 Kramer, 'Would You Take Your Child to See This Film?: The Cultural and Social Work of The Family Adventure Movie', pp. 294–311.
52 Jennifer Holt, '1989: Movies and the American Dream', in Stephen Prince (ed.), *American Cinema of the 1980s: Themes and Variations* (New Brunswick and New Jersey: Rutgers University Press, 2007), pp. 210–231.
53 Kristin Thompson, *The Frodo Franchise: The Lord of the Rings and Modern Hollywood* (Berkeley and London: University of California Press, 2007), p. 5.
54 Allen, 'Home Alone Together: Hollywood and the "Family" Film', p. 121.

55 Kramer, '"The Best Disney Film Never Made": Children's Films and The Family Audience in American Cinema since the 1960s', p. 192.

56 Ibid.

57 Christopher Finch, *The Art of Walt Disney* (New York: Harry N. Abrams, Inc., 1995), p. 372.

58 Kramer, '"The Best Disney Film Never Made": Children's Films and The Family Audience in American Cinema since the 1960s', p. 193.

59 'Walt Disney Grows Up', *The Economist*, 23 July 1983, pp. 86–87.

60 'Theme Parks: The American Dream and the Great Escape', *The Economist*, 11 January 1986, pp. 83–84.

61 Royle, 'Steven Spielberg in His Adventures on Earth', p. 86.

62 Nigel Morris, *The Cinema of Steven Spielberg: Empire of Light* (London: Wallflower, 2007), p. 81.

63 Prince, 'Introduction: Movies and the 1980s', in *American Cinema of the 1980s: Themes and Variations*, pp. 1–21.

64 Ibid, pp. 9–10.

65 Myra Forsberg, 'Spielberg at 40: The Man and the Child', *Steven Spielberg: Interviews*, pp. 126–132.

66 Ibid, p. 131.

67 Balio, *Hollywood in the Age of Television*, p. 262.

68 Ibid, p. 268.

69 Cook, *Lost Illusions: American Cinema in the Shadow of Watergate and Vietnam, 1970–1979*, p. 65.

70 Thompson, *The Frodo Franchise: The Lord of the Rings and Modern Hollywood*, p. 219.

71 Ibid.

72 Stephen Prince: 'Timeline: the 1980s', in *American Cinema of the 1980s: Themes and Variations*, p. xi.

73 Ibid.

74 Royle, 'Steven Spielberg in His Adventures on Earth', p. 87; Prince, 'Timeline: the 1980s', p. xiv.

75 Morris, *The Cinema of Steven Spielberg: Empire of Light*, pp. 84–85.

76 Landon Y. Jones, *Great Expectations: America and the Baby Boom Generation* (New York: Coward, McCann & Geohagan, 1980), p. 2.

77 Ibid, p. 73.

78 Ibid, p. 1.

79 Ibid.

80 Reynolds Farley, *The New American Reality* (New York: Russell Sage Foundation, 1996), p. 113.

81 Ibid, p. 110.

82 See Stephanie Coontz, *The Way We Really Are: Coming to Terms with America's Changing Families* (New York: Basic Books, 1998); Caplow et al., *Middletown Families: Fifty Years of Change and Continuity*; Jones, *Great Expectations: America and the Baby Boom Generation*, pp. 1–2.

83 Jones, *Great Expectations: America and the Baby Boom Generation*, p. 212.

84 Ibid, p. 207.

85 Irving Louis Horowitz, *Ideology and Utopia in the United States 1956–1976* (London, Oxford and New York: Oxford University Press, 1977), p. 46.

86 Jimmy Carter, 'The "Crisis of Confidence" Speech', 15 July 1979: <http://www.pbs.org/wgbh/amex/carter/filmmore/ps_crisis.html> [accessed 24 February 2007].

87 Michael Schaller, *Reckoning with Reagan: American and its President in the 1980s* (Oxford: Oxford University Press, 1992), pp. 66, vii.

88 Ibid, pp. 49, 76.

89 Ibid, pp. 3, 72.

90 Ibid, p. 75.

91 Ibid, p. 76.

92 Ibid, p. 66.

93 Wood, *Hollywood from Vietnam to Reagan*, p. 162.

94 Cook, *Lost Illusions: American Cinema in the Shadow of Watergate and Vietnam, 1970–1979*, p. xi.

95 Edward Reiss, *The Strategic Defence Initiative* (Cambridge: Cambridge University Press, 1992), pp. 39–40.

96 Ibid, p. 37.

97 Ibid.

98 Ibid, p. 38.

99 Ibid, p. 153.

100 Ibid, p. 159.

101 Timothy Shary, *Generation Multiplex: The Image of Youth in Contemporary American Cinema* (Austin: University of Texas Press, 2002), pp. 2, 181–208.

102 Mick Broderick, 'Rebels with a Cause: Children versus the Military Industrial Complex', in Timothy Shary and Alexandra Seibel (eds), *Youth Culture in Global Cinema* (Austin: University of Texas Press, 2007), pp. 37–56.

103 Ibid, p. 38.

104 Wood, *Hollywood from Vietnam to Reagan*, p. 164.

105 Kramer, 'Would You Take Your Child to See This Film?: The Cultural and Social Work of The Family Adventure Movie', p. 297.

106 Toby Miller et al., *Global Hollywood 2* (London: BFI Publishing, 2005), p. 266; Morris, *The Cinema of Steven Spielberg: Empire of Light*, p. 85.

107 Morris, *The Cinema of Steven Spielberg: Empire of Light*, p. 85.

108 Coontz, *The Way we Really Are: Coming to Terms with America's Changing Families*, pp. 33–43.

109 Ibid, p. 33.

110 Andrew J. Cherlin, 'The Changing American Family and Public Policy', in Andrew J. Cherlin (ed.), *The Changing American Family and Public Policy* (Washington: The Urban Institute Press), 1988, pp. 1–29.

111 Schaller, *Reckoning with Reagan: America and its President in the 1980s*, p. 57.

112 Coontz, *The Way we Really Are: Coming to Terms with America's Changing Families*, p. 6.

113 Frank F. Furstenberg, 'Good Dads – Bad Dads: Two Faces of Fatherhood', in *The Changing American Family and Public Policy*, pp. 193–218.

114 Ibid, p. 200.

115 Ibid, p. 204.

116 Janet Wasko, *Hollywood in the Information Age: Beyond the Silver Screen* (Cambridge: Polity Press, 1994), p. 34.

117 'New plan to put Warners in Family Way', *Variety*, 9 December 1991, pp. 1–3.

118 Ibid.

119 Christian Moerk, 'Family Volume at WB', *Variety*, 14 May 1993, p. 3; Kathleen O'Steen, 'Matoian Makes Fox His Family', *Variety*, 8 November 1993, p. 1.

120 Moerk, 'Family Volume at WB'.

121 Ibid.

122 Michael Dare, 'MAJORS NOW MINOR IN FAMILY PIX DIVISIONS', *Variety*, 30 June 1994, pp. 10, 28.

123 Ryan Murphy, 'The Kids Are All Right: PG Flicks – "The Secret Garden" and "Free Willy" Are Among the Family-Oriented Films On Which Studios are Setting Their Sights', *Entertainment Weekly*, 6 April 1993: <http://www.ew.com/ew/article/0,,20218929,00.html> [accessed 29 October 2009].

124 Elaine Dutka, 'A Startling New Concept: Family Films with Money Tight and Criticism of Sex and Violence High, Studios are Looking at PG's Power', *The Los Angeles Times*, 22 March 1993, p. F1.

125 Ibid.

126 Bernard Weinraub, 'Hollywood is Testing Family Values' Value', *The New York Times*, 12 November 1992: <http://www.nytimes.com/1992/11/12/movies/hollywood-is-testing-family-values-value.html> [accessed 24 March 2010].

127 Dare, 'MAJORS NOW MINOR IN FAMILY PIX DIVISIONS'.

128 Tino Balio, 'Hollywood Production Trends in the Era of Globalisation, 1990–1999', in Steve Neale (ed.), *Genre and Contemporary Hollywood*, pp. 165–184.

129 Morris, *The Cinema of Steven Spielberg: Empire of Light*, p. 176.

130 Ana Maria Bahiana, 'Hook', *Steven Spielberg: Interviews*, pp. 151–156.

131 Ibid, p. 154.

132 Morris, *The Cinema of Steven Spielberg: Empire of Light*, pp. 176, 178.

133 Ibid, p. 179.

134 Susan Faludi, *Backlash: The Undeclared War Against Women* (London: Vintage, 1993), p. 2.

135 Maltby, *Hollywood Cinema*, p. 223.

136 Judy Brennan, 'Summer School Lessons', *The Los Angeles Times*, 12 September 1996, p. F1.

137 Bernard Weinraub, 'Movies for Children, and Their Parents, Are Far From "Pollyanna"', *The New York Times*, 22 July 1997: <http://www.nytimes.com/1997/07/22/movies/movies-for-children-and-their-parents-are-far-from-pollyanna.html?sec=&spon=&pagewanted=all> [accessed 14 May 2009].

138 Ibid.

139 Ibid.

140 Balio, 'Hollywood Production Trends in the Era of Globalisation, 1990–1999', p. 165.

141 Ibid, p. 171.

Chapter 7: The Family Audience and the Global Media Environment

1 Paul Grainge, *Brand Hollywood: Selling Entertainment in a Global Media Age* (London and New York: Routledge, 2008), p. 6.

2 Kramer, '"It's Aimed at Kids – the Kid in Everybody": George Lucas, *Star Wars* and Children's Entertainment', pp. 366–367.

3 Allen, 'Home Alone Together: Hollywood and the "Family" Film', pp. 109–134.

4 'All Time Worldwide Box Office Grosses', *Box Office Mojo*. Box office statistics, particularly before the 1970s, are notoriously unreliable, particularly if distorted further by accounting for inflation.

5 '2009 MPAA Theatrical Market Statistics', *Motion Picture Association of America*, 2009, p. 11.

6 Sharon Waxman, 'Study Finds Film Ratings are growing more lenient', *The New York Times*, 14 January 2004: <http://www.nytimes.com/2004/07/14/movies/study-finds-film-ratings-are-growing-more-lenient.html?fta=y> [accessed 24 August 2009].

7 Gabriel Snyder, 'Don't Give me an "R": Film Rating Slips in Light of Political Climate', *Variety*, 21 February 2005, p. 8.

8 Ibid.

9 'Entertainment Industry Market Statistics', *Motion Picture Association of America*, 2007, p. 13.

10 'All Time Worldwide Box Office Grosses'.
11 Jennifer Geer, 'J. M. Barrie Gets the Miramax Treatment: Finding (and Marketing) Neverland', *Children's Literature Association Quarterly*, vol. 32, no. 3 (Fall 2007), pp. 193–212.
12 Snyder, 'Don't Give me an "R": Film Rating Slips in Light of Political Climate'.
13 'All Time Worldwide Box Office Grosses'.
14 Torben Grodal, *Embodied Visions: Evolution, Emotion, Culture, and Film* (Oxford: Oxford University Press, 2009), p. 4.
15 Geoff King, 'Spectacle, Narrative, and the Spectacular Hollywood Blockbuster', in *Movie Blockbusters*, pp. 114–127.
16 Dave McNary, 'Fantasy Movies a Hit Overseas: "Compass" is Latest Family-Friendly Pic to Thrive', *Variety*, 7 March 2008: <http://www.variety.com/article/VR1117982057.html?categoryid=19&cs=1> [accessed 28 August 2009].
17 Thompson, *The Frodo Franchise: The Lord of the Rings and Modern Hollywood*, p. 84.
18 Grainge, *Brand Hollywood: Selling Entertainment in a Global Media Age*, p. 59.
19 Jonathan Bing and Cathy Dunkley, 'Kiddy Litter Rules H'Wood: Tyke Tomes Ascendant in Studios' Post-Potter Parade', *Variety*, 7 January 2002, pp. 1, 3.
20 Ibid.
21 Dade Hayes, 'Kudos Crown a Rich Run for "Shrek": Toon Nabs Inaugural Oscar for Best Animated Feature', *Variety*, 25 March 2002, p. 6.
22 Carl Plantinga, *Moving Viewers: American Film and the Spectator's Experience* (Berkeley, Los Angeles and London: University of California Press, 2009), p. 2.
23 Ibid, p. 34.
24 Ibid, p. 39.
25 Ibid.
26 Dave McNary, 'Family Fare Golden around Globe: "Ice Age", "Narnia" Trump Conventional B.O. Wisdom and Join $100 Mil Club', *Variety*, 19 June 2006, p. 26.
27 Adam Dawtrey, '"Compass" Spins Foreign Frenzy: Film's Overseas Success Raises Questions in U.S.', *Variety*, 10 March 2008, p. 7.
28 Ibid.
29 Ibid.
30 Ibid.
31 McNary, 'Fantasy Movies a Hit Overseas: "Compass" is Latest Family-Friendly Pic to Thrive'.
32 Dade Hayes, *Anytime Playdate: Inside the Preschool Entertainment Boom, or How Television Became My Baby's Best Friend* (New York, London, Toronto and Sydney: Free Press, 2008), p. 122.

33 Anthony Kaufman, 'Heavenly Features: Moving into the Mainstream, the Christian Right Tells Hollywood to Have a Little Faith', *Village Voice*, 29 November 2005: <http://www.villagevoice.com/2005-11-29/film/heavenly-features/> [accessed 30 October 2009].

34 Shawn Levy, '"Avatar" is a Movie-Movie That Might Just Change All Movies', *The Portland Oregonian*, 17 December 2009: <http://blog.oregonlive.com/madaboutmovies/2009/12/review_--_avatar_is_a_movie-mo.html> [accessed 12 March 2010]; Scott Foundas, 'Avatar: On Top of a Distant World', *LA Weekly*, 17 December 2009: <http://www.laweekly.com/2009-12-17/film-tv/avatar-on-top-of-a-distant-world> [accessed 12 March 2010].

35 The phrase coined by Warner Bros. executive Robert Daly to describe the synergistic expansion of the company in 1997, and quoted in Grainge, *Brand Hollywood: Selling Entertainment in a Global Media Age*, pp. 54–56.

36 Kenneth Turan, 'Avatar', *The Los Angeles Times*, 17 December 2009:<http://www.calendarlive.com/movies/reviews/cl-et-avatar17-2009dec17,0,7145753.story> [accessed 12 March 2010].

37 Ibid.

38 Foundas, 'Avatar: On Top of a Distant World'; Levy, '"Avatar" is a Movie-Movie That Might Just Change all Movies'.

39 Mark Graser, 'Warner Bros. Creates DC Entertainment: Studio Taps Premiere Exec Diane Nelson as Chief', *Variety*, 9 September 2009: <http://www.variety.com/article/VR1118008299.html?categoryid=1236&cs=1> [accessed 29 September 2009].

40 Heather Hendershot, 'Introduction: Nickelodeon and the Business of Fun', in Heather Hendershot (ed.), *Nickelodeon Nation: The History, Politics and Economics of America's only TV Channel for Kids* (New York and London: New York University Press, 2004), pp. 1–12.

41 Hayes, *Anytime Playdate: Inside the Preschool Entertainment Boom, or How Television Became My Baby's Best Friend*, p. 127.

42 Sam Thelman, 'High-End Toys are Aimed at Adults: Sales of Action Figures are Up 8% This Year', *Variety*, 25 February 2008, p. 6.

43 Ibid.

44 See Ben Fritz, 'EA Develops Hasbro Properties: Upcoming Games Will Include "G.I. Joe" Tie-In', *Variety*, 11 February 2008: <http://www.variety.com/article/VR1117980627.html?categoryid=1079&cs=1> [accessed 30 September 2009]; and Ben Fritz, 'Hollywood Sees Star Qualities in Classic Games and Toys', *The Los Angeles Times*, 28 September 2009: <http://www.latimes.com/business/la-fi-ct-brands28-2009sep28,0,1264698.story> [accessed 1 October 2009].

45 'Game Player Data', *Entertainment Software Association*: <http://www.theesa.com/facts/gameplayer.asp> [accessed 5 September 2011].

46 Ibid.

47 Ben Fritz and Pamela McClintock, 'Animation World Gets Competitive: Studios Challenging Pixar for Toon Throne', *Variety*, 21 March 2008: <http://www.variety.com/article/VR1117982758.html?categoryid=1019&cs=1> [accessed 16 October 2009].

48 Ibid.

49 Janet Wasko and Eileen R. Meehan, 'Dazzled By Disney? Ambiguity in Ubiquity', in Janet Wasko, Mark Phillips and Eileen R. Meehan (eds), *Dazzled By Disney: The Global Disney Audiences Project* (London and New York: Leicester University Press, 2001), pp. 329–343.

50 Ibid.

51 Frederick Wasser, *Veni, Vidi, Video: The Hollywood Empire and the VCR* (Austin: University of Texas Press, 2002), pp. 163–164.

52 Ibid.

53 Kenneth M. Chanko, 'Who Says a Movie Sequel Can't be Made for Home Video?', *The New York Times*, 19 June 1994: <http://www.nytimes.com/1994/06/19/movies/film-who-says-a-movie-sequel-can-t-be-made-for-home-video.html?scp=3&sq=return%20to%20jafar&st=cse> [accessed 17 October 2009].

54 Ibid.

55 Scott Hettrick, 'Video Bows Mint Coin: Pic Franchises Mine Straight-to-Video Gold', *Variety*, 23 June 2000: <http://www.variety.com/article/VR1117782996.html?categoryid=20&cs=1> [accessed 1 November 2009].

56 Marc Graser, 'H'Wood's Direct Hits: DVD Preems Boffo, But Biz Frets over Sequel-Mania', *Variety*, 13 September 2004, p. 1.

57 Thomas McLean, 'Family Fare Does Well in Down Market: In Tough Economy, Original DVD Titles Chug Along', *Variety*, 6 January 2009, p. 22.

58 Adam Dawtrey, 'U.K. Trio Funds Family Pix: BBC, Film Council, Children's Foundation Pool Cash', *Variety*, 13 October 2003, p. 14.

59 Ibid.

60 *Children's Film and Television Foundation:* <http://www.cftf.org.uk/> [accessed 5 September 2011].

61 Michaela Boland, 'FCC Broadening its Scope by Calling the Shots: Org Wants to Fund More Broad-Appeal Movies, Children's Pics', *Variety*, 7 May 2006: <http://www.variety.com/article/VR1117942616.html?categoryid=2226&cs=1> [accessed 28 August 2009].

62 Ibid.

63 Nick Vivarelli, 'Scandi Markets Drive Kidpic Biz: Laws Set Aside Coin for Children's Films', *Variety*, 5 February 2007, p. 60.

64 Richard Katz, 'Showtime Ups Production of Kidvid Originals', *Variety*, 29 June 1998, p. 18.

65 Lily Oei, 'ABC, Disney Net in Kiddie Synergy: Quartet to Announce P'gramming Skeds', *Variety*, 18 March 2004, p. 5.

66 Dade Hayes, 'Kids Play in Fractured Media Playground: "Fun for All Ages" Label Doesn't Apply Anymore', *Variety*, 3 October 2008, p. 21.

67 Hayes, *Anytime Playdate: Inside the Preschool Entertainment Boom, or How Television Became My Baby's Best Friend*, pp. 5–6.

68 David Bloom, 'Targeting Those Tricky Teenagers: 20-Million Strong "Tweens" an In-Demand Demo', *Variety*, 29 April 2002, p. 45.

Conclusion

1   King, 'Spectacle, Narrative, and the Spectacular Hollywood Blockbuster', p. 119.

2   Miller et al., *Global Hollywood 2*, pp. 190–191.

3   Edward A. Gargan, 'Waiting for China: Anxious Artists – Flowering in the Face of a Giant Unknown', *The New York Times*, 16 February 1997, p. 31.

4   Ben Child, 'Avatar Smashes Chinese All-Time Box-Office Record', *The Guardian*, 19 January 2010: <http://www.guardian.co.uk/film/2010/jan/19/avatar-smashes-chinese-record> [accessed 21 March 2010].

5   Ibid.

6   Tim Arango, 'U.S. Media See a Path to India in China's Snub', *The New York Times*, 3 May 2009: <http://www.nytimes.com/2009/05/04/business/media/04media.html> [accessed 23 March 2010]; Anupama Chopra, 'Stumbling toward Bollywood', *The New York Times*, 20 March 2009: <http://www.nytimes.com/2009/03/22/movies/22chop.html> [accessed 23 March 2010].

7   Carrie Rickey, 'Americans Are Seeing Fewer and Few Foreign Films', *The Philadelphia Inquirer*, 9 May 2010: <http://www.philly.com/inquirer/entertainment/20100509_Americans_are_seeing_fewer_and_fewer_foreign_films.html#axzz0r7gJ2McM> [accessed 17 June 2010].

8   Derek Bose, *Brand Bollywood: A New Global Entertainment Order* (New Delhi: Sage India, 2006), pp. 207–208.

9   Peter J Dekom, 'The Global Market', pp. 418–430.

10 Miller et al., *Global Hollywood 2*, p. 11; Celestine Bohlen, 'Reality Conspires to Undo Russian Films', *The New York Times*, 28 February 1994: <http://www.nytimes.com/1994/02/28/movies/reality-conspires-to-undo-russian-films.html> [accessed 12 April 2010]; Elizabeth Guider and Tom Birchenough, 'H'w'd Heat Hits Russia', *Variety*, 3 February 2006, p. 1.

11 Michael Curtin, *Playing to the World's Biggest Audience: The Globalisation of Chinese Film and TV* (Berkeley, Los Angeles and London: University of California Press, 2007), pp. 284–285.

12   Miller et al., *Global Hollywood 2*, pp. 10, 25.

13   Ibid.

14   Jonathan A. Knee, Bruce C. Greenwald and Ava Seave, *The Curse of the Mogul: What's Wrong with the World's Leading Media Companies* (New York: Portfolio, 2009), p. 169; 'Theatrical Market Statistics 2009', *The Motion Picture Association of America:* <http://www.mpaa.org/> [accessed 17 June 2010].

15   Rickey, 'Americans Are Seeing Fewer and Fewer Foreign Films'; Miller et al., *Global Hollywood 2*, p. 94.

16   Correspondence between the author and Andy Bird, 26 March 2009.

17   'SDCC Redux: Disney's Head of Production, Oren Aviv', *Comingsoon.net*, 3 August 2009: <http://www.comingsoon.net/news/movienews.php?id=57634> [accessed 26 October 2010].

18   Geer, 'J. M. Barrie Gets the Miramax Treatment: Finding (and Marketing) Neverland', pp. 193–212.

19   Ben Fritz, 'Disney Animation Gets Pixar-ization: Catmull Thinks a Radical Shift is needed', *Variety*, 24 February 2007: <http://www.variety.com/article/VR1117960093.html?categoryid=1019&cs=1> [accessed 29 September 2011].

20   Gomery, *The Hollywood Studio System: A History*, p. 272.

21   Knee, Greenwald and Seave, *The Curse of the Mogul: What's Wrong with the World's Leading Media Companies*, p. 3.

SELECT FILMOGRAPHY

Abbott and Costello Meet Frankenstein. Dir Charles Barton. Universal: 1948.

Addams Family, The. Dir Barry Sonnenfeld. Paramount: 1991.

Ah, Wilderness! Dir Clarence Brown. MGM: 1935.

Aladdin. Dir Ron Clements and John Musker. Buena Vista: 1992.

Alice in Wonderland. Dir Norman Z. McLeod. Paramount: 1933.

Alice in Wonderland. Dir Tim Burton. Disney: 2010.

A Midsummer Night's Dream. Dir Max Reinhardt, William Dieterle. Warner Bros: 1935.

Are We There Yet? Dir Brian Levant. Columbia: 2005.

Around the World in 80 Days. Dir Michael Anderson. United Artists: 1956.

Asterix and Obelix vs. Caesar. Dir Claude Zidi. Canal Plus: 1999.

Avatar. Dir James Cameron. Twentieth Century Fox: 2009.

Babes in Toyland. Dir Gus Meins and Charley Rogers. MGM: 1934.

Back to the Future. Dir Robert Zemeckis. Universal Pictures: 1985.

Bambi. Dir James Algar et al. RKO: 1942.

Barefoot Boy. Dir Karl Brown. Monogram: 1938.

Batman. Dir Tim Burton. Warner Bros.: 1989.

Bedknobs and Broomsticks. Dir Robert Stevenson. Buena Vista: 1971.

Benji. Dir Joe Camp. Mulberry Square Productions: 1974.

Big. Dir Penny Marshall. Twentieth Century Fox: 1988.

Biscuit Eater, The. Dir Stuart Heisler. Paramount: 1940,

Black Beauty. Dir Max Nosseck. Twentieth Century Fox: 1946.

Black Hole, The. Dir Gary Nelson. Buena Vista: 1979.

Blue Bird, The. Dir Walter Lang. Twentieth Century Fox: 1940.

Born Free. Dir James Hill. Columbia: 1966.

Bright Eyes. Dir David Butler. Twentieth Century Fox: 1934.

By the Light of the Silvery Moon. Dir David Butler. Warner Bros.: 1953.
Charlie and the Chocolate Factory. Dir Tim Burton. Warner Bros.: 2005.
Cheaper by the Dozen. Dir Walter Lang. Twentieth Century Fox: 1950.
Cheaper by the Dozen. Dir Shawn Levy. Twentieth Century Fox: 2003.
Chitty Chitty Bang Bang. Dir Ken Hughes. United Artists: 1968.
Chronicles of Narnia, The: The Lion, the Witch and the Wardrobe. Dir Andrew Adamson. Buena Vista: 2005.
Cinderella. Dir James Kirkwood. Paramount: 1914.
Clash of the Titans. Dir Desmond Davis. MGM: 1981.
Close Encounters of the Third Kind. Dir Steven Spielberg. Columbia: 1977.
Coraline. Dir Henry Selick. Universal: 2009.
Courtship of Eddie's Father, The. Dir Vincente Minnelli. MGM: 1963.
David Copperfield. Dir George Cukor. MGM: 1935.
Destry Rides Again. Dir Benjamin Stoloff. Universal: 1932.
Dog of Flanders, A. Dir James B. Clark. Twentieth Century Fox: 1960.
Educating Father. Dir James Tinling. Twentieth Century Fox: 1936.
Escape To Witch Mountain. Dir John Hough. Buena Vista: 1975.
E.T.: The Extra Terrestrial. Dir Steven Spielberg. Universal: 1982.
Family Affair, A. Dir George B. Seitz. MGM: 1937.
Fantasia. Dir James Algar et al. RKO: 1940.
Fantastic Voyage. Dir Richard Fleischer. Twentieth Century Fox: 1966.
Father of the Bride. Dir Vincente Minnelli. MGM: 1950.
Finding Nemo. Dir Andrew Stanton, Lee Unkrich. Buena Vista: 2003.
5,000 Fingers of Dr. T., The. Dir Roy Rowland. Columbia: 1953.
Flash Gordon. Dir Mike Hodges. Universal: 1980.
Ghost Busters. Dir Ivan Reitman. Columbia: 1984.
Golden Compass, The. Dir Chris Weitz. New Line: 2007.
Goonies, The. Dir Richard Donner. Warner Bros.: 1985.
Gremlins. Dir Joe Dante. Warner Bros.: 1984.
Gulliver's Travels. Dir Dave Fleischer. Paramount: 1939.
Harry Potter and the Sorcerer's Stone. Dir Chris Columbus. Warner Bros.: 2001.
Harry Potter and the Deathly Hallows – Part II. Dir David Yates. Warner Bros.: 2011.
Has Anybody Seen My Gal? Dir Douglas Sirk. Universal: 1952.
Home Alone. Dir Chris Columbus. Twentieth Century Fox: 1990.
Hook. Dir Steven Spielberg. TriStar Pictures: 1991.
Huckleberry Finn. Dir Norman Taurog. Paramount: 1931.
Huckleberry Finn. Dir J. Lee Thompson. United Artists: 1974.
Human Comedy, The. Dir Clarence Brown. MGM: 1943.
I Remember Mama. Dir George Stevens. RKO: 1948.
Ice Age. Dir Chris Wedge. Twentieth Century Fox: 2002.
Independence Day. Dir Roland Emmerich. Twentieth Century Fox: 1996.

Indiana Jones and the Kingdom of the Crystal Skull. Dir Steven Spielberg. Paramount: 2008.

Iron Giant, The. Dir Brad Bird. Warner Bros.: 1999.

It's A Wonderful Life. Dir Frank Capra. RKO: 1947.

Jason and the Argonauts. Dir Don Chaffey. Columbia: 1963.

Jaws. Dir Steven Spielberg. Universal: 1975.

Jungle Book, The. Dir Wolfgang Reitherman. Buena Vista: 1967.

Jurassic Park. Dir Steven Spielberg. Universal Pictures: 1993.

Kid, The. Dir Charles Chaplin. Warner Bros.: 1921.

King Kong. Dir Merian C. Cooper and Ernest B. Schoedsack. Universal: 1933.

Lassie Come Home. Dir Fred M. Wilcox. MGM: 1943.

Life with Father. Dir Michael Curtiz. Warner Bros.: 1947.

Little Lord Fauntleroy. Dir John Cromwell. United Artists: 1936.

Little Mermaid, The. Dir Ron Clement and John Musker. Buena Vista: 1989.

Little Princess, The. Dir Walter Lang. Twentieth Century Fox: 1939.

Little Women. Dir George Cukor. RKO Pictures: 1933.

Lord of the Rings, The: The Fellowship of the Ring. Dir Peter Jackson. Warner Bros.: 2001.

Love Bug, The. Dir Robert Stevenson. Buena Vista: 1969.

Mary Poppins. Dir Robert Stevenson. Buena Vista: 1964.

Meet Me In St. Louis. Dir. Vincente Minnelli. MGM: 1944.

Miracle on 34th Street. Dir George Seaton. Twentieth Century Fox: 1947.

Mrs. Doubtfire. Dir Chris Columbus. Twentieth Century Fox: 1993.

My Fair Lady. Dir George Cukor. Warner Bros.: 1964.

My Friend Flicka. Dir Harold D. Schuster. Twentieth Century Fox, 1943.

Mysterious Island. Dir Cy Endfield. Columbia: 1961.

Nancy Drew, Reporter. Dir William Clemens. Warner Bros.: 1939.

National Velvet. Dir Clarence Brown. MGM: 1945.

NeverEnding Story, The. Dir Wolfgang Petersen. Warner Bros.: 1984.

Night at the Museum. Dir Shawn Levy. Twentieth Century Fox: 2006.

Old Yeller. Dir Robert Stevenson. Buena Vista: 1957.

Oliver! Dir Carol Reed. Columbia: 1968.

One Hundred Men and a Girl. Dir Henry Koster. Universal: 1937.

On Moonlight Bay. Dir Roy Del Ruth. Warner Bros.: 1951.

Our Town. Dir Sam Wood. United Artists: 1940.

Peter Pan. Dir Hamilton Luske et al. RKO: 1953.

Pinocchio. Dir Hamilton Luske and Ben Sharpsteen. RKO: 1940.

Pirates of the Caribbean: The Curse of the Black Pearl. Dir Gore Verbinski. Buena Vista: 2003.

Pollyanna. Dir David Swift. Buena Vista: 1960.

Poor Little Rich Girl. Dir Irving Cummings. Twentieth Century Fox: 1936.

Princess Bride, The. Dir Rob Reiner. Twentieth Century Fox: 1987.

Raiders of the Lost Ark. Dir Steven Spielberg. Paramount: 1981.
Return of Jafar, The. Dir Tad Stones. Buena Vista: 1994.
Romeo and Juliet. Dir George Cukor. MGM: 1936.
Run Wild, Run Free. Dir Richard Sarafian. Columbia: 1969.
RV: Runaway Vacation. Dir Barry Sonnenfeld. Columbia: 2006.
7 Faces of Dr. Lao, The. Dir George Pal. MGM: 1964.
7th Voyage of Sinbad, The. Dir Nathan Juran. Columbia: 1958.
Shrek. Dir Andrew Adamson and Vicky Jenson. Paramount: 2001.
Simpsons Movie, The. Dir David Silverman. Twentieth Century Fox: 2007.
Skippy. Dir Norman Taurog. Paramount: 1931.
Snow White and the Seven Dwarfs. Dir David Hand. RKO: 1937.
Sound of Music, The. Dir Robert Wise. Twentieth Century Fox: 1965.
Sounder. Dir Martin Ritt. Twentieth Century Fox: 1972.
Spider-Man. Dir Sam Raimi. Columbia: 2002.
Star Wars. Dir George Lucas. Twentieth Century Fox: 1977.
Steamboat Willie. Dir Ub Iwerks. Celebrity Productions: 1928.
Stepmom. Dir Chris Columbus. Columbia: 1998.
Summer Holiday. Dir Rouben Mamoulian. MGM: 1948.
Superman. Dir Richard Donner. Warner Bros.: 1978.
Swiss Family Robinson, The. Dir Ken Annakin. Buena Vista: 1960.
Tarzan the Ape Man. Dir W. S. Van Dyke. MGM: 1932.
Thief of Bagdad, The. Dir Ludwig Berger et al. United Artists: 1940.
Three Smart Girls. Dir Henry Koster. Universal: 1936.
Time Bandits. Dir Terry Gilliam. Handmade Films: 1981.
Tom Sawyer. Dir John Cromwell. Paramount: 1930.
Tom Sawyer. Dir Don Taylor. United Artists: 1973.
tom thumb. Dir George Pal. MGM: 1958.
Toy Story. Dir John Lasseter. Buena Vista: 1995.
Transformers. Dir Michael Bay. Paramount: 2007.
Treasure Island. Dir Victor Fleming. MGM: 1934.
Treasure Island. Dir Byron Haskin. RKO Pictures: 1950.
Tron. Dir Steven Lisberger. Buena Vista: 1982.
20,000 Leagues under the Sea. Dir Richard Fleischer. Buena Vista: 1954.
Uncle Buck. Dir John Hughes. Universal: 1989.
Up. Dir Pete Docter and Bob Peterson. Disney: 2009.
Weekend with Father. Dir Douglas Sirk. Universal: 1951.
What A Life. Dir Theodore Reed. Paramount: 1939.
Who Framed Roger Rabbit. Dir Robert Zemeckis. Warner Bros.: 1988.
Willy Wonka & the Chocolate Factory. Dir Mel Stuart. Warner Bros.: 1971.
Wizard of Oz, The. Dir Victor Fleming. MGM: 1939.
Yearling, The. Dir Clarence Brown. MGM: 1946.

SELECT BIBLIOGRAPHY

Allen, Robert C., 'Home Alone Together: Hollywood and the "Family Film"', in Melvyn Stokes and Richard Maltby (eds), *Identifying Hollywood's Audiences: Cultural Identity and the Movies* (London: British Film Institute, 1999), pp. 109–134.

Austin, Bruce A., *Immediate Seating: A Look at Movie Audiences* (Belmont, CA: Wadsworth, 1989).

Babington, Bruce and Peter William Evans, *Blue Skies and Silver Linings: Aspects of The Hollywood Musical* (Manchester: Manchester University Press, 1985).

———, *Biblical Epics: Sacred Narrative in the Hollywood Cinema* (Manchester: Manchester University Press, 1993).

Balio, Tino, *United Artists: The Company That Changed the Film Industry* (Madison, Wisconsin: University of Wisconsin Press, 1987).

——— (ed.), *Hollywood in the Age of Television* (Boston: Unwin Hyman, 1990).

———, *Grand Design: Hollywood as a Modern Business Enterprise, 1930–1939* (Berkeley, Los Angeles and London: University of California Press, 1993).

Barrier, Michael, *Hollywood Cartoons: American Animation in its Golden Age* (Oxford: Oxford University Press, 2003).

Bazalgette, Cary and Terry Staples, 'Unshrinking The Kids: Children's Cinema and the Family Film', in Cary Bazalgette and David Buckingham (eds), *In Front of the Children* (London: British Film Institute, 1995), pp. 92–108.

Booker, Keith M, *Disney, Pixar and the Hidden Messages of Children's Films* (California: Praeger, 2010).

Brown, Noel, *Hollywood, the Family Audience and the Family Film, 1930–2010* (PhD Thesis submitted to Newcastle University, June 2010).

Considine, David M., *The Cinema of Adolescence* (Jefferson, N.C.: McFarland, 1985).

Cook, David A., *Lost Illusions: American Cinema in the Shadow of Watergate and Vietnam, 1970–1979* (Berkeley, London and Los Angeles: University of California Press, 2000).

Coontz, Stephanie, *The Way We Never Were: American Families and the Nostalgia Trap* (New York: Basic Books, 1992).

Crafton, Donald, *The Talkies: American Cinema's Transition to Sound, 1926–1931* (Berkeley and London: University of California Press, 1999).

Curtin, Michael, *Playing to the World's Biggest Audience: The Globalisation of Chinese Film and TV* (Berkeley, Los Angeles and London: University of California Press, 2007).

Dale, Edgar, *Children's Attendance at the Motion Pictures* (New York: Macmillan, 1935).

Dale, Edgar et al., *Motion Pictures in Education*: *A Summary of the Literature: Sourcebook for Teachers and Administrator* (New York: H. W. Wilson, 1937).

deCordova, Richard, 'Ethnography and Exhibition: the Child Audience, the Hays Office and Saturday Matinees', in Gregory A. Waller (ed.), *Moviegoing in America: A Sourcebook in the History of Film Exhibition* (Oxford: Blackwell Publishers, 2002), pp. 159–169.

Doherty, Thomas, *Teenagers and Teenpics: The Juvenilization of American Movies in the 1950s* (Philadelphia: University of Temple Press, 2002).

Edgerton, Gary R., *American Film Exhibition and an Analysis of the Motion Picture Industry's Market Structure, 1963–1980* (London: Garland Publishing, 1983).

Farber, Stephen, *The Movie Rating Game* (S.I.: Public Affairs Press, 1972).

Finler, Joel W., *The Hollywood Story* (London and New York: Wallflower Press, 2003).

Ford, Richard, *Children in the Cinema* (London: Allen and Unwin, 1939).

Geraghty, Lincoln and Mark Jancovich (eds), *The Shifting Definitions of Genre: Essays on Labelling Films, Television Shows and Media* (London: McFarland, 2008).

Gilby, Ryan, *It Don't Worry Me: Nashville, Jaws, Star Wars and Beyond* (London: Faber and Faber, 2003).

Goldstein, Ruth M. and Edith Zornow, *The Screen Image of Youth: Movies about Children and Adolescents* (Metuchen: Scarecrow, 1980).

Gomery, Douglas, *Movie History: A Survey* (Belmont, California: Wadsworth Publishing, 1991).

———, *Shared Pleasures: A History of Movie Presentation in the United States* (Madison: University of Wisconsin Press, 1992).

———, *The Hollywood Studio System: A History* (London: British Film Institute, 2005).

Grant, Barry Keith (ed.), *Film Genre Reader III* (Austin: University of Texas Press, 2003).

Grieveson, Lee, '"A Kind of Recreative School for the Whole Family": Making Cinema Respectable, 1907–09', in *Screen* 42, no. 1 (2001), pp. 64–76.

Grodal, Torben, *Embodied Visions: Evolution, Emotion, Culture, and Film* (Oxford: Oxford University Press, 2009).

Guback, Thomas H., *The International Film Industry: Western Europe and America since 1945* (Bloomington: Indiana University Press, 1969).

Harryhausen, Ray and Tony Dalton, *An Animated Life: Adventures in Fantasy* (London: Aurum, 2003).

Hays, Will H., *The Memoirs of Will H. Hays* (New York: Doubleday, 1955).

Hickman, Gail Morgan, *The Films of George Pal* (South Brunswick and New York: A. S. Barnes and Company, 1977).

Hine, Thomas, *The Rise and fall of the American Teenager* (New York: Bard Books, 1997).

Jackson, Kathy Merlock (ed.), *Walt Disney: Conversations* (Jackson: University Press of Mississippi, 2006).

Jackson, Kenneth, *Crabgrass Frontier: The Suburbanisation of the United States* (New York: Oxford University Press, 1985).

Jones, Gerard, *Honey, I'm Home! Sitcoms: Telling the American Dream* (New York: Grove Weidenfeld, 1992).

Jones, Landon Y., *Great Expectations: America and the Baby Boom Generation* (New York: Coward McCann and Geohegen, 1980).

Jowett, Garth S., *Film: The Democratic Art* (Boston: Little, 1976).

Jowett, Garth S., Ian C. Jarvie and Kathryn H. Fuller, *Children and the Movies: Media Influence and the Payne Fund Controversy* (Cambridge: Cambridge University Press, 1996).

King, Geoff, *Spectacular Narratives: Hollywood in the Age of the Blockbuster* (London and New York: I.B.Tauris, 2000).

Knee, Jonathan A., Bruce C. Greenwald and Ava Seave, *The Curse of the Mogul: What's Wrong with the World's Leading Media Companies* (New York: Portfolio, 2009).

Koszarski, Richard, *An Evening's Entertainment: The Age of the Silent Feature Picture, 1915–1928* (New York: Scribner, 1993).

Kramer, Peter, 'Would You Take Your Child to See This Film?: The Cultural and Social Work of the Family Adventure Movie', in Steve Neale and Murray Smith (eds), *Contemporary Hollywood Cinema* (London: Routledge, 1998), pp. 294–311.

———, '"The Best Disney Film Never Made": Children's Films and The Family Audience in American Cinema since the 1960s', in Steve Neale (ed.), *Genre And Contemporary Hollywood* (London: British Film Institute, 2002), pp. 185–200.

———, '"It's Aimed at Kids – the Kid in Everybody": George Lucas, Star Wars and Children's Entertainment', in Yvonne Tasker (ed.), *Action and Adventure Cinema* (London: Routledge, 2004), pp. 358–370.

————, 'Disney and Family Entertainment', in Linda Ruth Williams and Michael Hammond (eds), *Contemporary American Cinema* (Maidenhead: Open University Press, 2006), pp. 265–271.

Lahue, Kalton C., *Continued Next Week: A History of The Moving Picture Serial* (Norman: University of Oklahoma Press, 1964).

Lynd, Robert S. and Helen Merrell Lynd, *Middletown: A Study in Contemporary American Culture* (London: Constable, 1929).

Maltby, Richard, 'The Production Code and the Hays Office', in Tino Balio (ed.),*Grand Design: Hollywood as a Modern Business Enterprise, 1930–1939* (Berkeley, Los Angeles and London: University of California Press, 1993), pp. 37–72.

————, 'Sticks, Hicks and Flaps: Classical Hollywood's Generic Conception of its Audiences', in Melvyn Stokes and Richard Maltby (eds), *Identifying Hollywood's Audiences: Cultural Identity and the Movies* (London: British Film Institute, 1999), pp. 23–47.

————, *Hollywood Cinema* (Oxford: Blackwell, 2003).

Miller, Don, *B Movies* (New York: Ballantine, 1973).

Miller, Toby et al., *Global Hollywood 2* (London: BFI Publishing, 2005).

Mitchell, Alice Miller, *Children and Movies* (Chicago: University of Chicago Press, 1929).

Monti, Daniel J., *The American City: A Social and Cultural History* (Oxford and Massachusetts: Blackwell Publishing, 1999).

Morris, Timothy, *You're Only Young Twice: Children's Literature and Film* (Urbana: University of Illinois Press, 2000).

Olsen, Scott Robert, *Hollywood Planet: Global Media and the Competitive Advantage of Narrative Transparency* (Hoboken: Lawrence Erlbaum Associates, 1999).

Plantinga, Carl, *Moving Viewers: American Film and the Spectator's Experience* (Berkeley, Los Angeles and London: University of California Press, 2009).

Postman, Neil, *The Disappearance of Childhood* (New York: Vintage Books, 1994 (1982)).

Rubin, Joan S., *The Making of Middlebrow Culture* (Chapel Hill: University of North Carolina Press, 1992).

Sammond, Nicholas, *Babes in Tomorrowland: Walt Disney and the Making of the American Child, 1930–1960* (London: Duke University Press, 2005).

Schatz, Thomas, *The Genius of the System* (London: Faber and Faber, 1998).

Schickel, Richard, *The Disney Version: The Life, Times, Art and Commerce of Walt Disney* (Chicago: Elephant Paperbacks, 1997).

Seldes, Gilbert, *The Great Audience* (New York: Viking, 1950).

Shary, Timothy, *Generation Multiplex: The Image of Youth in Contemporary American Cinema* (Austin: University of Texas Press, 2002).

Smoodin, Eric, *Animating Culture: Hollywood Cartoons from the Sound Era* (Oxford: Roundhouse, 1993).

Spigel, Lynn, *Make Room for TV: Television and the Family Ideal in Postwar America* (Chicago: University of Chicago Press, 1992).

Staples, Terry, *All Pals Together: The Story of Children's Cinema* (Edinburgh: Edinburgh University Press, 1997).

Stedman, Raymond William, *The Serials* (Norman: University of Oklahoma Press, 1970).

Stokes, Melvyn, 'Female Audiences of the 1920s and early 1930s', in Melvyn Stokes and Richard Maltby (eds), *Identifying Hollywood's Audiences: Cultural Identity and the Movies* (London: British Film Institute, 1999), pp. 42–60.

Thompson, Kristin, *Exporting Entertainment: America in the World Film Market 1907–1934* (London: British Film Institute, 1985).

————, *The Frodo Franchise: The Lord of the Rings and Modern Hollywood* (Berkeley and London: University of California Press, 2007).

Thomson, David, *A Biographical History of Film* (London: Andre Deutsch, 1994).

Thorp, Margaret Farrand, *America at the Movies* (New Haven: Yale University Press, 1939).

Vasey, Ruth, *The World According to Hollywood, 1918–1939* (Madison: The University of Wisconsin Press, 1997).

Wasser, Frederick, *Veni, Vidi, Video: The Hollywood Empire and the VCR* (Austin, Texas: University of Texas Press, 2002).

Watts, Steven, *The Magic Kingdom: Walt Disney and the American Way of Life* (Columbia: University of Missouri Press, 1997).

Wojcik-Andrews, Ian, *Children's Films: History, Ideology, Pedagogy, Theory* (New York and London: Garland Publishing, 2000).

Wood, Robin, *Hollywood from Vietnam to Reagan* (New York: Columbia University Press, 1986).

Wyatt, Justin, *High Concept: Movies and Marketing in Hollywood* (Austin: University of Texas Press, 1994).

Zierold, Norman J., *The Child Stars* (New York: Coward-McCann, 1965).

INDEX

The Hollywood Family Film